A PORTRAIT OF
WILLIAM COWPER

A PORTRAIT OF WILLIAM COWPER

His Own Interpreter
in
Letters and Poems

LOUISE B. RISK

BENT BRANCH PUBLISHERS
GLEN ECHO, MARYLAND

Risk, Louise B., 1925-
    A portrait of William Cowper : his own interpreter in letters and poems / Louise B. Risk.
      p. cm.
    Includes bibliographical references and index.
    ISBN 0-9633934-1-3

    1. Cowper, William, 1731-1800. 2. Poets, English—18th century—Biography. 3. Cowper, William, 1731-1800—Biography. 4. Cowper, William, 1731-1800—Correspondence. 5. Cowper, William, 1731-1800—Poetry. 6. Cowper, William, 1731-1800—Criticism and interpretation. I. Title.
PR3383.R5 2004
921—dc22

                        2004104384

Bent Branch Publishers
P.O. Box 427
Glen Echo, Maryland 20812

Printed in the United States of America

Copyediting and proofreading by PeopleSpeak.
Book design and composition by Carolyn Wendt.
Cover design by Desktop Miracles.

First Edition
08 07 06 05 04   10 9 8 7 6 5 4 3 2 1

GOD IS HIS OWN INTERPRETER,
AND HE WILL MAKE IT PLAIN.

Contents

Illustrations

FIGURES

LIGHT SHINING OUT OF DARKNESS

Since the last decades of the twentieth century, there has been a strong resurgence of interest in the British poet William Cowper (1731–1800). The backbone of new research and writing on Cowper is the five-volume authoritative edition of Cowper's letters and prose writings edited by James King and Charles Ryskamp as well as the three-volume edition of Cowper's poetry edited by John D. Baird and Charles Ryskamp.

These landmark volumes form the basis of the present work, the subtitle of which is "His Own Interpreter in Letters and Poems." In his authentic voice Cowper has told the story of his life, the relationship between his life and his work, as well as the meaning and purpose of his poetry. As much as any writer, Cowper has provided his own biography.

Although much has been written about Cowper since his death two centuries ago, some writers, conforming to their own biases, have slanted the record left by Cowper himself. Omission of major themes in Cowper's life and the imposition of personal points of view have created a picture of Cowper unrecognizable to the modern reader of the complete letters and poems.

One central theme in Cowper's life was his Christian faith. For his friend William Unwin, Cowper summarized his spiritual journey: he found a God and was permitted to worship him; he was deprived of this privilege; he had no hope of recovering (*L*, 2:133).[1] Thus he had experienced an evangelical conversion to Christ as savior but later felt totally abandoned by God. In *A Critical History of English Poetry,* Cowper's faith was scorned. "But first and foremost Cowper is an Evangelical preacher. If England is in trouble it is that God is punishing her sins. . . . Neither Cowper's piety nor his patriotism interests us to-day."[2]

Contrariwise, other writers tried to give Cowper strong beliefs he only rarely enjoyed. As early as the 1816 preface to Cowper's *Memoir,* the writer, clearly evangelical himself, falsely stated, "In William Cowper was a lively example of that righteousness, peace and joy in the Holy Ghost which constitute the Kingdom of God in the hearts of men; of that faith which overcomes the world and purifies the heart."[3] But Cowper rarely enjoyed peace or joy in believing.

Another central theme in Cowper's life was his chronic melancholy, serious depressions, and intervals of insanity. Again some nineteenth-century writers trivialized his mental illnesses or ignored them altogether. The 1816 preface struggled to describe Cowper's "unhappy malady," said to be understandable in a bodily form that was nervous and irritable, a "mind particularly timid and assaulted with gloomy thoughts led on by spleen," and a character of "natural timidity and feminine softness."[4]

The critical history cited above made light of Cowper's religion and illnesses in two sentences. "He combines the egotism of the invalid with that of the pious. The things he likes are those which all men ought to like."[5] Lord Byron presented in venomous short form the nineteenth-century scorn for Cowper, "the maniacal and Calvinist poet."[6]

In addition to Cowper's own meticulously detailed accounts of his struggles with faith and illness, my portrait of Cowper has also benefited from new books about the evangelical revival in England and the influence of John Newton. Even more important to my portrait has been the work of modern psychiatrists whose special field is the relationship between creativity and depression.

Other subjects vital to an appreciation of Cowper both as man and author are his enjoyment of country life and his love for many friends and family members. Cowper had an astonishing gift for intimacy. In these areas Cowper's letters and poems are inexhaustible sources of information and understanding. To help organize such a wealth of material, the chapters of my book have titles in Cowper's own words and are arranged chronologically. This is more difficult than ordering his biography by subject as has often been done. The chronology helps the reader understand how Cowper's disciplined writing schedule affected his friendships.

A central purpose of this book is to show that Cowper was brave and unyieldingly determined to overcome the greatest odds. This book attempts finally to lay to rest the view of Cowper presented in David Cecil's excellent biography of 1930, *The Stricken Deer, or the Life of William Cowper.* This title used Cowper's own words.

> I was a stricken deer that left the herd
> Long since; with many an arrow deep infixt
> My panting side was charged, when I withdrew
> To seek a tranquil death in distant shades.
>
> (*P,* 2:165)

Cecil's presentation of Cowper as a stricken and often pathetic figure was so influential that literary critics long continued to patronize him.

The strong resurgence today of interest in William Cowper, both the writer and the man, is fueled by a new appreciation of Cowper's poetry. The *Monthly Review* in 1816 had said, even while Cowper was still the most popular poet in England, "Defects would exclude Cowper from a high station in the list of poets." Some such defects were judged to be "familiar and *vulgar* language" and "rough unmeasured cadences of song" by way of proof that, in Cowper, "Verse is no longer a dignified and mysterious gift."[7] In dramatic contrast, *Eighteenth Century Poetry: An Annotated Anthology* of 1999 says of Cowper, "Our selections include two great poems of despair; but these stand out from the bulk of Cowper's work. What strikes the reader forcibly is the sense and sanity of his poetry, its alertness to variety, and commitment to the strenuous moral life. We remember that it was Cowper's energy and boldness that struck the readers of the next generation. . . . Cowper's strength of character underlay his timidity."[8]

There are growing resources for Cowper scholars such as the recently announced gift to Lehigh University Special Collections of works of William Cowper. The gift includes about three hundred volumes representing over 250 separate editions, ranging from eighteenth-century first editions to modern-day reprints. My own work has benefited immeasurably from ready access to the Library of Congress, especially the Rare Book Room.

The foundation of the present volume throughout is William Cowper, explaining himself in his authentic voice. One of Cowper's best known hymns is "Light Shining Out of Darkness." In a memorial sermon after Cowper's death, Samuel Greatheed said that this hymn was written while Cowper was walking in the fields "having received some presentiment" of his coming breakdown of 1773. Cowper presents a bewildering God, a frowning providence with a smiling face.

God moves in a mysterious way,
His wonders to perform;
He plants his footsteps in the Sea,
And rides upon the Storm.

Deep in unfathomable Mines
Of never failing Skill,
He treasures up his bright designs,
And works his Sovereign Will.

Ye fearfull Saints, fresh courage take,
The clouds ye so much dread,
Are big with Mercy, and shall break
In blessings on your head.

Judge not the Lord by feeble sense
But trust him for his Grace,

Behind a frowning Providence
He hides a Smiling face.

His purposes will ripen fast,
Unfolding ev'ry hour,
The Bud may have a bitter taste,
But *wait, to smell the flower.*

Blind unbelief is sure to err,
And scan his work in vain;
God is his own Interpreter,
And he will make it plain.

(P, 1:174)

In this hymn God was his own interpreter. Cowper became *his* own interpreter in letters and poems.

BIRTHPLACE OF THE POET COWPER.

p. 16.

FIGURE 1. The rectory of St. Peter's Church, Berkhamsted, from Samuel Greatheed, *Home and Haunts of Cowper: Sixteen Illustrations* (Philadelphia: Lindsay & Blakiston c. 1801). Courtesy of the Library of Congress.

PART ONE

A
MOTHERLESS
CHILD

1

ATTACHMENT AND LOSS
1731–1741

In 1731 Berkhamsted was a Hertfordshire town of about fifteen hundred inhabitants twenty-six miles from London. It was a pleasant place of hills and woods, meadows and farms—a prosperous market center. William Cowper always remembered his earliest years.

> What peacefull Hours I then enjoy'd!
>   How Sweet their Memr'y still!
> But they have left an Aching Void,
>   The World can never fill.
>   (*P,* 1:139)

Several hundred houses clustered around High Street and Castle Street. At the center of town was the imposing St. Peter's Church; its rectory was the home of the Reverend John Cowper. In 1731 he was in his ninth year as rector, his third as a married man. At age thirty-seven he was widely admired as a scholar, a writer, and a member of one of Hertfordshire's most illustrious landholding families.

In November 1731 John Cowper's wife, Ann Donne Cowper, was awaiting the imminent birth of another child. Her first son, Spencer, had been born in 1729, the year after her marriage. He died at five weeks of age. Nine months later Ann gave birth to twins, Ann and John, who died within two days. Now, one year later, she was waiting again. On November 15 William Cowper was born.

When William was one and a half, his sister Theodora Judith was born. He was barely three when his brother Thomas was born and died in less than two weeks. Soon after, his two-year-old sister Theodora Judith died. When William was a week shy of his sixth birthday, his brother John was born. Six days later his mother, Ann, died.

The appalling emotional and physical toll of her nine-year marriage and six pregnancies led to Ann's death at twenty-eight. His mother's death left an emotional toll on William that overshadowed the remaining years of his life.

The story of the Reverend John Cowper's family was far from unique in eighteenth-century England. In his invaluable book, *The Family, Sex, and Marriage in England 1500–1800,* Lawrence Stone writes that in mid-century "between a quarter and a third of all children of English peers and peasants were dead before they reached the age of fifteen."[1] For many complex and often unclear reasons, slow change for the better was observed. "After 1750 in England the level of infant and child mortality began to fall, and the expectation of life at birth to rise."[2]

Stone's discussion of the use of contraception may well apply to John Cowper's family. Very slowly after 1750 contraception came to be "theologically and morally acceptable" and sexual pleasure within marriage "a legitimate aspiration without relation to the objective of reproduction."[3] Previously, Anglican theology had categorically denied that contraception was acceptable in God's sight.

Even more slowly, especially among the economically and culturally advantaged, wives began to question sexual resignation and husbands "to share in the anxieties and sufferings of their wives with repeated pregnancies and painful childbirth."[4]

The earliest formal tribute to Ann Donne Cowper was carved on the monument erected by her husband in St. Peter's Church at Berkhamsted. The words, composed by her young niece, Lady Walsingham, convey no sense of human remorse let alone any hint of divine purpose. This is what Ann's family remembered about the "comforts of a life well-spent."

Here lies, in early years bereft of life,
The best of mothers, and the kindest wife.
Who neither knew, nor practic'd any art,
Secure in all she wish'd, her husband's heart.
Her love to him still prevalent in death
Pray'd Heaven to bless him with her latest breath.

    Still was she studious never to offend,
And glad of an occasion to commend:
With ease would pardon injuries receiv'd,
Nor e'er was chearful when another griev'd.
Despising state, with her own lot content,
Enjoy'd the comforts of a life well-spent.
Resign'd when Heaven demanded back her breath,
Her mind heroic 'midst the pangs of death.

    Whoe'er thou art that dost this Tomb draw near,
O stay awhile, and shed a friendly tear,
These lines, tho' weak, are as herself sincere.[5]

Not until her son William's authentic voice was heard in prose and poetry would Ann's life be remembered on a higher plane of art and love.

As the year 1737 was coming to a close, in the rectory at Berkhamsted were Reverend John Cowper, his infant son, John, his six-year-old son, William, and servants, including no doubt a wet nurse. What would be his father's plan for William? On the one hand, at midcentury most noble families were educating children at home and responding to their children's needs for love, time, and parental effort. On the other hand, "many aristocratic children still went off to boarding-school as early as the age of seven, and did not return home again for decades, spending their holidays with close relations."[6]

John Cowper made unfortunate decisions about William's education. Boarding school would be the place for him. At the time many country rectors operated schools for extra income. Having known each other at universities and ecclesiastical conferences, Anglican rectors sent their sons to each others' schools. Unfortunately, some clergymen were more fit for the pulpit or the study than for the schoolroom. One school in Berkhamsted was so troubled that a lawsuit had been initiated by Reverend John Cowper himself.

At Aldbury, only a few miles away from Berkhamsted, was a school run by the Reverend William Davis, a friend of John Cowper. Little William was sent there only briefly. Was his father dissatisfied with the school or had Reverend Davis been displeased with William?

Next, the six-year-old William was taken from home and sent to boarding school in Markyate Street on the Bedfordshire-Hertfordshire border. The headmaster, again well known to John Cowper, was the Reverend William Pittman, a fellow of King's College, Cambridge, and a prominent classical scholar. As became evident in William's case, he was not qualified to supervise boys, nor aware of their personal problems. In later years, William described his plight.

> Here I had hardships of various kinds to conflict with. . . . But my chief affliction consisted in being singled out from all the children in the school by a lad about fifteen years of age as a proper subject upon whom he might let loose the cruelty of his temper . . . He had by his savage treatment of me imprinted such a dread of his very figure upon my mind that I well remember being afraid to lift my eyes upon him higher than his knees, and that I knew him by his shoe buckles better than by any other part of his dress. . . . The cruelty of this boy, which he had long practiced in so secret a manner that no creature suspected it, was at length discovered; he was expelled from school, and I was taken from it. (*L*, 1:5,6)

The next two years would be even more lonely and terrifying than William's first two years away from the nursery and from his home environment of fields and woods. Almost half a century later, he still remembered Berkhamsted. "There was neither tree nor grate, nor stile, in all that country, to which I did not feel a relation, and the house itself I preferred to a palace" (*L*, 3:42). William was taken, alone, to London. His father's decision for his eighth and ninth years was that he live in the city with Mrs. Disney and her husband, prominent oculists.

Again we have William's words to tell the story. On April 6, 1792, he wrote to his friend and, later, biographer, William Hayley.

> I have been all my life subject to inflammations of the eye, and in my boyish days had specks on both that threatened to cover them. My father alarmed for the consequences, sent me to a female Oculist of great renown at that time in whose house I abode two years, but to no good purpose. From her I went to Westminster school, where at the age of fourteen the small-pox seized me, and proved the better oculist of the two, for it delivered me from them all. — Not however from great liableness to inflammation, to which I am in a degree still subject, tho' much less than formerly, since I have been constant in the use of a hot footbath every night, the last thing before going to rest. (*L*, 4:50–51)

Eighteenth-century ophthalmology was primitive. Those men and women who treated eye diseases often had no scientific education and no affiliation with any place resembling a hospital. Some who practiced freely and without licenses were quacks and charlatans. No standards existed for eye medications and there was little understanding of the functions of the different structures of the eye.

Modern pediatric ophthalmology recognizes the importance of the emotional response of patients and parents to the fear of blindness. Some parents and some children may exaggerate or, on the other hand, deny a threat to sight that actually exists. "The emotional response of the parent or patient to signs or symptoms of eye disease may be the most important aspect of the problems with which the ophthalmologist might deal. It may overshadow all aspects of the ocular problem."[7]

The Reverend John Cowper cannot be judged harshly for his "alarm for the consequences" of William's specks. Nor can we know what he had been able to learn about specks. James Wardrop, fellow of the Royal College of Surgeons, published in 1808 *Essays on the Morbid Anatomy of the Human Eye.* Chapter 11 is entitled "Of the Speck of the Cornea."[8] The sign of specks was dimness of vision, from the slightest perceptible cloudiness to dense opacity and from one speck to three or more distinct spots.

William Cowper's letter of April 6, 1792, to Hayley ends with the comment that he became less subject to eye inflammation after he began using a hot footbath every night. Even a century after Cowper's time and after the work of James Wardrop, primitive and irrelevant treatments such as footbaths were still described in reference books.

Cowper relied on Sir John Elliott's medicines, which may have been an ointment of mercuric oxide. He wrote to Joseph Hill on October 30, 1782, for a further supply: "Every time I feel the least uneasiness in either eye, I tremble lest my AEsculapius being departed my infallible remedy should be lost forever."[9]

Cowper's two boyhood years with the Disneys had been, as he said, to no good purpose. It is not known whether their regimen permitted visits home to Berkhamsted or whether his father ever visited William while his son lived alone in London. The first decade of William Cowper's life came to a close as he was once more "taken," this time from the Disneys to Westminster School.

2

A SEASON OF
CLEAR SHINING
1742–1749

Ten-year-old William Cowper was enrolled at Westminster School in April 1742. Questions immediately come to mind. Was he going to have the physical, mental, and emotional stamina to make his way in a noisy, competitive environment of nearly 350 boys? As it turned out, his Westminster School years were very satisfying for Cowper.

> When comforts are declining,
>   He grants the soul again
> A season of clear shining
>   To cheer it after rain.
>   (*P,* 1:188)

He wrote in one of his Olney hymns that he had enjoyed peaceful hours at home. But a child as finely attuned as he to the emotions of other people must have been grieved in his earliest years by the deaths in the Berkhamsted rectory of three infant siblings, a two-year-old sister, and finally his mother. Forty-two years after he entered Westminster, he wrote about her to a friend. "I can truly say that not a week passes, (perhaps I might with equal veracity say a day) in which I do not think of her" (*L,* 2:294).

This is a statement of unresolved grief. The worst imaginable circumstances in which the boy Cowper could have begun to accept his grief were at the school run by Dr. Pittman or at the London home of the Disneys. As Andrew Brink writes, "Cowper's authoritarian father decided that the boy should lose all the familiar physical elements of attachment at the moment of an overwhelming loss of his primary attachment object."[1] There was a sense in which Cowper lost not only his mother but his father as well. He remarried just as the boy was entering Westminster.

Cowper entered this school with "a sense of separation, isolation and desertion," which in his entire life he never entirely lost.[2] Post-Freudian psychiatry has provided striking insights into the lives of men who have experienced in early years the loss of a mother. These insights include the necessity for resolving and expressing this deep grief. David Aberbach writes, "The yearning and searching which subside in the normal grief process become chronic in pathological grief."[3]

In 1742, as in other significant turning points in his later life, William Cowper made a courageous new start. Notwithstanding the difficulties of his earliest years, Cowper demonstrated at Westminster bravery and determination. As an entering student, he called forth imaginative resources sufficient to understand what Westminster offered that he could embrace: scholarship, friendship, and his own identity.

A splendid era in the history of Britain's Westminster School corresponded with the headmastership of Dr. John Nicoll, 1733–1753. William Cowper was enrolled from 1742 to 1749. As Charles Ryskamp has written, "At this moment the first school in the land was Westminster."[4] A history of the school states, "Dr. Nicoll had great personal charm, and in many ways seems to have been ahead of his time. In that rod-ridden age he trusted 'his boys,' as he affectionately called them, and was content to leave the honor of the school in their hands."[5]

The classics were the basis of a Westminster education. Cowper and his classmates mastered the rules of Latin and Greek, memorized passages of ancient literature, knew the dates and crucial events of ancient history. But since the school had a ratio of one master to fifty boys, it was fortunate that private studies were encouraged and supervised by Dr. Nicoll.

Especially important to Cowper, the headmaster took trouble to prepare students for confirmation in the Church of England. "I believe most of us were struck by his manner, and affected by his exhortation" (*L*, 1:7).

At eighteen Cowper left Westminster an educated young man, the master of Latin, Greek, French, and Italian, widely read, head of his house, and the third-ranking scholar in the sixth form.

Considering Cowper's suffering when he was only eight at the hands of an older bully at Dr. Pittman's school, it was fortunate that a gradual change had come about in the English public school. Earlier, as Lawrence Stone writes, "In the first year the boy is a virtual slave at the mercy of the older boys." And when this same boy is older "in his turn acts as a cruel and arbitrary tyrant toward his juniors."[6]

Flogging by headmasters and teachers was the norm before the more civilized approach used by Dr. Nicoll. Earlier, in post-Restoration Westminster, "Dr. Busby was famous both for his pedagogic excess and for his enthusiasm for flogging." Indeed, he had been "notorious for savagery."[7]

Although the emotional health of Westminster students in Dr. Nicoll's time was much improved, living conditions varied greatly according to a boy's finances. Many were crowded into small rooms, and it was not uncommon for several to sleep in the same bed. These conditions were favorable for the spread of communicable diseases, especially smallpox, which Cowper contracted when he was twelve or thirteen. No specific information is available about how Westminster cared for victims of smallpox. Certainly masters, boys, and parents had every reason to be alarmed.

In the eighteenth century, bizarre theories of contagious diseases included "noxious miasms," and "venomous corpuscles," the most prominent advocate of this view being the renowned Dr. Hermann Boerhaave of Leyden. Lacking modern vaccination, "by 1800 smallpox still caused a third of all blindness and killed an estimated four hundred Europeans each year."[8] As Donald Hopkins points out, neither princes nor peasants were exempt.

London experienced epidemics in 1731, 1734, and 1736. As scientific knowledge grew, the popularity of inoculation grew as well. In 1746 the London Small-Pox and Inoculation Hospital was founded. In the middle of the eighteenth century, about one fourth of all mankind was being killed, blinded, or disfigured for life by smallpox.

Cowper wrote about the effect of smallpox on his eyes. There is no rational explanation for his idea that smallpox cured his eye troubles! What is factually certain is that smallpox has always severely damaged the eyes of many of its victims and blinded others while some patients' eyes simply improve and return to normal as the disease progresses.

In his Westminster years William Cowper began to experience the support and pleasure that would always come from his remarkable gift for friendship. At school Cowper swam and rode and excelled at cricket and football with his friends. His closest bonds were forged with young men who were, like himself, inveterate readers and writers, boys with "simple, amiable, gentle manners and with a similar relish for humour."[9]

The story of Cowper's friendship with Walter Bagot serves as one example. Cowper's earliest surviving letter was written in 1750 to his friend Watty Bagot who was still at Westminster while Cowper had moved on to Greville Street to study law at Mr. Chapman's house (*L*, 1:65). The law was an excellent choice for many gentlemen and scholars leaving Westminster, but it would be an ill-fated choice for William Cowper. He was still in good, boyish spirits, however, when he wrote to Bagot, joking that mail would only have to travel the mile and a half on London streets between them. To tell Watty about his new life, Cowper quoted Shakespeare's *Henry IV.* "I myself am an humble Servant to old Father Antick the Law" (*L*, 1:65).

Three decades passed before Cowper and Bagot had a real opportunity to renew their friendship. The intervening years were times of difficulty and isolation for Cowper. As to Bagot, he became rector of Blithfield and Leish, Staffordshire, in 1759. He married in 1773 and had seven children before his wife Ann died at age thirty-one in 1786.

In 1785 Bagot heard from Cowper, whose plan was being established to publish a new English edition of Homer by subscription. Bagot gave money and promised Cowper his support. Cowper received this news with pleasure. Soon Cowper, with the aid of his prodigious memory, was writing to Watty in his uniquely observant and personal way, "I remember your brother Richard most perfectly, and have his face and figure now before me; his light brown short curling hair, . . . his round plump face, and the smile that seldom deserted it" (*L*, 2:465).

The following month Cowper wrote again, expressing warmth and compassion as though he were talking face to face with his friend. Bagot's wife had just died, and the bereaved husband had quoted Job in Latin when he wrote to Cowper. "My harp is turning into mourning, and my music into the voice of weeping." Cowper replied, "Alas! Alas! My dear, dear friend, may God comfort you. . . . I feel for you as I never felt for man before!" (*L*, 2:486).

Cowper's gift for friendship enabled him to write of his own difficulties and sorrows in a uniquely candid, unreserved, and even self-mocking tone. In 1868 he wrote twice to Bagot from Olney at a critical juncture in his friendships with Mary Unwin and Lady Hesketh and before his proposed move to Weston Underwood.

"We [Cowper and Mary] have long lived a life perfectly recluse." He told Bagot in May that Lady Hesketh was coming to stay in the vicarage. "So that henceforth you must conceive of me no longer as a hermit, but as a man of the world. When the Winter rains come I shall probably relapse into my Cell again" (*L*, 2:554).

A sentence he wrote to Lady Hesketh highlights the simplicity and grace that characterized Cowper's many friendships. "I love Bagot sincerely because he has a singular affection for me" (*L*, 2:487). Four lines of verse illumine Cowper's understanding of true friendship.

> Long shine the star, what Star soere it be,
> That Tempers and inclines thine heart to me,
> For if a Star can temper and incline
> The heart to friendship, thou hast also thine.
> (P, 3:4).

Along with scholarship and friendship, Cowper carried throughout his life his identity as a gentleman as expressed in the code of Westminster

School. Later chapters will show the determination required for him to be such a gentleman in a town like Olney, where he had little money and few books and was isolated by emotional frailty from the gentleman's epicenter—London.

Being a gentleman was important because in the mideighteenth century "traditional society looked, above all, to two ideals: the ideal of a Christian, and the ideal of a gentleman."[10] That is to say that a gentleman was identified by the Anglican Church and by the aristocracy and gentry. William Cowper's parents were both from distinguished families. Not all family members had substantial money or extensive landholdings "but wealth could only outweigh birth within the ranks of those already known to be gentlemen."[11]

The unique characteristic of the English elite was "the solidarity not of a caste or of an economically-defined class but, principally, of a culturally-defined elite. Nowhere else in Europe was school education so important to the structure of the elite's code."[12] The great schools like Eton and Westminster demanded mastery of the classics in "preparing their charges to take their place within an aristocratic world of values by an acquaintance with the patrician ideals of classical civilization . . ."[13]

"Dr. John Nicoll, Headmaster of Westminster 1733–53, was admired because he . . . had the art of making his scholars gentlemen; for there is a court of honour in that school to whose unwritten laws every member of our community was amenable and which to transgress by any act of meanness that exposed the offender to public contempt was a degree of punishment, compared to which the being sentenced to the rod would have been considered as an acquittal or reprieve."[14]

3

O, ASK NOT WHERE CONTENTMENT MAY ABIDE

1750–1753

A t the age of eighteen, being tolerably furnished with grammatical knowledge but as ignorant in all points of religion as the satchel on my back, I was taken from Westminster and, having spent about three months at home, was sent to acquire the practice of the law with an attorney" (*L*, 1:8). For three years Cowper lived with a lawyer, Mr. Chapman, on Greville Street in the legal district of London. Then he moved to the Temple, London's center for the study and practice of the law. These were not years of contentment.

> O! ask not where Contentment may abide
> In whose still Mansion those true Joys abound
> That pour sweet Balm o'er Fortune's fest'ring Wound,
> On Honest Minds alone she deigns to wait.
>
> (*P*, 1:22)

Again, in his *Memoir*, Cowper used the words "taken" and "sent." It was not his plan but his father's that he become a lawyer. His letter to Mrs. King more than thirty years later told his life story. Of the years that his father intended as preparation for the law and even government,

Cowper wrote, "I was bred to the law. A Profession to which I was never much inclined, and in which I engaged rather because I was desirous to gratify a most indulgent Father, than because I had any hope of success in it myself. I spent 12 years in the Temple [including three with Mr. Chapman] where I made no progress in that science to cultivate which I was sent thither" (*L*, 3:120–21).

In a sharper vein he wrote to Frances Hill of the failure of his father's intentions: "My father intended to beget a Chancellor, and he begat instead, a Translator of Homer. It is impossible for the effect to differ more from the intention" (*L*, 2:525).

William Cowper barely pretended to be a law student. He took full advantage of a system so lax that failure to attend meetings or classes could be corrected by paying fines. James King's biography includes a telling description of legal education in Cowper's day:

> The Inns of Court, which included the two Temples, only provided the requisite paper qualifications to practice law. To become a lawyer in the eighteenth century was often a matter of patience and luck. The aspiring barrister or solicitor cultivated connections at the Inns of Court, England's "University in a state of decay." Such a young man might discuss law with his fellows, but the law was usually one topic among many. Sir William Holdsworth has put the matter well: Legal education in the eighteenth century is a very melancholy topic. . . . The law student was obliged to get his knowledge of law by means of undirected reading and discussion, and by attendance in chambers, in a law office, or in courts. At the Inns, there were many ceremonies which were leftovers from the past, but these events had become devoid of educational intent. Meaningless ritual had replaced legal training. The lack of strict regimen at the Temples allowed Cowper to do what came naturally: drift.[1]

As Cowper learned through his later periods of melancholy and madness, the natural and necessary life for him was to work long hours on a daily basis at reading and particularly writing. To drift was fatal for his emotional health. At Westminster it was the hard work in acquiring a classical education that had provided the first substantial happiness he had enjoyed since his mother's death.

Cowper, as his own interpreter, could put his need to work in simple yet powerful words. After a long separation from his beloved cousin Harriet Cowper Hesketh, he was quick to describe himself in his authentic voice: "My dear Cousin, Dejection of Spirits which I suppose may have prevented many a man from becoming an Author, made me one. I find constant employment necessary, and therefore take care to be constantly employ'd" (*L*, 2:382).

Three months later he returned to this theme. "To write was necessary to me." He told his cousin that his translation of Homer was not only a search for fame. Homer "served me for more then two years as an amusement, and as such was of infinite service to my spirits" (*L*, 2:462). To drift as he did at Mr. Chapman's and the Temple was not only bad for his spirits but also a failure in his own mind to honor his father's wishes and live a purposeful life.

In his last years Cowper enjoyed strong and mutually affectionate friendships with men many years younger. For example, he advised his beloved Johnny of Norfolk about the necessity of hard work for a satisfying career: "I was never a regular Student myself but lost the most valuable years of my life in an Attorney's office and in the Temple" (*L*, 3:385). In the same vein but in greater detail he wrote to Samuel Rose:

> Had I employed my time as wisely as you in a situation very similar to yours, I had never been a poet perhaps, but I might by this time have acquired a character of more importance in society, and in a situation in which my friends would have been better pleased to see me. But three years mis-spent in an attorney's office were almost of course followed by several more equally mis-spent in the Temple, and the consequence has been, as the Italian Epitaph says — Sto qui. The only use I can make of myself now, at least the best, is to serve in terrorem to others when occasion may happen to offer, that they may escape so far as my admonitions can have any weight with them, my folly and my fate. (*L*, 3:304–5)

During the three years at Mr. Chapman's, Cowper spent many hours, neither employed nor drifting but in the embrace of family life. Sometimes he went home to Berkhamsted to see his father, his stepmother of ten years, Rebecca, and his teenaged brother, John, a pupil at Felsted School. Cowper never described these visits in his letters. Only speculation can throw light on Cowper's possible visits during his father's life-threatening illness at age fifty-six.

Cowper had another home, again not in London, but in Norfolk, where his mother's brother Roger Donne was rector of Catfield. Roger and his wife, Harriet Judith Rival Donne, had five children—William Cowper's beloved Norfolk cousins. As he wrote years later to the youngest Donne cousin, Rose, his "days of Infancy" at Berkhamsted had been enjoyed with his playfellow Elizabeth, the oldest of the cousins and an only child for ten years. When William was five years old, Elizabeth was eleven, "making the parsonage ring with laughter." He wrote that Elizabeth "probably remembers more of my Childhood than I can recollect either of hers or of my own. But this I know, that the days of that period were happier than most that I have known since" (*L*, 3:430).

Cowper enjoyed visiting the Donne cousins in Catfield. In later childhood his favorite was Harriet, who later married Richard Balls, the second-oldest cousin. Five years William's senior, she was "an unaffected, plain-dressing, good-tempered, cheerful cousin and playmate" for "many an hour merry at Catfield." "Oh when shall we ride in a Whiskum-Snivel [old-fashioned gig] again, and laugh as we have done heretofore?" he asked her forty years after he had last seen her (*L*, 3:432).

In her fifties, Harriet Balls had to sell her extensive Catfield estate of eighty acres, the mansion house, and other buildings. William wrote to say that he wished she could have kept the property. "For of all places in the earth I love Catfield, and should then have had a chance of seeing it again" (*L*, 3:432).

Cowper visited his Donne relatives in Catfield in the early 1750s when he was living in London at Mr. Chapman's. But in these years the home and family most important to him lived at 30 Southampton Row in London. John Cowper, father of William and son of Judge Spencer

Cowper, was seven years older than his brother Ashley, William Cowper's uncle. Ashley and his wife, Dorothy Oakes, had eight children in ten years. Three daughters survived infancy: Harriet, born in 1733, Theodora Jane, born about a year later, and Elizabeth Charlotte, the youngest.

William Cowper's life was closely entwined with Ashley, Harriet, and Theodora. As related in Cowper's *Memoir,* the story of these complex relationships began when, having been "sent to acquire the practice of law," Cowper "was at liberty to spend my leisure time, which was well nigh all my time, at my uncle's at Southampton Row" (*L,* 1:8). Many years later he wrote in the same vein to Harriet, who had married Sir Thomas Hesketh. "I did actually live 3 years with Mr. Chapman a Solicitor, that is to say I slept three years in his house, but I lived, that is, spent my days in Southampton Row, as you very well remember. There was I, the future Lord Chancellor, constantly employed from morning to night in giggling and making giggle instead of Studying the Law" (*L,* 2:523).

The house at 30 Southampton Row was in a rural more than a city setting. As King wrote, "Ashley's house overlooked the gardens and fields of Bedford Estates and the open land stretched away to Hampstead." As Cowper put it, "I am now settled in my new territories commanding Bedford gardens, and all the fields as far as Highgate and Hampstead, with such a concourse of moving pictures as would astonish you; so rus-in-urbe-ish, that I believe I shall stay here . . . here is air and sunshine, and quiet . . . to comfort you."[2]

William Cowper and his uncle Ashley Cowper were already friends when the nineteen-year-old, uncommitted, drifting lawyer-to-be began to spend all his time at Ashley's house. Cowper had vacationed in younger days with Ashley and his family at Southampton, a popular spa resort. Freemantle House was a wooded estate in the east part of the city. Later, in 1765, Cowper wrote to Harriet Hesketh in reply to an invitation: "You cannot think how glad I am to hear you are going to commence lady and mistress of Freemantle. I know it well, and could go to it from Southampton blind-fold. You are kind to invite me to it, and I shall be so kind to myself as to accept the invitation, though I should not for a slight consideration be prevailed upon to quit my beloved retirement at Huntingdon" (*L*, 1:114–15).

The friendship between uncle and nephew was strained by William's unhappy love for Theadora and by Ashley's refusal to agree to their marriage. But William wrote to Joseph Hill when Ashley's wife died in May of 1783, conveying "affectionate respect" to his uncle. As always in commenting about a death in the family or of someone he loved, Cowper was gracious: "I feel for my Uncle, and do not wonder that his loss afflicts him. A connexion that had subsisted so many years could not be rent asunder without great pain to the Survivor" (*L*, 2:135).

Cowper appreciated Ashley's longtime encouragement of his own writing. In a letter to Harriet Hesketh in 1785 Cowper said: "It gives me the sincerest pleasure that my Uncle was so satisfied with my book. . . . He was always favorable to my versifying efforts, and upon the strength of his encouragements I began in very early days to think myself somebody" (*L*, 2:427–28).

Harriet Cowper was not yet twenty when William began to spend "well nigh all his time" at Southampton Row. Harriet played many complex roles in Cowper's life, the first one, at this time, as the sister of Cowper's sweetheart. Except for part of the 1760s and '70s when they were out of touch, Harriet devoted her time and notable energy to Cowper's welfare. A letter from Cowper to Thomas Park of July 15, 1793, summed up his feelings for Harriet: "When you saw Lady Hesketh, you saw the relation of mine with whom I have been more intimate, even from childhood than any other. She has seen much of the world, understands it well, and having great natural vivacity, is of course one of the most agreeable companions" (*L*, 4:369).

When Cowper wrote to Harriet at the time of her father, Ashley's, death, he was thinking as well of the possibility of her own death. "Be not hasty my Dear to accomplish thy journey, for of all that live thou art one whom I can least spare, for thou also art one who shall not leave thy equal behind thee" (*L*, 3:177).

As it turned out, Harriet died seven years after William. In the year before her passing, she confessed to Hayley that she had been in love with William Cowper. Now that she was old, she felt entitled to speak her sentiments. "There was no period of my life in which I should not have gloried in being known to the whole World as the decided Choice of Such a Heart as Cowper's!"[3]

In Cowper's last letter to Harriet before his complete breakdown of 1763, he wrote disparagingly of his attempt to prepare for the position of clerk of journals in the House of Lords. He said he had weaknesses and always disappointed expectations. "O, my good Cousin! If I was to open my heart to you, I could shew you strange sights." His last paragraph began, "Adieu, my dear Cousin! So much as I love you, I wonder how the Deuce it has happened I was never in love with you" (L, 1:94).

The numerous biographers of Cowper, writing shortly after his death in 1800 and continuing through the two hundred years since, have tried to decipher the feelings that William and Theadora, Harriet's sister, had for each other. Some claim flatly that William loved his cousin greatly. Others complicate the relationship to such a degree that romance is all but buried. When William and Thea (called Delia in his poems) were seeing each other virtually every day at Southampton Row, he was nineteen, she sixteen. While his early years have been well chronicled, little is known about Thea before the days of her romance with Cowper. Certainly she was beautiful, as he celebrated in "A Song."

> The sparkling eye, the mantling cheek,
> The polish'd front, the snowy neck,
>   How seldom we behold in one!
> Glossy locks, and brow serene,
> Venus' smiles, Diana's mien,
>   All meet in you, and you alone.
>   (P, 1:13)

Although one of Cowper's greatest gifts was to bring those he loved vividly to life with his pen as a paintbrush, he has left us no clear picture of his sweetheart. She seems out of focus, as vague as her sister Harriet is vivid.

In some of his first poems about Delia, Cowper sounded like an immature young man, falling in love with love, toying with a passing infatuation. He told Delia his symptoms: thinking only of her, trying in vain to read or to carry on a conversation. Once he didn't show her what he had written for fear of offending her. Their quarrels were as insubstantial as her refusal to give him a ringlet of her hair. But then there was a reason for childish disagreements:

> You knew, Dissembler! all the while,
> How sweet it was to reconcile
> > (*P,* 1:30)

Cowper wrote at this time several poems of a starkly different nature. In "Mortals! Around Your Destin'd Heads," he spoke of a Wreck'd Mariner, always his most tragic image of himself.

> Thus the Wreck'd Mariner may strive
> > Some Desart Shore to gain,
> Secure of Life, if he survive
> > The fury of the Main.

> But there, to Famine doom'd a prey,
> > Finds the mistaken Wretch,
> He but escaped the troubled Sea,
> > To perish on the Beach.
> > > (*P,* 1:26–27)

While toying with Delia and exploring the superficial aspects of young love, Cowper understood himself in a totally different way and was his own interpreter as he searched for contentment. He spoke of his mind as a mansion, perhaps using his prodigious memory to recall Shakespeare's phrase, "the mansion of my heart" (Cymbeline 3.4.70). He prefigured Wordsworth's "Tintern Abbey": "Thy mind shall be a mansion for all lovely forms."

O! ask not where Contentment may abide
   In whose still Mansion those true Joys abound
   that pour sweet Balm o'er Fortune's fest'ring Wound, . . .
   On Honest Minds alone she deigns to wait.

(P, 1:22)

Cowper's mind was honest enough to grasp the substance of his "fest'ring wound." His mother's death, the loneliness of a bereaved boy in boarding school and at the oculists, the separation from the only place where he had lived with his mother—the rectory at Berkhamsted.

The fest'ring wound was also a family matter. In his brief life story written in 1791 for Mrs. King, he included a telling reference to his "fits of dejection" and "melancholy." "But it pleased God that I should be born in a country where melancholy is the national characteristic, and of a house more than commonly subject to it" (*L*, 3:551). There is no way to know how many Cowpers in his and previous generations suffered from depression.

There is a mystery that in the great amount of information about the Cowpers and their families presented in William's own writings, as well as in the exhaustive research of his biographers, only two references have been found to Ashley's wife, Dorothy Oakes, the mother of his three surviving daughters and of the numerous other children who had died early in life. Dorothy was mentioned as being present at tea when Harriet first met William, then a student at Westminster. When Dorothy died, she was mentioned by William when he sent through Joseph Hill his condolences to Ashley.

Some facts are known about family melancholy in the cases of William, Ashley, and Theadora. Harriet Cowper Hesketh knew the whole story of family depressions, at times concealing the facts, at other times candid. She wrote to her cousin William in 1786: "You know both my father and sister never were fond of Company, and I think this has increased greatly upon him lately, even more I believe than even my Sister now finds pleasant, as he really does not wish to see even his nearest Relations."[4]

The year after William died and more than a decade after her father's death, Harriet was in close communication with William Hayley. She told him that

> tho' nobody had in general finer Spirits, or more Animation than her father yet he was subject to a degree of low Spirits, which wd sometimes hang upon him for months together, and which were almost as affecting to see as those which you & I Sir have witness'd with so much Pain! My dear Father's were different indeed in some respects, as he was always perfectly quiet and Composed, avoided Company, and never Join'd in any Conversation, but he was not apparently actuated by those horrors, which were permitted So cruelly to distress his Invaluable Nephew![5]

Whether thinking of his own fest'ring wound or of the melancholy of others in the family, William Cowper knew well that "the Grief of a wounded Spirit is of all the most dreadfull" (*L*, 1:156).

Like her father, Ashley, and her cousin William, Theodora was subject to debilitating depressions. Hers became an unlived life. Barely twenty when her father refused permission for her to marry William, her would-be husband recorded her promise to love him always.

> Fear not that time, where'er we rove,
> Or absence, shall abate my love.
>
> (*P,* 1:35)

As fuel to feed this promise, she kept all Cowper's letters, every piece of tangible evidence that he had once loved her. She lived a long life, twenty-four years more after William's death, clinging to her disappointment until she died in 1824. There was no question of her lifelong seclusion and wide evidence as well that her depression at times deepened into insanity.

Cowper told Hill in 1769 that Theodora had been, like himself, a patient at Dr. Cotton's asylum. "I find that the vacancy I left at St. Alban's is filled up by a near relation" (*L*, 1:207). In a letter of her old age to William Hayley, Theodora wrote, "I have long since been a Wander[er] and Vagabond upon the Face of the Earth. . . . By a long continuance of Sorrow, the Mind loses the power of being susceptible of Joy." On certain days she found it "difficult to hold a Pen."[6]

Unlike Ashley and Theodora, William Cowper recorded in all its terrible reality his own depressions and descents into madness. His *Memoir* described 1753, when the festering wound opened and all contentment was lost: "I was struck not long after my settlement in the Temple with such a dejection of spirits as none but they who have felt the same can have the least conception of. Day and night I was upon the rack, lying down in horrors and rising in despair. I presently lost all relish to those studies I have been before closely attached to; the classics have no longer any charm for me; I had need of something more salutary than mere amusement, but had none to direct me where to find it" (*L*, 1:8).

Cowper discovered the poems of George Herbert and "poured upon him all day long." He continued in a depressed state of mind "near a twelvemonth." He then went to Southampton for several months of vacation with Harriet, her fiancé Thomas Hesketh, and other friends. "I was also a Sailor, and being of Sir Thomas Hesketh's party, who himself was a born one, was often pressed into service." Cowper, not being a born sailor, disliked much "to be occupied in great waters unless in the finest weather. . . . Being surrounded with water I was as much continued in it as if I had been surrounded by fire" (*L*, 2:377).

He joked that he was as glad to get off the yacht as Noah was to leave the ark or Jonah to exit the whale. Soon after Cowper arrived at Southampton, his depression was much relieved: "After our arrival we walked together to a place called Freemantle about two miles from the town. The morning was clear and calm; the sun shone bright upon the sea; and the country upon the borders of it was the most beautiful I had ever seen. We sat down upon an eminence at that end of the arm of the sea which runs between Southampton and the New Forest. Here it was that of a sudden, as if another sun had been kindled that instant in the heavens on purpose to dispel sorrow and vexation of spirit, I felt the weight of all my misery taken off. My heart became light and joyous in a moment, and had I been alone, I could have wept with transport" (*L*, 1:9).

But the benefits of this vacation time were much exaggerated. His "light and joyous heart" returned to the problems of Berkhamsted and London, to his troubled romance with Theadora, and his empty life as a nonlawyer.

In the poem written at Berkhamsted that included Thea's promise of lifelong fidelity, Cowper wrote that the "change from joy to woe" was quick and brought on "dark clouds of sorrow, pain and care." He said succinctly, "Delia and I must separate" (*P*, 1:35). In another poem at this time he said that she had consulted "her parents' will, regardless of her own" (*P*, 1:48).

In another poem he fantasized about escaping with Delia to a sylvan shade where they could "gently spin out the silken thread of life" (*P*, 1:42). He called this place their Eden. Years later he wrote, "O yes I saw my Paradise before me—but I also saw the flaming Sword that must for ever keep me from it."[7] This was the "fiery sword" of Milton's angel, barring Adam and Eve from Eden.

When the blessing of Delia was "snatched from his arms," Cowper's emotional health worsened. He imagined himself with Delia trying to fly like embodied souls to their native sky.

> When lo! the force of some resistless weight
> Bears me straight down from that pernicious height;
> Parting, in vain our struggling arms we close;
> Abhorred forms, dire phantoms interpose;
> With trembling voice on thy lov'd name I call,
> And gulphs yawn ready to receive my fall.
>
> (*P*, 1:43)

Theadora's parents naturally were aware of Cowper's depression in 1753 and surely heard from Harriet whether or not the Southampton vacation had helped Cowper. The poems to Delia revealed Cowper's state of mind. It is difficult to see how Ashley and his wife could have permitted their young, very unsophisticated daughter to marry a desperate, unstable man with no immediate prospects of employment.

4

A FIERCE BANDITTI

1754–1763

After his emotional breakdown of 1753, Cowper returned to his London life at the Temple. He continued his pattern of idleness, still not applying himself to the study of the law. He assumed a jocular façade and imitated the life of a rake. But a new quality of hysteria was evident in his writing. An example was the first of a lifetime of letters Cowper wrote to his staunch friend and financial adviser, Joseph Hill. Cowper used doggerel to request that his rooms at the Temple be made ready by his laundress.

> To that Town I shall Trot
> (No I lie, I shall not,
> For to Town I shall Jog in the Stage)
> On October the Twentieth,
> For my Father consenteth
> To make me the Flower of the Age!
>
> So bid her prepare
> Every Table and Chair,
> And Warm well my Bed by the Fire,
> And if this be not done
> I shall break her Back bone
> As sure as I ever come nigh her.
> *(L, 1:77–8)*

Letters to Chase Price, his friend from Westminster, joke about which of them was a more genuine coxcomb. Cowper's sexual bravado is intermixed with descriptions of a life of all play and no work. "Dancing all last Night; In bed one half of the Day & Shooting all the other half, and now am going to—what? To kill a boding Screech Owl perch'd upon a—Walnut Tree just by my Window, have at you old Wise Acre!" (*L*, 1:74–75).

Cowper even tried to make light of his depression, claiming he was jovial and merry. The masquerade was unsuccessful. As his biographer King concisely put it, "William Cowper applied a hard veneer to his tender spirit."[1] In 1754 when Cowper was trying to cover his difficulties with a jocular façade, he wrote "An Epistle to Robert Lloyd, Esq." Here, as so many times in the future, he acknowledged that his purpose was not to show genius or wit,

> But to divert a fierce banditti
> (Sworn foes to every thing that's witty!),
> That, with a black infernal train,
> Make cruel inroads in my brain,
> And daily threaten to drive thence
> My little garrison of sense:
> The fierce banditti, which I mean,
> Are gloomy thoughts led on by Spleen.
> (*P*, 1:55)

On July 9, 1756, the death of Rev. John Cowper, William's father, was an overwhelming loss for the son. With John Cowper's passing, William felt that he had lost his native land, the only place where he had known his mother. As he later wrote to Samuel Rose,

> When my Father died I was young; too young to have reflected much. He was Rector of Berkhamstead, and there I was born. It had never occurred to me that a parson has no fee simple in the House and glebe he occupies. There was neither Tree nor Gate nor stile in all that country to which I did not feel a relation, and the House itself I preferred

to a palace. I was sent for from London to attend him in his last illness, & he died just before I arrived. Then, and not 'till then, I felt for the first time that I and my native place were disunited for ever. I sighed a long adieu to fields and woods from which I once thought I should never be parted, and was at no time so sensible of their beauties as just when I left them all behind me to return no more. (*L*, 3:42–43)

In June of the year following his father's death, Cowper was back in Berkhamsted undertaking with his brother the difficult and distasteful task of dividing up his father's property under the direction of his stepmother, Rebecca. He wrote to John Duncombe on July 16 saying how uncomfortable his former home was to him at that moment. "I believe no man ever quitted his Native Place with Less Regrett than myself." Except for a few friends, "I should never wish to see either the place or anything that belongs to it again." Obviously, Cowper wrote in the heat of a distressing moment! He asked that his father's gold sleeve buttons be sent to Duncombe because "My poor Father has often been the better for your Drollery." Duncombe had a knack for making Rev. John Cowper laugh (*L*, 1:78–79).

Cowper lost not only his native place but also the father who had been "taking" and "sending" his son for almost twenty years. After Ann Donne Cowper died, William had no choice about going at age seven to boarding school, then to live with oculists, next to Westminster, and finally to study law. Nor had the boy been given a choice about being in London rather than in the fields and woods around the modest Berkhamsted rectory, which he considered a palace.

On the other hand, William had also lost in his father an amiable and indulgent protector. Ten years later, he wrote to Mrs. Madan about seeing his native place from twelve miles away. The sight affected him greatly. His childhood and youth "passed in review before me . . . and these were followed by such a tender Recollection of my dear Father and all his Kindness to me, the Amiableness and Sweetness of his Temper & Character, that I went out into the Orchard and burst forth into Praise and Thanksgiving to God for having made me the son of a Parent whose remembrance was so sweet to me" (*L*, 1:183).

After his father died, Cowper did not turn decisively from his life as a law student. As his father's property was being divided, William bought chambers at the Inner Temple. He was still "sent."

In the year after his father died, Cowper wrote two poems of compelling power, speaking in an authentic voice of self-understanding. He described not a carefree law student in London, but a drowning seaman. He wrote not of a debonair playboy, but of a lost wanderer.

> The seaman thus, his shatter'd vessel lost,
>   Still vainly strives to shun the threat'ning death;
> And while he thinks to gain the friendly coast,
>   And drops his feet, and feels the sands beneath,
>
> Borne by the wave, steep-sloping from the shore,
>   Back to th' inclement deep, again he beats
> The surge aside, and seems to tread secure;
>   And now the refluent wave his baffled toil defeats.
>
> (*P*, 1:40)

These poems included expressions of his authentic feelings for Theadora.

> And Her—thro' tedious years of doubt and pain,
> Fix'd in her choice, and faithful—but in vain!
> O prone to pity, generous, and sincere,
> Whose eye ne'er yet refus'd the wretch a tear;
> Whose heart the real claim of friendship knows,
> Nor thinks a lover's are but fancied woes;
> See me—ere yet my destin'd course half done,
> Cast forth a wand'rer on a wild unknown!
> See me neglected on the world's rude coast,
> Each dear companion of my voyage lost!

Nor ask why clouds of sorrow shade my brow!
And ready tears wait only leave to flow!
Why all, that sooths a heart, from anguish free,
All that delights the happy—palls with me!
(P, 1:62–63)

Five years after his depression of 1753, Cowper was still not apply-ing himself to the law. In a letter of August 1758 to Clatworthy Rowley, he claimed that his idleness in London was to him "a most agreeable life." He knew better. He also boasted to his friend of "a blessed three days" in Greenwich where he claimed to have been "tortured with love."

"There I found that lovely and beloved little girl of whom I have often talked to you; she is at that age, sixteen, at which every day brings with it some new beauty to her form. No one can be more modest, nor (which seems wonderful in a woman) more silent; but when she speaks, you might believe that a Muse was speaking. Woe is me that so bright a star looks to another region; having risen in the West Indies, thither it is about to return, and will leave me nothing but sighs and tears. You see me tortured with love, I, you with lasciviousness" (*L,* 1:81–82).

An agreeable life in London would require money. In November 1758 he admitted the same to Duncombe but only in a jocular vein. He admitted to his longtime friend that his years of ignoring his law stud-ies worked against his own interest. "I am not fond of the Law, but I am very fond of the money that it produces" (*L,* 1:83).

Soon there was another death in William's family, that of his step-mother, Rebecca, on July 31, 1762. That very same day, he wrote to Harriet Hesketh about the fortune left "to be divided equally between my brother and myself . . . a division not very unlike splitting a hair . . ." This fragment of his letter was preserved by Harriet, who probably destroyed the last pages, which may have expressed Cowper's resentment of Rebecca (*L,* 1:89).

In September Cowper was still putting a lighthearted veneer on his diminishing resources. He told Rowley, "I have no Estate [as it] happens." He advised Rowley to adopt his own resolution "never to be melancholy while I have a hundred pounds in the world to keep up my Spirits." He said his basic need was for "clean Linnen and good Company" (*L*, 1:90–91).

The storm gathering around his lack of employment was described by Cowper in his *Memoir*. With all jocularity gone, he said he was "apprehensive of approaching want . . . there being no appearance that I should ever repair the damage by a fortune of my own getting" (*L*, 1:13). He would have to accept help. Ashley Cowper had long been clerk of the Parliaments. The position was a notorious sinecure, the duties performed by clerk assistants.[2] In the period leading up to William's crucial financial need in 1763, there had been a cloud around Ashley of reprimands and accusations of favoritism and dishonesty.

The final crisis for William was the result of his desire for the clerkship of journals, a post in which he could work in private, transcribing minutes into journals. The House of Lords insisted that he had to be examined and thus prove publicly that he was fit for this clerkship. But Cowper wrote that "they whose spirits are formed like mine, to whom a public exhibition of themselves on any occasion is mortal poison, may have some idea of the horror of my situation" (*L*, 1:15).

How was it that Cowper had "the feelings of a man when he arrives at the place of execution?" (*L*, 1:16). He was conflicted on every point. He had to prepare for the public examination, but he could not concentrate or study. He wanted the clerkship of journals for the money, but if he received the post, his beloved uncle might be accused of nepotism and thus disgraced. How could Cowper be saved from poverty and at the same time uphold Ashley's honor?

In September 1763 he went for a brief vacation to Margate where he enjoyed some cheerful company. According to his biographer Thomas Wright, this break from London was taken on the advice of Dr. William Heberden. In his later poem, "Retirement," Cowper remembered his physician and friend:

Virtuous and faithful HEBERDEN! whose skill
Attempts no task it cannot well fulfill,

Gives melancholy up to nature's care,
And sends the patient into purer air.

(P, 1:385)

Another biographer, David Cecil, wrote of Cowper's time in Margate: "For the time being it certainly did do him good. . . . As he lay on the sand, watching the irregular line of wave break sparkling, and recede, and break again, as far as eye could reach, his troubled spirit sank into a kind of tranquility. . . . But his outward agitation alone was stilled: The trouble that caused it was still as formidable to him as before."[3]

Cowper wrote vividly in his *Memoir* about his fears and despair at this time. "I looked forward to the approaching winter and regretted the flight of every moment that brought it nearer, like a man bourne away by a rapid torrent into a stormy sea from which he sees no possibility of returning, and where he knows he cannot subsist" (*L,* 1:16). This was an accurate preview of Cowper's impending fate, with "reason sunk beneath the storm" (*P,* 1:136). His descent into madness at the close of 1763 would change his life forever.

5

A SONG OF MERCY AND JUDGMENT

1763–1765

William Cowper wrote a spiritual autobiography unique in the literature of religious conversions. It encompasses the three decades from his boyhood to his move to Huntingdon in 1765. He characterized this work as an account of his search for God. Cowper's self-revelations are unusual because he claims to know the moral of the story of his insanity. "But blessed be the God of my salvation for every sigh I drew, for every tear I shed, since thus it pleased Him to judge me here that I might not be judged hereafter" (*L*, 1:34). As Max Byrd explains, "God punishes him for his sins with madness, and thereby redeems him."[1]

As to his sins, Cowper first "charges God with injustice: 'What sins have I committed to deserve this misery?'"(*L*, 1:17). Soon Cowper was tempted to the "dark and hellish purpose of self-murder" (*L*, 1:18). Having failed to kill himself by poison or drowning, he felt as sinful as a companion of devils and as the "just object of His boundless vengeance" (*L*, 1:22). He described himself as a decent, good-natured man in the eyes of the world, but as a rank atheist with a rotten rebellious heart in the eyes of God. Cowper then resumed futile attempts at suicide by knife and hanging, after which, being truly convicted of sin, he despised himself. "I delivered myself over to absolute despair" (*L*, 1:29).

Max Byrd, in his study of madness and literature in the eighteenth century, brilliantly identifies what is unique and authentic about Cowper's autobiography:

> After so many pages covering so many years, how astonishing that here at last is our first account of the experience of madness. Whatever reservations one might hold about Cowper's tone of voice or the nature of his delusions, surely we come here to a new moment, when the madman speaks to us—and we can hear and understand him . . . but now in Cowper's words we encounter, not imagined madness but undeniably madness itself, the voice of a human being speaking across some mysterious, still-dark divide.[2]

Following his suicide attempts, Cowper wrote to his brother John. Then one night, as Cowper's story continues:

> I laid myself down in bed, howling with horror, while my knees smote against each other. In this condition my brother found me; the first word I spoke to him (and I remember the very expression) was, "Oh brother, I am damned—damned." A long series of "still greater terrors" assailed the madman. My hands and feet became cold and stiff; a cold sweat stood upon my forehead; my heart seemed at every pulse to beat its last and my soul to cling to my lips as if upon the very point of departure.
>
> At eleven o'clock, my brother called upon me, and in about an hour after his arrival, that distemper of mind, which I had so ardently wished for, actually seized me. While I traversed the apartment in the most horrible dismay of soul, expecting every moment that the earth would open and swallow me up; my conscience scaring me, the avenger of blood pursuing me, and the city of refuge out of reach and out of sight; a strange and horrible darkness fell upon me. If it were possible, that a heavy blow could light on the brain, without touching the skull, such was the sensation I felt. I clapped my hand to my forehead, and cried aloud through the pain it gave me. At every stroke, my thoughts

and expressions became more wild and incoherent; all that remained clear was the sense of sin, and the expectation of punishment. These kept undisturbed possession all through my illness, without interruption or abatement. (*L,* 1:29–32)

Always, as his life unfolded, a sense of sin was a powerful problem for Cowper. The fundamental nature of his sin was never fully apparent to himself nor to his many biographers and interpreters. But Cowper was able to describe his suffering. "The accuser of brethren was ever busy with me night and day, bringing to my recollection in dreams the commission of long-forgotten sins and charging upon my conscience things of an indifferent nature as atrocious crimes" (*L,* 1:34).

At many junctures in his life, Cowper received the practical and emotional help he needed at the propitious time. In this first of Cowper's periods of insanity, his brother helped him. Also he asked his brother to find his friend and cousin, Martin Madan.[3]

The Reverend Martin Madan was the son of Cowper's Aunt Judith, his father's sister. A man of many interests and talents, he was educated at Westminster and Christ Church, Oxford. He had ambitious careers first as a lawyer and then as a churchman. Martin Madan's religious zeal was the outcome of an evening in 1750 when he heard John Wesley preach on the text, "Prepare to meet thy God." Having entered the meeting as a skeptical spectator, he left as a committed convert. His heart had been dramatically changed.

Not only a dynamic public figure and preacher, Martin Madan was also a kind and compassionate man, ready to respond to William Cowper's conviction, in the throes of madness, that "if there was any 'balm in Gilead' for me his [Madan's] hand must administer it" (*L,* 1:29). Indeed, as Cowper wrote, "Madan treated me with a truly Christian tenderness" (*L,* 1:30). Sitting on the bedside together, Madan explained the principles of Evangelicalism: All men have sinned, but in Christ's death is atonement for all sins. Every person, regardless of the past, may accept the gospel of salvation by living out a lively faith in Jesus as a free gift of God.

Madan's kind exhortations notwithstanding, Cowper's condition did not improve. His brother, in agreement with Madan and other friends, decided to take the patient to Dr. Nathaniel Cotton's asylum in St. Albans. Cowper started the journey in "a sudden ecstasy of joy," but on arriving at the doctor's house he became so afraid of close confinement that three or four people were needed to take him in (*L*, 1:33).

The first five months with Dr. Cotton, as Cowper writes, were "spent in continual expectations of the fatal moment when Divine Vengeance should plunge me into the bottomless abyss" (*L*, 1:37). Cowper said it would "be proper to draw a veil" over "the secrets of my prison house" (*L*, 1:33). But he does record his attempts at suicide, which required that he be "narrowly watched" (*L*, 1:34). Cowper's poem, "A Song of Mercy and Judgment" (*P*, 1:135–37) mentions the noises he heard, the visionary scenes he saw, "Flames of Hell and Screams of Woe." This poem drew no veil over some clinical details. Loathing food, he did not eat. His strength declined and his body wasted away. Being bound and watched, the doctor's asylum was to Cowper "a Pit of Roaring."

Martin Madan had been for Cowper a kind and compassionate pastor. Now Dr. Cotton of St. Albans was to be the physician Cowper needed at this desperate time in January 1764. Later, Cowper remembered his good fortune: "I was carried to Dr. Cotton" who treated him "with the greatest tenderness" and "with the utmost diligence. . . . I had so much need of a religious friend to converse with, to whom I could open my mind upon the subject without reserve, I could hardly have found a fitter person for the purpose" (*L*, 1:101).

Nathaniel Cotton was a physician and popular poet. He had studied medicine at the University of Leyden under the renowned Hermann Boerhaave. Cotton graduated from Leyden in 1730. Returning to England, he lived for forty-eight years in St. Albans during two marriages and in the company of eleven children.

The family home was on St. Peter's Street. Dr. Cotton's professional home was the Collegium Insanorum on Dagnall Street, where he cared in a humane manner for mentally disturbed patients. During his lifetime, Cotton's hospital was "one of the most discreet, exclusive and best-managed establishments of its kind, to which afflicted ladies and gentlemen of a pious nature could retire without fear of maltreatment or other abuses so common at that time in receptacles for lunatics."[4]

Nathaniel Cotton was a private man. An extraordinary coincidence in the life stories of doctor and patient was that both Cotton's and Cowper's mothers had died when their sons were six years old. Cotton never spoke even to his two wives or his many children about his own childhood, never telling where he had lived as a child or with whom. He preferred anonymity. In fact, his popular volume of poems for young readers, *Visions in Verse*, went through eleven editions without the author's name. He explained himself in the opening lines of the book:

> Authors, you know, of greatest Fame
> Thro' Modesty suppress their Name;
> And would you wish me to reveal,
> What these superior Wits conceal?
> Forego the Search, my curious Friend
> And husband Time to better End.
> All my Ambition is, I own,
> To profit and to please, unknown.[5]

Cotton's self-effacing nature was evident in the words he wanted carved on a tomb for himself and his wives: "Here are deposited the remains of Anne, Hannah and Nathaniel Cotton."

A man like this was exactly the person to help Cowper. Far more efficacious than any schedule or medication that Dr. Cotton might have been using was the physician's ability to talk to his patient in a manner more akin to the treatment of madness in the twentieth than the eighteenth century. As Cowper later wrote about Dr. Cotton, "I shall always respect him. He is truly a philosopher according to my judgment of the character, every tittle of his knowledge in natural subjects being connected in his mind with the firm belief of an Omnipotent agent" (*L*, 2:275).

The turning point of Cowper's hospitalization at the Collegium Insanorum came when, as his spiritual biography records, "he became capable of entering with some small degree of cheerfulness into conversation with the doctor" (*L,* 1:37). On July 25, 1764, Cowper's brother came from Cambridge. William told John that he was "as much better as despair can make me." When John suggested that William's dread of judgment was a delusion, the tormented patient burst into tears. At this point the pace of the autobiographical account quickens. Cowper records a dream of a sweet, dancing boy, surely himself (*L,* 1:38). Later that morning he read Romans 3:25. "Whom God hath set forth to be a propitiation through faith in his blood, to declare his righteousness for the remission of sins that are past, through the forbearance of God."

The tempo of Cowper's narrative again quickens. Immediately he believed. Immediately the sun of righteousness shone. In a moment he remembered all that Martin Madan had said and he believed it. The words of the autobiography take on a note of near hysteria, Cowper describing himself as being "choked with transport," and "overwhelmed with joy unspeakable" (*L,* 1:39–40).

With his usual good judgment, Dr. Cotton "began to fear lest the sudden transition from despair to joy should terminate in a fatal frenzy" (*L,* 1:40). Cowper himself inserts a detached and factual self-analysis: "I have known many a lifeless and unhallowed hour since—long intervals of darkness interrupted by short returns of joy and peace in believing" (*L,* 1:40). The patient stayed on with his doctor for another year, the two men conversing together every morning.

A modern reader cannot but regret that Cowper had firmly determined that his autobiography be restricted to his religious struggles. Of the time from October 1763 when Cowper became insane through June 1765 when he left St. Albans, many events and thoughts were omitted from his narrative. During the last year with Dr. Cotton, did they ever talk about the deaths of their mothers? Did poetry come into the conversation? An even more tantalizing subject for speculation is how Cowper spent all those days. Did he ever have visitors or write to family members? William's beloved Berkhamsted was only a few miles away. Did he visit the scene of his childhood, where, before his mother died, he was a sweet, dancing boy?

On a June day at four in the morning, William Cowper, age thirty-four, set out from St. Albans to Huntingdon by way of Cambridge. He was traveling alone except for Samuel Roberts, his attendant from the hospital. Throughout his life, Cowper always dreaded a change of place. His pattern of suffering with every move to a new home began when, not yet seven, he had been taken to boarding school and then to live with oculists in London. Abandonment was the fear he never conquered.

Now he traveled away from Dr. Cotton to a place where he would be alone. "I passed the whole time of my journey in silent communion with God" (*L,* 1:43). Perhaps William Cowper recalled his lines in "A Song of Mercy and Judgment," which best express the grace and mercy he sometimes experienced. The Savior speaks:

> I, he said, have seen thee grieving,
> Lov'd thee as I pass'd thee by;
> Be not faithless, but Believing,
> Look, and Live, and never Die.
> (*P,* 1:136)

6

FAR FROM THE WORLD
1765–1767

In late June of 1765 a solitary figure knelt in prayer in the corner of a field in Huntingdon. William Cowper was now absolutely alone. His brother had left to return to Cambridge. At Cowper's lodgings with him were a young orphan boy and Sam Roberts, who had taken care of Cowper at the Collegium Insanorum and, as he wrote, "waited on me with so much patience and gentleness that I could not bear to leave him behind" (*L*, 1:42).

Huntingdon was said in earlier times to have surpassed "all the neighboring towns in the pleasantness of its situation, and in its handsomeness and beauty."[1] At this time it was a simple community of less than two thousand inhabitants. The meadows through which the River Ouse meandered were still unspoiled. William Cobbett wrote that Huntingdon meadows were "by far the most beautiful that I ever saw in my life . . . Here are *bowling-greens* of hundreds of acres in extent, with a river winding through full to the brink."[2] But while he prayed in the meadows for God's help and companionship, Cowper felt "like a traveller in the midst of an inhospitable desert, without a friend to comfort or a guide to direct him" (*L*, 1:43). A year and a half later in January, always his darkest month, he wrote to Lady Hesketh. "My lot is cast in a Country where we have neither Woods nor Commons nor pleasant Prospects. All flat and insipid; in the summer adorned only with blue Willows and in the Winter covered with a Flood" (*L*, 1:156).

On his arrival at Huntingdon, Cowper wrote to Joseph Hill that "by the mercy of God, I am restored to perfect health, both of mind and body." But his loneliness was transcendent. No fervency of prayer in the meadows could sustain his hope that God would make his "solitude sweet" or that the wilderness could "bloom and blossom as the rose." Cowper summarized his status with stark simplicity: "I began to dislike my solitary situation and to fear that I should never be able to weather out the winter in so lonely a dwelling" (*L*, 1:44–45).

In August Cowper met the Unwin family and by November was living as a boarder in their home. The Reverend Morley Unwin was married to Mary Cawthorne Unwin, twenty years his junior. At the time they became Cowper's friends, their son William was twenty-one, their daughter Susanna, eighteen.

Of all Cowper's many close friends and relations, Mary Unwin became the most important. They would never be separated until her death in 1796. Over all these thirty-one years, Cowper wrote about Mary in letters and poems. He best captured the heart of his feeling four months after he became her boarder. "The Lady, in whose house I live is so excellent a Person, and regards me with a Friendship so truly Christian, that I could almost fancy my own Mother restored to Life again, to compensate me for all the Friends I have lost, and all my Connections broken" (*L*, 1:134).

After meeting the Unwins and preparing to move into their home, Cowper wrote a cheerful and optimistic letter to his uncle Major Cowper at the Park. "As to my own personal Condition, I am much happier than the day is long, and Sunshine and Candle light alike see me perfectly contented. I get Books in Abundance, as much Company as I chuse, a deal of *Comfortable Leisure*, and enjoy better Health, I think, than for many Years past. What is there wanting to make me Happy? Nothing if I can but be as thankful as I ought, and I trust that He who has bestowed so many Blessings upon me, will give me Gratitude to crown them All" (*L*, 1:120–21).

Cowper's subsequent letters from his Huntingdon days expressed his determination to start a new life, having left London and St. Albans forever behind. He saw himself permanently retired to the country with gardening as a wholesome pastime. The Olney Hymn "Retirement" expressed his expectations.

> Far from the World, O Lord I flee,
> From strife, and tumult far,
> From scenes, where Satan wages still
> His most successful war.
>
> (*P*, 1:186)

His letters of the midsixties also show that, blessings notwithstanding, he could not live content without his identity as a gentleman or without some contact with friends and family members he had been close to in earlier days. Nor could his all-too-human heart find peace in the barren soil of his distorted faith where judgment far overshadowed mercy.

Joseph Hill was of importance to Cowper as a friend and manager of his meager income. Hill knew William from their years at the Temple and was acquainted with Ashley Cowper and other members of the family. Hill was becoming a successful lawyer, handling the affairs of many wealthy clients. Loyal and infinitely patient with William, Hill struggled for years to help scrape up enough money for his friend to live in genteel poverty. Hill often gave Cowper money and forgave debts Cowper owed him. He was the instigator of gifts to Cowper from family members.

Cowper never took Hill for granted and accepted Hill's expressions of concern with good grace. Later, when Cowper was moving from Huntingdon to Olney, he wrote Hill: "Many more thanks are due to you for the tender and friendly manner in which you bring me acquainted with the Distress that attends my circumstances." He expressed his entire trust in his financial adviser, not harboring the least anxiety about payment but "because I abhor the thought of trespassing upon the Goodness of a faithful Friend" (*L*, 178–79).

Hill's loyalty was tested by Cowper's many letters that urged Hill to accept the gospel. But unlike other subjects of Cowper's insistent evangelism, Hill did not become resentful. Cowper wrote: "The Gentleness and Candour of your manner, engages my Affections to you very much! You answer with Mildness to a Admonition which would have provoked many to Anger" (*L*, 1:206–7).

Some interpreters of Cowper have suggested that he was cavalier about his lack of employment and a spendthrift as well, accepting handouts without compunction. But on becoming a boarder at the Unwins, he wrote to Hill: "It is my fixt purpose to Live upon my Income; in which Resolution I am supported by reflecting, that I have nothing else to Live upon" (*L*, 1:129). He acknowledged that "more Debts than Money has been my Distress this many a day and is likely to continue so. These Deficiencies of money frighten me, lest I should not be able to continue in this comfortable retreat" (*L*, 1:147).

He gave Hill an overview of his situation. When he left St. Albans, there had been special charges and expense for the journey. In his initial lodging there had been housekeeping expenses, some needlessly high because of his inexperience in managing domestic details. Then, too, he still owed money to Dr. Cotton. "I correspond with the little Man because I love him and have great Reason to do so" (*L*, 1:135).

Cowper projected his expenses at the Unwins: rent for his room, wages for Sam Roberts, board for the boy, who might have starved without Cowper's help, and bills from his tailor and draper. Some of Cowper's relatives complained that he was extravagant. But Roberts had known how to care for Cowper in the dire days at St. Albans. Spending money on clothes was the only means Cowper had to announce to the village world of Huntingdon—"I am a gentleman."

In early April of 1766, Cowper wrote to his cousin Mrs. Cowper giving what he called "a Peep into my vile and deceitful heart." He had arranged for William Unwin to call on her at the Park because he wanted Unwin to meet a member of the prominent Cowper family. All strangers at Olney are "suspected Characters, unless they bring their Credentials with them." The villagers had been speculating that he might not be a gentleman but "a mere vagabond." It was important to Cowper that Unwin see for himself the "splendid Connections at the Park" and thereby learn that his friend was not "that fellow Cowper" but a gentleman. Having made this admission in a cheerful enough voice, he concluded the letter by railing at his own "Pride of Heart, Indignation and Vanity." He anticipated that the blood of Christ would take away his "Guilt of Sin" (*L,* 1:162–63).

Ironically, he himself did fear becoming a vagabond, out of touch with friends and family in London. In a letter to Martin Madan, he speculated about the thoughts his friends might be entertaining: "Perhaps I have many friends who pity me, ruined in my profession—stript of my preferment—and banished from all my old acquaintance. They wonder I can sustain myself under those evils and expect that I should die broken hearted" (*L,* 1:129).

Cowper's letters to Lady Hesketh always included affectionate regards to his "connexion." He wondered if his friends were really curious about his situation. "If they really interest themselves in my welfare, it is a mark of their great charity for one who has been a disappointment and a vexation" (*L,* 1:108). His loneliness and sense of isolation were still strong a year later when he referred to the silence of many who "before the affliction that befell me, were ready enough to converse with me" (*L,* 1:132).

Cowper's most often expressed anxieties in the Huntingdon years had to do with lack of money and loss of friends. But his core anxiety was more serious. Having arrived in Huntingdon after a long hospitalization, he aspired to live as a new convert to the gospel of God's saving grace and mercy. He wrote explicitly to Martin Madan that before his conversion he had lived thirty-three years without God. Then God gave him affliction and subsequently took it away. Lastly, God gave two blessings—"faith in His Dear Son" and an "intimate and comfortable assurance of complete salvation" (*L,* 1:107). The agony of Cowper's soul was that he could not enjoy this assurance while imprisoned in his all-pervasive sense of sinfulness.

Cowper knew himself well and could write about himself with striking clarity. In June 1772 he wrote to Mrs. Madan, "Sin is my burthren." Years later, he acknowledged that it was the devil's work that made him regard himself as "the vilest sinner" (*L,* 1:253).

Two recipients of his letters at this time were his Aunt Judith Madan and her daughter Maria Frances Cecilia, wife of her cousin (and William's cousin) Major William Cowper of the Park. Both women were evangelicals along with Martin Madan, who was Judith's son and Maria's brother. To Mrs. Madan Cowper said that he was a wrath-provoking sinner, having lost, after he "came forth from the Furnace, his first love, when the Name of Jesus was like Honey and Milk upon my Tongue" (*L*, 1:168). To Maria Cowper he wrote that God had thundered curses into his heart. "I believed myself Sealed up under eternal Wrath and the Sentence of unspeakable Vengeance" (*L*, 1:138). Here already are words prophetic of Cowper's terrifying poem written seven years later, "Hatred and Vengeance, My Eternal Portion" (*P*, 1:209–10).

He also wrote back and forth with great urgency to Mrs. Cowper debating the theological issue of being able, or not able, to know family members and friends in the future state, that is to say, in heaven. He insisted that this be so. He needed future hope to make the present bearable. There can be no doubt that he lived for the possibility of reunion with his mother.

Over the course of Cowper's first year with the Unwins, he wrote *Adelphi*, his spiritual autobiography, which began with his childhood and continued through February 1767. While writing *Adelphi* and letters at the same time, his mind remained fixed on his sinfulness, on insanity or affliction, and on his religious conversion. With Lady Hesketh, who had little sympathy for "methodistical" or "enthusiastic" ways, he tried to use his life story to warn and threaten her about the day of judgment. God had "snatched me like a Brand out of the Burning," he wrote, then "great and grievous afflictions were applied to waken me out of this deep sleep" (*L*, 1:157).

When he permitted Lady Hesketh to read his autobiography, the lesson Cowper intended was to show her "the sovereignty of God's free Grace in the deliverance of a sinfull Soul from the nethermost Hell." Harriet Hesketh's response had a sharply rational edge. She could not see how such a life as Cowper's "could merit such bitter sufferings at the Hand of a Merciful God" (*L*, 1:195).

7

A TRANSIENT,
HALF-SPENT LIFE
1767–1770

The world of the Unwin family and their boarder William Cowper was shattered on July 2, 1767, when the Reverend Morley Unwin died suddenly and in great pain after falling from his horse and fracturing his skull. Before even a week had passed, William Cowper and Mary Unwin had made a decision about the future. As early as July 10, Cowper wrote to Mrs. Madan that he and Mrs. Unwin together would "seek an abode under the Sound of the Gospel." His explanation for the formation of this new household was that "I am a sort of adopted Son in this Family, where Mrs. Unwin has always treated me with Parental Tenderness: Therefore by the Lord's leave, I shall still continue a Member of it" (*L*, 1:170).

Four days after Morley Unwin died, William Cowper and Mary Unwin met John Newton. This meeting had an astonishing outcome: Cowper and Mary Unwin would live next door to John and Mary Newton in Olney for many years. The couples, one in a marriage of unusual devotion, the other in a friendship of love and mutual dependency, remained close through many joys and abundant sorrow.

In September 1767 when William Cowper and Mary Unwin moved into Orchard Side next door to the Olney vicarage, the first blessing the Newtons bestowed on them was a public welcome at church, at home, and in public and private prayers. This welcome was important because even before Morley Unwin died, there had been gossip in Huntingdon about Cowper's place in the Unwin home and the exact nature of his attachment to Mary. Cowper had written to Mrs. Madan that he was weary of Huntingdon. "Neighbors made shocking aspersions about our Names and Conduct, but Mr. and Mrs. Newton have Christian Tenderness and Affection towards us" (*L*, 1:176).

Devoted friends could hardly be more different than William Cowper and John Newton. In early boyhood they had experienced a common sorrow. Their mothers died when they were six. While William went on to insecurity and loneliness at boarding school, Newton's adolescence was shaped by his father's influence and life as a captain in the merchant marine.

Before he was forty years old, Newton wrote an autobiography, *Authentic Narrative*, which was so popular that he became "a public and international figure within the evangelical movement."[1] Newton's life story is still known today and his religious conversion celebrated around the world in the hymn "Amazing Grace." Newton said, "I know of no case more extraordinary than my own."[2]

While Cowper was studying classics at Westminster School and later toying with legal studies while living a desultory life in London, Newton was a slave trader on the high seas, with life-threatening crises too numerous to count—storms and shipwrecks, starvation and fevers. While Cowper won and lost the heart of an over-protected eighteen-year-old beauty, Newton fell passionately in love with Mary Catlett. After years of lengthy separations, they married, living together in happiness and devotion until her death in 1790.

Before conversion to the gospel, Newton's life by any standard could be called dissolute or sinful. But he embraced with joy the forgiveness offered in the doctrine of the Atonement. Cowper, too, wrote of his own conversion, but he was never able to overcome his guilt for sins that, by any standard, were abundantly forgivable.

As vicar at Olney, Newton's far-flung ministry was driven by his extraordinary level of energy. The essence of gospel service for him was "public preaching and private counseling."[3] On Sundays Newton habitually

OLNEY CHURCH.

Tall Spire, from which the sound of cheerfull bells
Just undulates upon the listning ear.

Vide the Task Book I.

Drawn by Ja.s Storer. Engrav'd by Ja.s Greig.

FIGURE 2. *Olney Church,* from *Cowper Illustrated by a Series of views in, or near, the Park of Weston-Underwood, Bucks.* (London: Verner and Hood, 1803). Courtesy of the Library of Congress.

preached an hour-long sermon at two services. This could be just the beginning. "On one single Sunday in 1765 he preached for a total of six hours at church and at home, commenting afterwards, 'if there was occasion I could readily go and preach again.'"⁴ For secular holidays and fair days Newton wrote sermons and hymns and prepared weekly lectures as well. At weddings and funerals, he was never known to forgo an opportunity to preach.

The meeting that brought Newton the most satisfaction was held on Sunday evenings after tea in the vicarage: "I think nothing has been more visibly useful to strengthen my heart, and to unite people closely together in the bonds of love."⁵

On weekday mornings in his study Newton became a profound student of the Bible and conversant with all the many permutations of evangelical theology. "He was a moderate on most matters of theological debate among evangelicals during the last half of the eighteenth century." Even as others disagreed with each other, John Wesley wrote to Newton, "You appear to be designed by Divine Providence for a healer of breaches."⁶

On weekday afternoons Newton made pastoral visits, seeing three or four families in a day. He comforted the sick and afflicted, not only with the gospel of Christ's love, but also with money made available by the wealthy merchant John Thornton. His parish extended far from Olney, generally within a triangle defined by Northampton, Bedford, and Newport Pagnell.

From William Cowper and Mary Unwin's arrival in Olney in 1767 until Cowper's descent into madness in 1773, there was a complex interplay between the activities and events in Cowper's life and his inner torments. After his conversion during his hospitalization at Dr. Cotton's, Cowper often expressed a desire to convert others to his evangelical faith, to "an effectual acquaintance with the Savior" (*L*, 1:191). He proselytized vigorously in letters to his beloved Harriet Hesketh and Joseph Hill. Only years later could he confess that he had been "imprudent, and, I doubt not, troublesome to many. Good is intended, but harm is done too often by the zeal with which I was at the time animated. But as in affairs of this life, so in religious concerns likewise, experience begets some wisdom in all who are not incapable of being taught. I do not now, neither have I for a long time, made it my practice to force the subject of evangelical truth on any . . . Pulpits for preaching, and the parlour, the garden, and the walk abroad for friendly and agreeable conversation" (*L*, 2:509).

Certainly Cowper required activities to relieve his religious preoccupations. Later in the 1770s and during the 1780s he developed the ideal avocation—that most solitary of occupations, writing. But during his first years in Olney, Cowper forced himself to imitate Newton, to pray and proselitize in public. It has been surmised that Newton was vigorously molding his friend to be a person he was not.

In whatever ways Newton deemed best, he took care of his troubled next-door neighbor, living out the Christian compassion he preached. After leaving Olney for the parish of St. Mary Woolnoth in London, Newton continued, even years later as a widower in old age, to correspond with Cowper and visit him as often as possible. Newton wrote to Cowper's beloved friend Johnny Johnson: "Next to the duties of my ministry, it was the business of my life to attend him."[7]

Cowper and Mary Unwin appreciated and accepted Newton's care. At the approach of his sixtieth birthday, Cowper wrote to Newton, "The years we have seen together will never be out of remembrance, and so long as we remember them we must remember you with affection. In the pulpit and out of the pulpit you have labor'd in every possible way to serve us" (*L*, 3:532).

Cowper often described his life in Olney as "unprofitable." He was unable to do what he intended. His uselessness was at "the Root of that Evil Tree which the world Good naturedly calls Bashfulness." He wrote Mrs. Madan about the challenge of leading family prayers when he arrived in Olney. He was torn between fear of praying in public and belief that God required it. He was trembling, harassed, and sick. The conflict was resolved when "the Lord brought me to that point, to choose Death rather than a Retreat from Duty" (*L*, 1:191). Gradually his fears abated, and he sometimes prayed aloud in meetings.

On the surface, the autumn months of 1767 passed smoothly. Mary Unwin and Mary Newton were good friends. John Newton's ministry flourished. Although William Cowper no longer corresponded with Harriet Hesketh, he did exchange letters with his aunt Judith Madan. They readily shared insights into their evangelical faith. He confessed to her the burden of his sins and failures, his dullness of spirit and lack of zeal.

Cowper had a clear appreciation of two blessings of his life at Olney. Having left "a world full of tempest and commotion," he knew "the value of the creek I have put into, and the snugness it affords me" (L, 1:118). And there was Mary, "the chief Blessing I have met with in my Journey since the Lord was pleased to call me" (L, 1:187).

Less than three months after moving to Orchard Side, Mary Unwin became gravely ill. This was not surprising for a middle-aged woman who had moved only ten weeks after her husband's accidental death and who was adjusting to life with a man as complex and volatile as Cowper. Together they went to consult Dr. Cotton at St. Albans. He did not expect medicines to be helpful in her case. Cowper told Mrs. Madan that Mary's disorder was a "Nervous Atrophy attended with violent spasms of the Chest and Throat" (L, 1:187).

Although Cowper despaired of Mary's recovery, three months later she was much better. In a letter to Mrs. Madan, Cowper expressed in hysterical tones the wish that he be able to rejoice in God's will even if that meant accepting Mary's death. Included with the letter was Cowper's poem, "Walking with God," later published as Olney Hymn Number One. Here Cowper's tone is calm as he seeks serenity in his pilgrimage to heaven. He remembers the blessedness and peace of the early days after his conversion and longs for the return of the Holy Spirit, who had been driven away by Cowper's sins.

> What peacefull Hours I then enjoy'd,
>   How sweet their Mem'ry still!
> But they have left an Aching Void
>   The World can never fill.
>   (P, 1:139–40)

In years to come, during Mary Unwin's frequent illnesses, Cowper was always threatened with the "aching void." In 1790 he wrote to Newton about the possibility of Mary's death. "I have one comfort and only one; bereft of that, I should have nothing left to lean on: for my spiritual props have long since been struck from under me" (*L*, 3:424).

By 1770 Cowper had lived five years in the country. The second stanza of his hymn "Retirement" expressed his love of country life.

> The calm retreat, the silent shade,
>   With prayer, and praise agree;
> And seem, by thy sweet bounty made,
>   For those, who follow Thee.
>   (*P,* 1:186)

He never regretted his decision to forego city life. Declining Hill's invitation to visit London, Cowper said he was "long accustom'd to Retirement" and unwilling to revisit noisy and crowded scenes "which I never loved, and which I now abhor" (*L*, 1:210).

However, his retreat was seldom calm. In retirement Cowper habitually looked backward, as he told Mrs. Madan, and saw dangers, precipices, and a bottomless pit. He relived his days of insanity at St. Albans, not occasionally, but every day. "The Recollection of what passed there and the Consequences that followed it, fill my Mind continually, and make the Circumstances of a poor transient half-spent Life, so insipid and unaffecting, that I have no Heart to think or write much about them" (*L*, 1:198).

To Mrs. Madan and Mrs. Cowper, he elaborated on what he meant by a half-spent life in Olney. Though knowing what he should do, nevertheless he was "prone to trifle and let Time and every good thing run to waste." He felt barren, dead, and unprofitable. From January to August of 1769, he wrote no letters. Unfulfilled was his purpose, to glorify God amongst Men "by a Conduct suited to his Word and Will. I am miserably defective in this Holy and blessed Art" (*L*, 1:203). While Cowper still believed in the future as "an everlasting inheritance in light," he derided himself for weakness in faith and love (*L*, 1:189).

In one Olney Hymn, "Peace After a Storm," Cowper writes that when his faith is taxed,

> I find myself a learner yet,
> Unskilful, weak, and apt to slide.

He concludes with the couplet,

> Thou, therefore, all the praise receive,
> Be shame, and self abhorrence, mine.
>   (*P,* 1:180–81)

In "Lovest Thou Me?" Cowper speaks in Jesus' voice. The Savior says that Cowper is healed and forgiven, sought out for salvation by God's unchanging love. Then Jesus poses a question: "Say, poor sinner, lov'st thou me?" Cowper cannot respond without qualifications.

> Lord, it is my chief complaint,
> That my love is weak and faint;
> Yet I love thee and adore,
> Oh for grace to love thee more!
>   (*P,* 1:157–58)

8

I HAD A BROTHER ONCE
1770–1773

On March 20, 1770, William Cowper's brother died at the age of thirty-three. Coming at a time when Cowper was self-deprecating and tormented with doubt, this loss moved him onto a steeper slope downward toward his breakdown in January of 1773.

> I had a brother once.—
> Peace to the mem'ry of a man of worth,
> A man of letters, and of manners too.
> Of manners sweet as virtue always wears,
> When gay good-nature dresses her in smiles.
> He graced a college in which order yet
> Was sacred, and was honor'd, lov'd and wept
> By more than one, themselves conspicuous there.
> (*P,* 2:158–59)

John Cowper was born in Berkamsted a few days before his mother's death. Having been sent off shortly afterward to boarding school and London, William saw little of John in childhood. John became a distinguished scholar of Corpus Christi College, Cambridge, graduating in 1754 with prizes and medals. When John died in Cambridge, the bishop of Cloyne wrote, "We have lost the best classic and most liberal thinker in our University."[1]

For Cowper, his brother

was a man of a most candid and ingenuous spirit, his temper remarkably sweet, and in his behaviour to me he had always manifested an
uncommon affection. His outward conduct, so far as it fell under my
notice or I could learn it by others, was perfectly decent and unblame-
able. There was nothing vicious in any part of his practice, but being of
a studious, thoughtful turn, he placed his chief delight in the acquisition of learning and made such acquisitions in it that he had but few
rivals in that of a classical kind. He was entirely skilled in the Latin,
Greek, and Hebrew languages, was beginning to make himself master of the Syriac, and perfectly understood the French and Italian, the
latter of which he could speak fluently. Learned, however, as he was,
he was easy and cheerful in his conversation, and entirely free from
that stiffness which is generally contracted by men devoted to such
pursuits. (*L*, 1:50)

William Cowper wrote at length about the circumstances of John's
death and conversion in *A Narrative of the Memorable Conversion of the
Revd. John Cowper, M.A.* There are letters as well, written between
February and June 1770 to John Newton, Mrs. Unwin and her son
William, Joseph Hill, Mrs. Cowper, and Mrs. Madan. These letters
record William Cowper's depth of distress. His turmoil was centered on
the question of whether before he died, John would experience an evangelical conversion, be born again of God, so that he would enter paradise and William would meet him there, "never more to be divided."
Cowper saw himself as a laborer praying his brother "out of Darkness
into marvellous Light" (*L*, 1:227).

This labor was extreme in its emotional intensity. Cowper described
himself to Mary Unwin as "toss'd upon Waves of Hope and Fear," thinking about his brother all day and praying for him in dreams. "I go to
sleep in a Storm, imagining that I hear his Cries, and wake in Terrour
lest he should be just departing." Cowper himself wanted to die, he
wrote, because the "World was a Wilderness" to him. His desire was to

be in a better country where "God shall wipe away all Tears from the Eyes of his People" (*L*, 1:214–16).

John was, in fact, converted shortly before his death. Cowper's joy over his brother's new faith was as intense as had been his previous turmoil. "My joy will not suffer me to sleep" (*L*, 1:217).

Notwithstanding Cowper's joy at his brother's conversion, it had been harrowing to sit for many days with a dying man, too weak to move, often delirious, whose statements gradually declined from complex theological language to "speech like that of an infant" (*L*, 1:225). When at last John died, fast asleep, lying perfectly still, William immediately left Cambridge to return to Olney. Considering his emotional state, it is hardly surprising that, as William wrote, "it was not judged proper that I should attend the Funeral" (*L*, 1:226).

A year later Cowper reported to Newton about his state of mind. Newton had written of a bustle of activity in London. Cowper said, "I am equally hinder'd by a Bustle within. The Lord I trust will give peace in his own time, but I can truly say that for the most part my Soul is among Lions" (*L*, 1:241). As rare as it was for Cowper to mention his parish activities, he said he had interpreted the Fifty-first Psalm in a morning service and an evening meeting. But, unlike St. Paul, Cowper was not content with God's grace.

The next year, in June 1772, Cowper told Mrs. Madan that his soul was "almost swallowed up in spiritual distress." He believed he was required by God to welcome adversity. Nevertheless, he wearied himself with "ineffectual struggles" against God's will. Most alarming was his image of a storm at sea in which he was a seaman, not "busy amongst the tackling aloft," but terrified, hovering down in the hold (*L*, 1:253).

For four years he stopped writing letters. The final letters he wrote were to Joseph Hill in November 1772. He was very short of money having lost some income since his brother's death. Again, Hill had invited him to London. Again, Cowper declined while declaring his love for Hill. "You have my Prayers, the only Return I can make you, for your many Acts of still continued Friendship" (*L*, 1:258).

During these four years without writing letters, William Cowper and Mary Unwin lived together at Orchard Side in a remarkable relationship of interdependency and mutual affection. Years later, after Mary's health had failed and Cowper's mind was faltering, he wrote in the language of the heart that Mary was "a friend whose life is dearer to me than my own" (*L*, 4:353).

As had been the case in Huntingdon, some Olney villagers and churchgoers gossiped about Mary and William. Now changes were imminent in Mary's family. Her son, William Unwin, a Cambridge graduate with a master's degree, had been serving as curate in Comberton, Cambridgeshire. In 1769 he was ordained a priest and became rector of Stock in Essex. He subsequently married and had three children. Clearly, he would in the future spend very little time in Olney. William Cowper and William Unwin had become good friends and would exchange frequent letters in the coming years.

Mary's daughter Susanna was rarely mentioned in Cowper's letters. About the time of her brother's move to Stock, Susanna became engaged and later married Matthew Powley, an Oxford graduate who was curate of Slaithwaite, Yorkshire, and soon to be named vicar of Dewsbury. Some evidence remains of Susanna's disapproval of Cowper, especially his financial dependence on her mother.

Two contemporary sources indicate that another family wedding was being considered. Mary Unwin and William Cowper were for a brief period engaged to be married, according to John Newton's fragmentary life of Cowper and Samuel Greatheed's memoirs of Cowper. Although never mentioned in Cowper's letters, this plan has been the source of extensive speculation by modern biographers of Cowper. Whatever may be conjectured about the circumstances of the engagement and its termination or whether Mary and William ever viewed it as more than a formality, it is certain that they made their decisions together.

The depth of reciprocity in their friendship was expressed by Cowper when he went to see his dying brother and Mary remained in Olney. He wrote to her, "I Never intentionally failed in any point where your Peace & Happiness are concern'd. . . . Let nothing that I

OLNEY BRIDGE.

That with its wearisome but needful length,
Bestrides the wintry flood. —— *Vide the Task, Book IV.*

FIGURE 3. *Olney Bridge,* from *Cowper Illustrated by a Series of views in, or near, the Park of Weston-Underwood, Bucks.* (London: Verner and Hood, 1803). Courtesy of the Library of Congress.

have said distress you, your Peace is as dear to me as my own, and I cannot grieve You, without suffering myself" (*L*, 1:215).

Susanna Unwin and Matthew Powley were married in Olney on May 15, 1774, in a service conducted by John Newton. On their wedding day, William Cowper was in the throes of his most harrowing mental breakdown.

Later, the personalities of the Powleys came to life in Cowper's letters. At Christmastime in 1780, Cowper wrote to William Unwin that his poor sister and Mr. Powley had no ear for humor and "can't laugh at our jokes" (*L*, 1:427). In late 1784 Cowper wrote about Mrs. Powley's serious nervous disorder, noting that by December she had less frequent and less violent fits. By the spring of 1786, Mrs. Powley was still far from well but planning to visit with "affectionate impatience for another sight of Olney" (*L*, 2:507). After another visit from the Powleys in June 1788, Cowper wrote to Newton: "Her we found much improved in her health & spirits, and him, as always, affectionate and obliging. It was an agreeable visit" (*L*, 3:172).

With all the unselfish and sometimes debilitating care that Mary Unwin lavished on William Cowper, it was fortunate that she remained in close touch with her daughter and son-in-law and with her son, daughter-in-law, and their children as well. Astonishing, in light of her poor health, the childless Susanna Powley died at the age of ninety, having outlived her husband by thirty years.

William Cowper and Mary Unwin had arrived in Olney in 1767. As urgently as Cowper sought peace with God, he did not find it. In June 1772 he told Mrs. Madan that he was like a terrified seaman in a storm. For the rest of his life, the storm at sea was Cowper's metaphor for his spiritual condition.

The storm that overwhelmed Cowper in 1773 never entirely abated. Its initial ferocity required all the strength that Mary Unwin could muster as well as all the devotion that Mary and John Newton could summon forth to care for their afflicted friend.

9

A HEART HOPELESS
AND DESERTED

1773

At the beginning of January 1773, William Cowper suffered a mental and spiritual breakdown from which he never entirely recovered. He found himself "in the belly of this Hell, compared with which Jonah's was a palace, a temple of the living God" (*L*, 2:83).

In his *Memoir* Cowper had described in harrowing detail his earlier breakdown of 1763. He had believed that his afflictions at Dr. Cotton's had been sent by God to accomplish the salvation of a sinner. After recovery, Cowper had been obsessed with his inadequate gratitude to God and his continuing predilection for sinfulness.

The breakdown of 1773 was different. Until his death almost thirty years later, Cowper's fixation was on the meaning of God's abandonment and the immutability of his Creator's hatred and vengeance. "God's ways are mysterious, and he giveth no account of his matters" (*L*, 2:200). What God had done to Cowper seemed clear enough, banishing him "to a remoteness from His presence in comparison with which the distance from East to West is no distance" (*L*, 3:165).

Long after the events of 1773, Cowper told his story to Lady Hesketh, who had been living in Europe and out of touch with her cousin at the time.

Know then that in the year 73 the same scene that was acted at St. Albans, opened upon me again at Olney, only covered with a still-deeper shade of melancholy, and ordained to be of much longer duration. I was suddenly reduced from my wonted rate of understanding to an almost childish imbecility. I did not indeed lose my senses, but I lost the power to exercise them. I could return a rational answer even to a difficult question, but a question was necessary, or I never spoke at all. This state of mind was accompanied, as I suppose it to be in most instances of the kind, with misapprehension of things and persons that made me a very untractable patient. I believed that every body hated me, and that Mrs. Unwin hated me most of all; was convinced that all my food was poisoned, together with ten thousand megrims of the same stamp. I would not be more circumstantial than is necessary. Dr. Cotton was consulted. He replied that he could do no more for me than might be done at Olney, but recommended particular vigilance, lest I should attempt my life:—a caution for which there was the greatest occasion. At the same time that I was convinced of Mrs. Unwin's aversion to me, could endure no other companion. The whole management of me consequently devolved upon her, and a terrible task she had; she performed it, however, with a cheerfulness hardly ever equalled on such an occasion; and I have often heard her say, that if ever she praised God in her life it was when she found that she was to have all the labour. She performed it accordingly, but, as I hinted once before, very much to the hurt of her own constitution. It will be thirteen years in little more than a week, since this malady seized me. (*L*, 2:455)

The most important point in Cowper's breakdown came in late January 1773. He had a dream "before the recollection of which, all consolation vanishes, and, as it seems to me, must always vanish" (*L*, 2:385). In the dream God spoke: *"Actum est de te, periisti."* ("It is all over with thee, thou hast perished.")[1] John and Mary Newton were summoned from the vicarage to Orchard Side at four in the morning. John stayed until eight, Mary all day.

In April the Newtons took Cowper into their own home where he remained for fourteen months. "He could not then be safely left by himself, he was seldom a minute at a time, out of the sight of one or other of us, by night or day, while he staid under our roof."[2] Cowper told Lady Hesketh that Mary Unwin sat up with him and even resorted to sleeping in her clothes on a bed in his room.

Finally, in October, Cowper was somewhat improved. When the Newtons were able to go out of town, Mary Unwin advised them not to hurry home and gave them a progress report.

> The Lord is very gracious to us; for though the cloud of affliction still hangs heavy on Mr. Cowper yet he is quite calm & persuadable in every respect. He has been for these few days past more open & communicative than heretofore. It is amazing how subtilly the cruel adversary has worked upon him & wonderfull to see how the Lord has frustrated his wicked machinations; for though He has not seen good to prevent the most violent temptations & distressing delusions, yet He has prevented the Mischeivous effects the enemy designed by them. A most Marvellous story will this Dear Child of God have to relate when by His Almighty power he is set at liberty. As nothing short of Omnipotence could have supported him through this sharp Affliction so nothing less can set him free from it. (*L*, 1:260)

Cowper never forgot his sufferings at Orchard Side and the vicarage. "Never was the mind of man benighted to the degree that mine has been; the storms that have assailed me would have overset the Faith of every man that ever had any, and the very real remembrances of them, even after they had been long pass'd by, makes Hope impossible" (*L*, 3:37).

Neither did Cowper ever forget the daily, unselfish, and compassionate care he received from Mary and John Newton and Mary Unwin. He expressed his gratitude in poems and letters until the end of his life.

A poem for Mary Unwin, "The Winter Nosegay," one of Cowper 's favorites, concluded with the lines,

And the winter of sorrow best shows
    The truth of a friend, such as you.
            (*P,* 1:426–27)

Cowper's last extant letter was written to John Newton. Recalling in profound sadness the days when he had thought himself secure of eternity, Cowper concluded, "Adien, Dear Sir, whom in those days I call'd Dear Friend, with feelings that Justified the appelation—" (*L,* 4:466).

For Newton, Cowper wrote two blunt, concise summaries of his life. The beginning of his life was spent in sin, the latter part has been "poisoned with Despair" (*L,* 1:393). Five months later, he described a life that began with a classical education at Westminster. "Then I learn'd the truth, and then I lost it, and there ends my History" (*L,* 1:444). Cowper's most vivid and heart-wrenchingly short life story was written for William Unwin on a Sunday morning as church bells were ringing. Cowper's had been a life in three parts, he wrote: he found a God and was permitted to worship him; he was deprived of this privilege; he had no hope to recover it (*L,* 2:133).

As Cowper well knew, such a life was impossible in terms of an evangelical theology that claimed that an acceptance of Christ as Savior could not be reversed. Newton, or any like-minded theologian, would question "that a man whose views of the Scripture are just like his own, who is a Calvinist from experience, & knows his election, should be furnished with a Shield of despair impenetrable to every argument by which he might attempt to comfort him" (*L,* 1:393). "That a Calvinist in principle, should know himself to have been Elected, and yet believe that he is lost, is indeed a Riddle" (*L,* 1:341).

The only solution to this theological dilemma was proposed by Cowper in many letters to Newton: Cowper's case was unique. "The dealings of God with me, are to myself utterly unintelligible; I have never met, either in books or in conversation, with an experience at all similar to my own" (*L,* 2:581).

"If God is still my Father, his paternal severity has toward me been such that I have reason to account it unexampled" (*L,* 2:547). Of his evangelical friends like Newton, "they think it necessary to the existence of divine truth, that he who once had possession of it should never finally lose it. I admit the solidity of this reasoning in every case but my own" (*L,* 2:200).

From a modern perspective, William Cowper's entire life after 1737 when his mother died was a search for hope that he had not been abandoned forever. Every move to a new lodging or a new town, every loss of contact with a friend or family member, especially every death, destroyed another segment of Cowper's frail hope and fortified his horror of being left alone. The single most devastating aspect of his lost faith was the lost hope of reunion in heaven with his mother and all those he passionately loved.

In the mid-1780s, concurrent with his renewed correspondence with Lady Hesketh, Cowper experienced glimpses of hope. "The light that reaches me cannot be compared either to that of the sun or of the moon. It is a flash in a dark night, during which the heavens seem open'd only to shut again" (*L,* 2:357).

Some months later, he was more optimistic. "My spirits are somewhat better than they were. In the course of the last month I have perceived a very sensible amendment. The hope of better days seems again to dawn upon me, and I have now and then an intimation, though slight and transient, that God has not abandoned me for ever" (*L,* 2:412).

The return of Lady Hesketh as a correspondent and as an anticipated visitor to Olney immediately focused Cowper's hope on hope of heaven. "For you must know that I should not Love you half so well if I did not believe that you will be my friend to Eternity. There is not room enough for friendship to unfold itself into full blow, in such a nook of a Life as this. Therefore I am and must and will be—Yours for ever—Wm. Cowper" (*L,* 2:553).

Two years later, when Lady Hesketh's father died, his nephew William Cowper wrote of the joyful interviews that Ashley Cowper would be having with those who had gone before. "The truth of the matter is, my Dear, that they are the happy ones, and that we shall never be such ourselves till we have joined their party. Could I hope for that felicity myself I should consider neither your parents nor my own as lost to me, but expect speedily to rejoin them" (*L,* 3:176).

But William Cowper was never able to escape for long the conviction of damnation as expressed most horribly in his poem of 1774.

HATRED AND VENGEANCE, MY ETERNAL PORTION

Hatred and vengeance, my eternal portion,
Scare can endure delay of execution:—
Wait, with impatient readiness, to seize my
    Soul in a moment.

Damn'd below Judas; more abhorr'd than he as,
Who, for a few pence, sold his holy master.
Twice betray'd, Jesus me, the last delinquent,
    Deems the profanest.
Man disavows, and Deity disowns me.
Hell might afford my miseries a shelter;
Therefore hell keeps her everhungry mouths all
    Bolted against me.
Hard lot! Encompass'd with a thousand dangers,
Weary, faint, trembling with a thousand terrors,
Fall'n, and if vanquish'd, to receive a sentence
    Worse than Abiram's:
Him, the vindictive rod of angry justice
Sent, quick and howling, to the centre headlong;
I, fed with judgments, in a fleshly tomb, am
    Buried above ground.

                (*P,* 1:209–10)

Even though Cowper had been able to record in May of 1786 his belief that he and Lady Hesketh would be friends to eternity, only three months later he told Newton that his hopes were blasted. "God gave them to me in derision and took them away in vengeance" (*L,* 2:581).

FIGURE 4. Portrait of William Cowper by Lemuel Francis Abbott, 1792. Courtesy of the National Portrait Gallery, London.

PART TWO

A WRITER IN THE COUNTRY

10

STUDENT OF MANY ARTS
1775–1780

In the mid-1770s William Cowper was living with Mary Unwin at Orchard Side, next door to the Newtons in the vicarage. Cowper's mental health was gradually improving. Against all odds and with unsurpassed courage, Cowper created a life and embarked on his career as a poet and letter writer.

At the conclusion of his essay on Cowper, Andrew Brink writes, "Only the struggle fully to take his place in life, and to possess the strength to meet it face on, could engender creative efforts of the importance we find in Cowper's poetry."[1]

Living in Olney, Cowper began to see nature as displaying the unambiguous footsteps of God, the bounteous giver of life. In the hymn "Retirement," Cowper envisions God's people escaping the evils of city life to enjoy the goodness of country life.

> The calm retreat, the silent shade,
> With prayer and praise agree;
> And seem, by thy sweet bounty made,
> For those, who follow Thee.
>
> (*P*, 1:186)

Thus, in nature, the presence of God was revealed.

Most importantly, retirement to a world of natural beauty gave poetic inspiration. "Oh nature! . . . Be thou the great inspirer of my strains" (*P,* 1:383). "Everything I see in the fields is to me an Object, and I can look at the same rivulet or at a handsome tree every day of my life with new pleasure" (*L,* 2:178). Cowper's appreciation of rural beauty was formed in early childhood at Berkhamsted while he lived in the embrace of his mother's love. Throughout life, he continued the habit of rural walks. "Scenes that sooth'd or charm'd me young, no longer young, I find still soothing and of pow'r to charm me still" (*P,* 2:120).

Cowper's victory in Olney over his breakdown of 1773 began in his garden and continued in the modest house where he put pen to paper in the morning and read his verses to Mary in the evening. He made a heroic effort to use poetry to "allay the perturbations of the mind."[2]

William Cowper had first taken up gardening while he was living in Huntingdon. From there, in a lighthearted, self-mocking vein, he wrote to Mrs. Cowper at the Park and to Joseph Hill about his new occupation. He told his cousin, "I am become a great florist and shrub doctor," and asked her for a small packet of seeds for a garden with "little else besides Jessamine and Honey Suckle" (*L,* 1:161). He warned that he had meager gardening skills and needed seeds easy to manage. Two months later he described himself to Joe as a student of the arts of pruning, sowing, and planting. He was growing melons and cabbages, cauliflowers and broccoli (*L,* 1:166).

At Olney Cowper's interest in the garden increased and soon extended to all its inhabitants. He told Lady Hesketh, "I commenced carpenter," making cupboards, boxes and stools, followed by birdcages, squirrel houses, and rabbit hutches (*L,* 2:455). He loved the smallest of his garden companions. "All the sounds that nature offers are delightful," including bees, birds, and insects, each with their concerts, "a very observable instance of providential kindness to man" (*L,* 2:278). Avian visitors to the garden were a part of his routine. "I have 8 Pair of tame Pigeons—when I first Enter the Garden in a Morning, I find them Perched upon the Wall, waiting for their Breakfast, for I feed them always upon the Gravel Walk" (*L,* 1:303).

Some companions normally found outdoors moved inside. Cowper's hares were part of his family and have been immortalized in a stained-glass window at St. Nicholas Church, East Dereham. The escapades of

Bess, Puss, and Tiney were a feature of Cowper's letters and occasionally appeared in his poetry.

EPITAPH ON A HARE

Here lies, whom hound did ne'er pursue
    Nor swifter Grey–hound follow,
Whose foot ne'er tainted morning dew
    Nor ear heard huntsman's hallo',

Old Tiney, surliest of his kind,
    Who, nurs'd with tender care
And to domestic bounds confined,
    Was still a wild Jack-hare.

Though duly from my hand he took
    His pittance ev'ry night,
He did it with a jealous look,
    And, when he could, would bite.

His diet was of wheaten bread
    And milk, and oats, and straw,
Thistles, or lettuces instead,
    With sand to scour his maw.

On twigs of hawthorn he regaled,
    On pippins' russet peel,
And, when his juicey sallads fail'd,
    Sliced carrot pleased him well.

A Turkey carpet was his lawn
    Whereon he lov'd to bound,
To skip and gambol like a fawn,
    And swing his rump around.

His frisking was at evening hours,
    For then he lost his fear,
But most before approaching show'rs
    Or when a storm drew near.

Eight years and five round rolling moons
    He thus saw steal away,
Dozing out all his idle noons,
    And ev'ry night at play.

I kept him for his humour' sake,
    For he would oft beguile
My heart of thoughts that made it ache,
    And force me to a smile.

But now, beneath this walnut-shade
    He finds his long last home,
And waits in snug concealment laid
    'Till gentler Puss shall come.

He, still more aged, feels the shocks
    From which no care can save,
And, part'ner once of Tiney's Box,
    Must soon partake his grave.
                (*P,* 2:19–20)

Cowper was devoted to larger and more conventional companions as well. The bulldog Mongo was fearless in thunderstorms: "The moment that he heard the thunder, which was like the blast of a great gun, with a wrinkled forehead and with eyes directed to the cieling whence the sound seemed to proceed, he barked. But he barked exactly in concert with the thunder" (*L,* 2:364).

The spaniel Beau was given a poem by way of gratitude for having presented Cowper with a water lily from the Ouse.

I saw him with that Lily cropp'd
    Impatient swim to meet
My quick approach, and soon he dropp'd
    The treasure at my feet.

Charm'd with the sight, the world, I cried,
    Shall hear of this thy deed,
My dog shall mortify the pride
    Of Man's superior breed.
                    (*P*, 3:28–29)

Of all his garden accomplishments, Cowper's greenhouse gave him the greatest pleasure. After receiving a letter from William Bull about his recent seaside vacation, Cowper replied, "Why should we envy any man? Is not our greenhouse a cabinet of perfumes? It is at this moment, fronted with carnations and balsams, with mignonette and roses, with jessamine and woodbine, and wants nothing but your pipe to make it truely Arabian, a wilderness of sweets" (*L*, 2:269).

For John Newton he described the greenhouse at its best in autumn. "But now I sit with all the windows and doors wide open, and am regaled with the scent of every flower in a garden as full of flowers as I have known how to make it" (*L*, 2:278).

Cowper's finest tribute to his greenhouse was "The Winter Nosegay," which he wrote for Mary to celebrate her true love and friendship. Cowper said that writing this poem had given him unsurpassed pleasure.

THE WINTER NOSEGAY

What nature, alas! has denied
    To the delicate growth of our isle,
Art has in a measure supplied,
    And winter is deck'd with a smile.
See Mary what beauties I bring
    From the shelter of that sunny shed,

Where the flow'rs have the charms of the spring,
　　Though abroad they are frozen and dead.

'Tis a bow'r of Arcadian sweets,
　　Where Flora is still in her prime,

A fortress to which she retreats,
　　From the cruel assaults of the clime.
While earth wears a mantle of snow,
　　These pinks are as fresh and as gay,
As the fairest and sweetest that blow,
　　On the beautiful bosom of May.

See how they have safely surviv'd
　　The frowns of a sky so severe,
Such Mary's true love that has liv'd
　　Through many a turbulent year.
The charms of the late blowing rose,
　　Seem grac'd with a livelier hue,
And the winter of sorrow best shows
　　The truth of a friend, such as you.
　　　　　　　　　　　　　(*P,* 1:426–27)

In April and May of 1780, Cowper wrote about a very different accomplishment, landscape drawing. He told William Unwin of this "most Amusing Art, and like every other Art, requires much Practise and Attention." He spoke of his "surprizing Proficiency in the Art considering my total Ignorance of it two months ago." He said Mary "is all Admiration and Applause" (*L,* 1:338–39). He told John Newton, "I draw mountains, valleys, woods and streams and ducks and dabchicks. I admire them myself and Mrs. Unwin admires Them, and her praise and my praise put together are fame enough for me" (*L,* 1:335).

In *The Dynamics of Creation,* Anthony Storr points out that, with the passage of time, a writer's memory of past events can germinate and

THE RUSTIC BRIDGE.

——————— *upon a rustic bridge*

We pass a gulph ————————

Vide the Task, Book I.

FIGURE 5. *The Rustic Bridge,* from *Cowper Illustrated by a Series of views in, or near, the Park of Weston-Underwood, Bucks.* (London: Verner and Hood, 1803). Courtesy of the Library of Congress.

bring forth their meaning.[3] This was often the case with Cowper. After ten years passed, he was able to write a concise, explicit explanation of his devotion to gardening, carpentry, and landscape drawing. In a letter to Mrs. King, he said he had found it necessary to adopt all these practices "that I might escape the worst of all evils both in itself and its consequences, an idle life." He told his new friend that "the Greenhouse, Verse excepted, afforded me amusement for a longer time than any expedient of all the many to which I have fled for refuge from the misery of having nothing to do" (*L*, 3:221–22).

But Cowper came to know that his "Verse" was far more than an amusement. It was poetry that would make him famous in England. Not long after these years of pursuing various hobbies, he would be a published author. In another letter of 1788 to Mrs. King, he celebrated his victory. "I send you, my dear Madam, the poem I promised you, and shall be glad to send you any thing and every thing I write, as fast as it flows. Behold my two volumes!" (*L*, 3:220).

11

THE INTERIOR SELF
1775–1780

The year 1780 was an unlikely time for William Cowper to embrace fully his career as writer. Early in this year, John and Mary Newton moved out of the vicarage, never to return except for brief visits at Orchard Side. Newton became vicar at St. Mary Woolnoth Church in London, where he preached to far larger and more prestigious congregations than those in Olney.

Always subject to feelings of abandonment, Cowper expressed his dire distress in a letter to Mary Newton.

> The Vicarage became a Melancholy Object, as soon as Mr. Newton had left it: When You left it, it became more melancholy. Now it is actually occupied by another family. Even I cannot look at it without being shocked. As I walked in the Garden this Evening I saw the Smoke rise from the Study Chimney, and said to myself, that used to be a Sign that Mr. Newton was there, but it is so no longer. . . . If I were in a Condition to leave Olney too, I certainly would not stay in it, it is no Attachment to the Place that binds me here, but an Unfitness for every other. I lived in it once, but now I am buried in it, and have no Business with the World on the Outside of my Sepulchre. (*L*, 1:321–22)

Cowper wrote an affecting poem inviting Newton to visit Olney.

To the Rev. Mr. Newton,
an Invitation into the Country

The swallows in their torpid state,
    Compose their useless wing,
And bees in hives as idly wait
    The call of early spring.

The keenest frost that binds the stream,
    The wildest wind that blows,
Are neither felt nor fear'd by them,
    Secure of their repose.

But man all feeling and awake
    The gloomy scene surveys,
With present ills his heart must ach,
    And pant for brighter days.

Old winter halting o'er the mead,
    Bids me and Mary mourn,
But lovely spring peeps o'er his head,
    And whispers your return.

Then April with her sister May,
    Shall chase him from the bow'rs,
And weave fresh garlands ev'ry day,
    To crown the smiling hours.

And if a tear that speaks regret
    Of happier times appear,
A glimpse of joy that we have met
    Shall shine, and dry the tear.
                      (*P,* 1:429–30)

Instead of grieving the year away, by December Cowper was working on several long poems. Exactly two years after the Newtons' departure, Cowper became the published author of a book of poetry, *Poems by William Cowper, of the Inner Temple, Esq.*

In letters to William Unwin in 1780, Cowper explained his motivation to write. Since Unwin was himself writing poetry, Cowper gave him some practical advice. "Touch and retouch" is "the secret of almost all good writing, especially in verse" (*L*, 1:359). Cowper said that he writes for his own amusement and if the reader is amused as well, it is like a second crop in a garden, "the more valuable because less expected!" (*L*, 1:365). Cowper returned to the subject of writing as relief in times of low spirits and dejection. "Having no Fool or Jester at hand, I resolved to be my own" (*L*, 1:404).

At the end of the year, a letter to John Newton summarized Cowper's theme of poetry as entertainment: "At this season of the year, & in this gloomy, uncomfortable climate, it is no easy matter for the owner of a mind like mine, to divert it from sad subjects, & fix it upon such as may administer to its amusement. Poetry, above all things, is useful to me in this respect. While I am held in pursuit of pretty images, or a pretty way of expressing them, I forget every thing that is irksome, &, like a boy that plays truant, determine to avail myself of the present opportunity to be amused, & to put by the disagreeable recollection that I must after all, go home & be whipt again" (*L*, 1:425).

As Andrew Brink concludes, "Writing verse was the best thing Cowper ever did, a continuation on the deepest possible level of the self-revelation and accommodation to reality carried on in conversation and in letters."[1]

Cowper's self-understanding was gradually changing, as was his view of poetry. Verse was not simply amusement to brighten the dark corners of his soul. The poetic music of language was indeed helpful in drowning out inner sounds of despair. But in his letters he began to speak of more substantial reasons for writing poetry. In "The Task" he later described himself as a poet with important business. "Cowper knew very well how the poetic process worked with him; he knew all about its origin and likely outcome."[2] Here is Cowper's authentic voice as he becomes his own interpreter:

> He that attends to his interior self,
> That has a heart, and keeps it; has a mind
> That hungers and supplies it; and who seeks
> A social, not a dissipated life,
> Has business. Feels himself engag'd t' achieve
> No unimportant, though a silent task.
>
> (*P*, 2:172)

Five years earlier, he had written Mary Newton that he was buried in Olney with no business outside his tomb. Now he offers a complex presentation of himself as a writer with business. His thoughts anticipate the work of psychologists and psychiatrists two centuries later who are exploring creativity and its relationship to the interior self.

Anthony Storr was a psychiatrist and writer of many popular books. "He expressed a belief in the creative possibilities inherent in mental suffering and the potential for self-healing to be found in artistic and intellectual creativity."[3] His affinity for Cowper may have grown out of his own lonely, depressive childhood and the bullying and misery he, like Cowper, experienced after he was sent away to school at a very early age.

In his book *Solitude*, Storr considers the lives and accomplishments of Cowper and other creative people subject to depression. He postulates that the creative process can protect an individual against being overwhelmed and also repair "the self damaged by bereavement."[4]

In *The Dynamics of Creation*, Storr deals with the lifelong problems experienced by some who have lost their mothers in early childhood. As adults, their hold on self-esteem and self-worth is never permanent but often short-lived. "No amount of external success compensates for what has not been incorporated in early childhood."[5]

Storr refers to the work of Andrew Brink on the particular struggles of creative people experiencing in childhood the loss of their mothers. While many Cowper scholars have been reluctant to give a modern clinical diagnosis of the poet's mental illness, Brink uses the terminology "reactive depression." He postulates that the death of his mother, casting a permanent shadow, was the most important fact about Cowper's life.

Brink's book *Loss and Symbolic Repair* includes the chapter, "William Cowper and the Elusive Object." Brink believes that "Cowper was the first English poet to give sustained attention to the intrapsychic meaning of grief."[6] Brink, as well as a colleague, John Bowlby, stress the significant layers of meaning inherent in Cowper's concept of "the void, the great emptiness or 'gone place.'" Cowper's other recurring poetic image is of a lifelong sea journey culminating in the death of Cowper, himself the castaway.

Brink's detailed interpretation of Cowper's poem, "On the Receipt of My Mother's Picture Out of Norfolk" (*P,* 356–60), as well as his interpretation of passages in the poem "The Task" has given Cowper scholarship a new direction from which there will be no turning back. Studies such as Roderick Huang's of 1957, which centers on Cowper's nature poetry, are no longer credible.[7] Huang discusses Cowper's reactions to nature as though they were unrelated to his intrapsychic self-understanding. He calls the poet's life "pathetic."

On the contrary, although Cowper certainly understood a turning point had occurred in 1780 when he lost the Newtons as next-door neighbors, yet he found interior strength to enter a season of satisfaction as a poet.

> When comforts are declining,
>   He grants the soul again
> A season of clear shining
>   To cheer it after rain.
>   (*P,* 1:188)

12

THE WRITER
WITH BUSINESS
1781–March 1782

In January 1781 William Cowper was working hard on his first book. *Poems by William Cowper, of the Inner Temple, Esq.* would be published on March 1, 1782. His unflagging determination to become a published poet was evident during these fourteen months. He wrote of his ambition in numerous letters to John Newton.

For time to write, Cowper had the advantage of a quiet life at Orchard Side, sharing his home, greenhouse, and garden with Mary Unwin. This period was undisturbed by any sad personal news from London or the wider world.

In the summer months of 1780, Cowper had been consolidating his thoughts about himself as a writer. In letters to Newton, Unwin, and Mrs. Cowper he recognized that writing relieved his melancholy, a chronic mood in which "cold Winds and dark Clouds intercept every Ray of Sunshine" (*L*, 1:368). Writing a letter, or "conversation on paper," could intrude upon his dreary thoughts like "a harlequin with a corpse" or "a kitten playing with its tail" (*L*, 1:367). He could be witty about his deep distress. With few subjects to write about, he wrote, he was like an artist with only one face to paint. "A Painter who should confine himself in the Exercise of his Art to the Drawing of his own Picture, must be a Wonderful Coxcomb if he did not soon grow Sick of his Occupation, and be particularly fortunate, if he did not make others as Sick as Himself" (*L*, 1:369).

Cowper recognized a particular advantage in the writing of letters—they could be accomplished in small steps, the way a walk is accomplished by putting one foot forward and then the other. "A letter is written, as a Conversation is maintained, or a Journey perform'd, not by preconcerted, or premediated Means, by a New Contrivance, or an Invention never heard of before, but merely by maintaining a Progress, and resolving as a Postillion does, having once Set out, never to Stop 'till we reach the appointed End. If a Man may Talk without thinking, why may he not Write upon the same Terms?" (*L*, 1:374).

As the year 1781 began, Cowper was energetically writing poetry. But just as an artist is reluctant to show others an incomplete painting, so Cowper did not readily share his intent to publish a volume of poetry. John Newton was his confidant as early as January 1781. Without reserve, John Newton lavished on Cowper both encouragement and advice, sending his friend an average of two letters a month until Cowper's poetry was published. The two men worked in harmony. Any lines to which Newton objected were not defended by Cowper. Any length for a given poem was acceptable to Newton, who understood the complex balance Cowper was seeking.

> A poet in my Circumstances has a difficult part to act. One minute obliged to bridle his Humor if he has any, and the next, to clap a Spur to the Sides of it. Now ready to weep from a Sense of the Importance of his subject, and on a sudden constrain'd to Laugh lest his gravity should be mistaken for Dullness. If this be not violent Exercise for the mind I know not what is, and if any man doubt it, let him try. Whether all this management and contrivance be necessary I do not know, but am inclined to suspect that if my Muse was to go forth clad in Quaker color, without one bit of Ribband to enliven her Appearance, she might walk from one end of London to the other, as little noticed as if she were one of the Sisterhood indeed. (*L*, 1:445)

After a productive winter, when spring 1781 came, Cowper was able to tell Joseph Hill, "I am in the press" (*L*, 1:470). Cowper had plans for the good weather ahead. "My appetite for fame is not keen enough to combat with my love of fine weather, my Love of Indolence, and my Love of gardening Employments" (*L*, 1:462). His chosen schedule was to garden in the morning, rest until tea, walk, and rest again. The hour from four to five was put aside for writing. Obviously, a book of poetry could not be prepared for the printer on such a schedule. But he told Hill that his poems were "principally the production of the last Winter. . . . The Season of the Year which generally pinches off the flowers of poetry, unfolds mine such as they are, and crowns me with a Winter garland" (*L*, 1:470–71).

Having confided his publication plans to Newton in January and to Hill in May, Cowper had not said a word about his book of poems to William Unwin. One possible explanation for this is that to publish poems can be of a deeper significance than to write them. In *Loss and Symbolic Repair*, Andrew Brink has explained the significance for a writer of a book's publication.[1] A sense of identity is achieved when a painter has an exhibition or a musician gives a public concert. Just so, the publication of a book reinforces the ego of a writer who has worked so long in solitude.

Cowper's ongoing secretiveness is also explained by Anthony Storr. Writers are afraid of talking about or showing others their work too soon: "Creative people learn, often through bitter experience, to be secretive. As we said before, new ideas are tender plants better not exposed too soon to comment. They wither under criticism, and are often dispelled and diluted by premature revelation."[2]

When the first day of May arrived, Cowper finally decided to tell William Unwin, "I am in the press." Cowper did his best to soothe Unwin's feelings about having been left in the dark. After all, most of the poems, having been composed during the past winter, had not been kept secret very long. Moreover, the poet had not been sure himself, until a few days past, that any printer would take a financial gamble on an unpublished writer. "But Johnson has heroically set all peradventures at defiance, and takes the whole charge upon himself—so Out I come" (*L*, 1:469).

Unwin's return letter expressed pain as well as jealousy of Newton's central role in the process of publication. In three more letters during May, Cowper gave Unwin sometimes superficial or limp explanations about the silence regarding his book. But these letters always implied faith in their enduring friendship. In kind, Unwin was magnanimous. Thus their intimacy was deepened rather than damaged by the poet's previous secretiveness. Cowper's poem, "To the Rev. William Cawthorne Unwin," was written as if to a brother.

An union form'd as mine with thee,
    Not rashly or in sport,
May be as fervent in degree,
    And faithful in its sort,
And may as rich in comfort prove,
    As that of true fraternal love.
                    (P, 1:437)

While Cowper was writing to Unwin about the proposed volume of poetry, he was corresponding with John Newton about a preface. Cowper suggested that his poem "Truth" might be offensive to readers who were not familiar with or sympathetic to evangelical Christian doctrine. He felt Newton would be the ideal person to write a preface to "Truth" or indeed to the entire volume (L, 1:462–63). Newton's preface would stimulate interest in Cowper's work.

By autumn Newton had sent a draft of a preface, which Cowper characterized as an affectionate introduction. This preface offered a brief biography of Cowper, including his early days in London, his religious conversion, and subsequent retreat to rural life. There was mention of his "long indisposition." Newton said the overall aim of Cowper's volume was "to communicate his own perceptions of the truth, beauty, and influence of the religion of the Bible." After extolling this faith as "the grand desideratum," Newton gave his personal testimony: "We are now certain that the gospel of Christ is the power of God unto salvation, to every one that believeth" (P, 1:159–70).

As Cowper's volume of poems was just about to be published, a final decision was made about the preface. Joseph Johnson thought it disadvantageous to the success of the book. He asked for and received Cowper's permission to negotiate with Newton about omitting the preface. While Newton's preface was included in a few copies of the first edition, it was not routinely a part of the poems until the fifth edition of 1793.

Cowper hoped that Newton would be easily persuaded to sacrifice, if necessary, the preface "to the interests of the book" (*L*, 2:26). Cowper wrote a conciliatory letter to John and Mary Newton in mid-March. On the one hand, he wrote to praise the preface again and to deplore the fact that the present times no longer accepted a faith that "every rational creature must admit to be true." On the other hand, he spoke highly of Johnson, who had made discerning changes to some lines of Cowper's poetry. Cowper was grateful to both Newton and Johnson (*L*, 2:36–37).

After publication, Cowper did not write to Newton for many months. It must be inferred that Newton had not been "easily persuaded" to remove his preface! In November Cowper thanked Mrs. Newton for sending fish and helping sell his book. By the following year, Cowper's letters to Newton again became frequent and give evidence that Newton had visited Cowper in Olney the previous summer. A letter in February 1783 was calm and affectionate: "Mrs. Unwin thanks Mrs. Newton for her kind letter and for executing her commissions. She means to answer next week by the opportunity of a basket of Chickens. We truly Love you both, think of you often, and one of us prays for you —the other will, when he can pray for himself" (*L*, 2:106).

By September Cowper was again describing his dejection and baring his soul to Newton, the friend of his heart, as he was able to do with no other correspondent.

> I have indeed been lately more dejected and more distressed than usual. More harrass'd by dreams in the night, and more deeply poison'd by them in the following day. I know not what is portended by an alteration for the worse after eleven years of misery, but firmly believe that it is not designed as the Introduction of a change for the better.

You know not what I suffer'd while you were here nor was there any need you should. Your friendship for me would have made you in some degree a partaker of my woes, and your share in them would have been encreas'd by your inability to help me. Perhaps indeed they took a keener edge from the consideration of your presence; the friend of my heart, the person with whom I had formerly taken sweet counsel, no longer usefull to me as a Minister, no longer pleasant to me as a Christian, was a spectacle that must necessarily add the bitterness of mortification to the sadness of despair. I now see a long Winter before me, and am to get through it as I can. (*L*, 2:160–61)

In May 1781 it became clear that Joseph Johnson would not be able to ready the book for the reading public until the winter of '82. In the summer London's book publishers and the reading public were out of the city. Cowper told Newton, "I had much rather therefore proceed leisurely as he advises (if he will indeed go on to print at his leisure) and so avail myself of the complete opportunity that Winter will bring with it, than open my Stall just when the Fair is over" (*L*, 1:478).

At first the delay in publication did not seem to dampen Cowper's spirits as was evident in a letter to Unwin.

If a Writer's friends have need of patience, how much more the Writer! Your desire to see my Muse in public, and mine to gratify you, must both suffer the Mortification of delay. I expected that my Trumpeter would have inform'd the world by this time of all that it is needfull for them to know upon such an Occasion, and that an advertizing Blast blown through every Newspaper, would have said, the Poet is coming! But Man, especially Man that writes verse, is born to disappointments, as surely as Printers and Booksellers are born to be the most dilatory and tedious of all Creatures. — The plain English of this magnificent preamble is, that the Season for publication is just elapsed, that the Town is going into the Country every day, and that my book cannot appear till they return, that is, to say, not 'till next Winter. (*L*, 1:480)

In July and August Cowper and Newton were continuing to work with Johnson to determine the number of poems and their order as well as to resolve a multitude of questions about wording and style. Cowper himself was correcting the proof sheets to avoid mistakes or careless tinkering with his text. A nagging issue was the slow pace of the printer. Cowper told Newton, "Johnson sent me lately a sort of Apology for his printer's negligence, with his promise of greater diligence for the future. . . . Still I see that there is time enough before us, but I see likewise that no length of time can be sufficient for the accomplishment of a work that does not go forward" (*L*, 1:508).

By late August other letters to Newton were more cheerful about the pace of the printer's work. "Thus we Jog on together comfortably enough" (*L*, 1:513). But by October Cowper's patience was almost exhausted. "Unless he proceeds with more Celerity, the publishing moment will escape us this year as it did the last" (*L*, 1:526).

Then came more encouragement. "Johnson sent me two sheets in the course of the last ten days, to my great astonishment. I complimented him upon his alacrity in hopes that encouragement might insure the continuance of it" (*L*, 1:535). After publication, he wrote Johnson that he was "highly Satisfied with the Printing" (*L*, 2:21). There were few errata.

During the previous April, Cowper had believed that the season ahead would enable him to indulge his love of fine weather, indolence, and gardening. But indolence had not been a possibility as he skillfully and persistently guided his book of poetry toward publication with the help of William Unwin, John Newton, and Joseph Johnson.

In early July, very suddenly, life in Olney changed. Lady Austen "waiving all forms" came to visit William Cowper and Mary Unwin (*L*, 1:494). The newcomer was staying nearby with her sister Martha in the parsonage at Clifton where her husband, Thomas Jones, served as curate. Ann Austen, at this time in her early forties, had been a widow for a decade. Her husband had been thirty years her senior and for much of their married life they had lived in Sancerre, France.

Ever since Cowper had left London for Huntingdon and Olney almost twenty years before he had written about his sorrow for lost connections with family and London friends. In retirement he grieved especially for his Westminster School comrades. "Of Seven or Eight whom I had Selected for Intimates out of above 300, in 10 Years' time not One was left me" (*L*, 1:398). Of the period between Newton's departure for London and Lady Austen's arrival, Cowper wrote: "there was not in the Kingdom a retirement more absolutely such than ours" (*L*, 1:515).

Lady Austen made a vivacious addition to life at Olney. Her visit lasted from July until she returned to London in December, an interval well chronicled in Cowper's letters to Unwin and Newton. The poet said she was "a person that has seen much of the world and understands it well, has high spirits, a lively fancy and great readiness of Conversation" (*L*, 1:515). Cowper praised her capacity for gratitude. "Discover but a wish to please her, and she never forgets it; not only thanks you, but the tears will start into her Eyes at the recollection of the smallest Service" (*L*, 1:523).

One day there was a picnic from noon to eight, surely a first for Cowper and Mary Unwin! The setting was the Spinney, which belonged to Maria Throckmorton. The picnickers included Cowper, Mrs. Unwin, Lady Austen, her sister, Rev. Jones, and two young ladies. Servants hauled a wheelbarrow with "eatables and drinkables to the scene of our fête champêtre" (*L*, 1:499–500, 502-3). Everyone ate in an open shed used for storing root vegetables and lined with moss and ivy. A board on top of the wheelbarrow served as a table.

The first hint that Lady Austen might actually move permanently to Olney came in Cowper's letter to Unwin the end of July. "She is a most agreable woman, and has fallen in love with your mother and me, insomuch that I do not know but she may settle at Olney" (*L*, 1:502). A month later Cowper told Newton that Lady Austen was "determined to settle here" and would repair and furnish the part of Orchard Side that had been the vicarage. Although Cowper said he was pleased on Mrs. Unwin's account, he was not sure the plan would ever become reality. "But these things are all at present in the clouds, two years must intervene, and in two years not only this project, but all the projects in Europe may be disconcerted" (*L*, 1:510–11).

Cowper conveyed this same news to Unwin, emphasizing that Lady Austen "loves your Mother dearly" and, as another woman in Olney, would be on hand to assist Mary in case of illness. Cowper's tone of voice was ambiguous as he concluded. "But if this plan is effected, we shall be in a manner one family, and I suppose never pass a day without some intercourse with each other" (*L*, 1:515).

Lady Austen left the vicinity of Olney in mid-December. Undoubtedly, she could discern that Cowper was busy with business and with Joseph Johnson and deeply preoccupied with the impending publication of his book.

At her departure Lady Austen herself "proposed a correspondence," and Cowper further said to Unwin, "Because writing does not agree with your Mother [she] proposed a correspondence with me" (*L*, 2:18). To say good-bye, Cowper wrote a poem rather than a letter because poetry, he said, derives from "the centre of a glowing heart." In the poem Cowper said he could not have dreamed of a visitor from Sancerre or the Loire choosing a cottage on the banks of the Ouse. He wrote that God's plans are deep and mysterious, producing a friendship that made three people one. The closing line of the poem was not an accurate prediction: "A three-fold cord is not soon broken" (*P*, 1:453–56).

In February Cowper wrote two letters to Unwin describing a fracas—the unraveling, for the time being, of the "three-fold cord." This was a fracas by mail. Lady Austen had been displeased by something Cowper had written. He apologized. Then she began expressing "a sort of romantic idea of our merits" (*L*, 2:18). Cowper reminded her that he was a mortal, not an idol, and that she was embellishing him with colors "taken from her own fancy." Cowper read his letter to Mary, who approved. Soon Cowper was to receive from Lady Austen some shirt ruffles, and she was to receive a copy of his book. However, Cowper's conclusion was that when "confidence which belongs only to true friendship, has been once unrooted, plant it again with what care you may, it is very difficult if not impossible to make it grow" (*L*, 2:24).

In March, one week after the publication of Cowper's poems, he declared that the connection with Lady Austen was "not altogether compatible with our favorite plan, with that silent Retirement in which we have spent so many years, and in which we wish to spend what are yet before us. . . . Her vivacity was sometimes Too much for us; occasionally perhaps it might refresh and revive us, but more frequently exhausted us" (*L*, 2:32–33).

The year 1782 began for Cowper in a spirit of dullness. Earlier in the fall he had told Newton, "I am almost weary of composing, having spent a year in doing nothing else" (*L*, 1:526). He had never allowed himself "more than a fortnight's respite." Yet without writing, he was bored. He said his "chief occupation at this season of the year, is to walk ten times in a day from the fire-side to his Cucumber frame and back again" (*L*, 2:12).

Writing was infinitely more to Cowper's interior self than a means of defeating boredom. He wrote Newton with candor and self-understanding. "The quieting and composing effect of writing was such, and so totally absorbed have I sometimes been in my rhiming occupation, that neither past nor the future . . . had any longer a share in my contemplation" (*L*, 2:20).

The Olney winter of '82 was the worst in the almost two decades that Cowper and Mrs. Unwin had lived there. They were not able to walk in the fields. Mrs. Unwin's health suffered. "Air and Exercise, her only remedies are almost absolutely necessary" (*L*, 2:31–32).

Cowper had too much time to ruminate about the reception of his book. He cared deeply about public opinion but tried to protect himself by remembering that he had intended well and done his best. He would be satisfied if only Newton and several others would say "well done" (*L*, 2:15).

In the closing months of 1781, as publication drew near, Cowper tried to open his inner self to Newton and Unwin. But the words to his friends were in part a defense against possible disappointment. "No man ever wrote such quantities of verse as I have written this last year, with so much indifference about the Event, or rather with so little ambition of public praise" (*L*, 1:508).

While claiming indifference to fame, he said that if it came, he had taken "the utmost pains to deserve it," polishing and retouching his poems "with the utmost care" (*L*, 1:528). Cowper contrasted his former with his present attitude. In the past he would have been worried about committing his name to the public and his reputation "to the hazard of their Opinion." Now he claimed it a matter of little consequence "whether the world's verdict shall pronounce me a Poet, or an empty Pretender to the title" (*L*, 1:538).

In a letter to Unwin, Cowper claimed that he was perfectly at ease about the approaching publication. "If I had not been pretty well assured beforehand that my tranquility would be but little endangered by such a measure, I would never have engaged in it, for I cannot bear disturbance." Cowper wrote in his most authentic voice about two conflicting sides of his inner self. "Though my life has long been like that of a Recluse, I have not the temper of one." He had made a choice in favor of a quiet nook, a snug fireside, and a diminutive parlor even though he was "not in the least an Enemy to cheerfullness and good humor" (*L*, 1:527).

Poems by William Cowper, of the Inner Temple, Esq. was published in 1782 by Joseph Johnson of St. Paul's Church Yard, London. The volume consisted of eight long essays, which became known as the Moral Satires. These poems contain a wide variety of subject matter addressed in many different tones of voice. Cowper attacks institutions and individuals. He can be both aggressive and sarcastic and knows how to use humor in his biting criticisms. In "Expostulation" he condemns England:

> Kneel now, and lay thy forehead in the dust,
> Blush if thou canst; not petrified, thou must:
> And but an honest and a faithful part,
> Commune what then thou wast, with what thou art.
>
> (P, 1:311)

In "Charity" he is particularly effective in condemning slavery and also in trivializing any knowledge if the source is human, not divine.

> Whether the space between the stars and us,
> Whether he measure earth, compute the sea,

Weigh sunbeams, carve a fly, or spit a flea,
The solemn trifler with his boasted skill
Toils much, and is a solemn trifler still.

(P, 1:346)

"The Progress of Error" includes an unsavory assemblage of characters. Cowper begins with the Serpent, "the pois'nous, black, insinuating worm" (P, 1:262). Then the reader meets "a cassock'd huntsman and a fiddling priest" (P, 1:265). Writers are not exempt from Cowper's scorn.

Ye novellists, who mar what ye would mend,
Sniv'ling and driv'ling folly without end.

(P, 1:270)

As to the press, it is the "God of our idolatry," an "ever-bubbling spring of endless lies" (P, 1:275). As to critics,

Like trout pursued, the critic in despair
Darts to the mud and finds his safety there.

(P, 1:276)

Nature is a subject of great importance to Cowper and is treated in "Charity," "Conversation," and "Retirement." Cowper closely allies nature to the highest virtue, charity.

Th' o'erflowing well of Charity springs here!
Hark! 'tis the music of a thousand rills,

Tis truth divine exhibited on earth,
Gives Charity her being and her birth.

(P, 1:346)

The gift of nature is part of God's "grand design" to enoble all of life.

Where'er it winds, the salutary stream
Sprightly and fresh, enriches every theme.
(P, 1:376)

Nature speaks to Cowper of perfection at the time of creation.

Traces of Eden are still seen below,
Where mountain, river, forest, field, and grove,
Remind him of his Maker's pow'r and love.

The happiness of retirement is in escaping the city,

To trace, in nature's most minute design,
The signature and stamp of pow'r divine.
(P, 1:378–79)

The most important insights found in Cowper's volume of poems are views into the heart of the poet himself. Few writers have had such clarity about themselves, let alone the ability to illuminate their inner experiences in poetry. In his first published volume, Cowper describes himself as a poet with the modest aim of pleasing and informing his readers while earning a modicum of praise for himself. He writes that it is better to be a trivial than a pretentious writer.

I judg'd a man of sense could scarce do worse,
Than caper in the morris-dance of verse.
(P, 1:255)

Compared to the greatest poets such as Homer and Milton, Cowper is a poor grasshopper.

I, and such as I,
Spread little wings, and rather skip than fly.
(P, 1:256)

Cowper's deep regret is that he is not able to "speak the wisdom of the skies," to be the bard of God's story. A truly fruitful poet would be able to sing God's theme,

> That he, who died below, and reigns above
> Inspires the song, and that his name is love.
>
> (*P,* 1:261)

Unwilling to be a hypocrite, Cowper gives an accurate, poignant account of the state of his soul.

> The Christian in whose soul, though now distress'd,
> Lives the dear thought of joys he once possess'd,
> When all his glowing language issued forth
> With God's deep stamp upon its current worth,
> Will speak without disguise, and must impart
> Sad as it is, his undissembling heart,
> Abhors constraint, and dares not feign a zeal,
> Or seem to boast a fire he does not feel.
>
> (*P,* 1:372)

In the final lines of his book, Cowper returns to the subject of himself as poet. He writes with focus and precision.

> Me poetry (or rather notes that aim
> Feebly and vainly at poetic fame)
> Employs, shut out from more important views,
> Fast by the banks of the slow-winding Ouse,
> Content, if thus sequester'd I may raise
> A monitor's, though not a poet's praise,
> And while I teach an art too little known,
> To close life wisely, may not waste my own.
>
> (*P,* 1:398)

About his published volume, Cowper writes that he aims "feebly and vainly at poetic fame," but in some passages in "Retirement" and "Truth" he far outreached this goal. The poetry has undeniable power and lasting effects, especially in passages about the poet's search for God's love.

Cowper writes an unforgettable description of the posture and silence of a walking statue, a victim of melancholy. (After his descent into madness in 1773, his doctors were left with only one recommendation, that Cowper walk in the lanes and fields of Olney.) He summons pity and sympathy for an illness that "claims most compassion." Recalling the vicious jokes and torments heaped on mental patients of his time, Cowper cautions,

> But with a soul that ever felt the sting
> Of sorrow, sorrow is a sacred thing.

On his country walks, the man is a moving statue because he has lost all ability to respond to nature. Cowper builds to a crescendo as he lists the sights unseen by the melancholic: hills, waters, parks, gardens, blooming groves. No matter in the blaze of noon or in the purple evening, nothing penetrates his cloud or

> Can call up life into his faded eye,
> That passes all he sees unheeded by.

At the end, Cowper introduces the possibility of a second birth, in which the beauties of nature may, by grace, offer "delights unfelt before" (P, 1:387).

In the central portion of the poem "Truth," Cowper writes a taut and terrifying fable of a storm, the herald of God's vengeance. While from youth to old age Cowper frequently recalled storms at sea, in "Truth" the idea of God's vengeance comes to full power. This vengeance precludes mercy.

In "Truth" a horse and rider are caught in rain, thunder, and lightning. The situation becomes hopeless. The rider drops the reins. Beyond all expectation, a neat, elegant mansion appears. As the hospitable owner offers warmth, security, and rest, the rider's terror changes to joy. This is Cowper's story of a sinner living in a storm of fear that God's vengeance requires spiritual death. But God speaks above the thunder:

> The remedy you want I freely give,
> The book shall teach you, read, believe and live.
>
> (P, 1:286–87)

This passage contains Cowper's most optimistic lines about his faith and God's mercy. After the poet's breakdown of 1763, followed by his conversion under the influence of Martin Madan and Dr. Cotton and then his first years in Olney with Mary Unwin and John Newton, Cowper's life became gradually warped by his unquenchable, more and more irrational, conviction of his own sinfulness. After the breakdown of 1773, he was less blighted by imagined sins but more certain of the reality of God's condemnation. His perception of God's abandonment and inexplicable vengeance led Cowper to the conviction that all hope of mercy was eternally lost.

The possibility must be entertained that at the moment he was writing the conclusion of "Truth" in 1781 he felt genuinely restored to God's love and mercy. As he wrote "All joy to the believer," that person of faith may have been Cowper himself. Certainly, he had earlier condemned the idea that a Christian poet would feign zeal "or seem to boast a fire he does not feel" (P, 1:372).

The proposition that Cowper ever felt restored to God's mercy is contrary to many lines Cowper later wrote and opposite to the received wisdom of Cowper's interpreters. But here in "Truth," Cowper's voice in the first person seems as authentic as it ever would be. His dependence on God "is what it was." It never failed before, so it does not fail now while he struggles "in the vale of tears."

> All joy to the believer! He can speak—
> Trembling yet happy, confident yet meek.
> Since the dear hour that brought me to thy foot,

And cut up all my follies by the root,
I never trusted in an arm but thine,
Nor hop'd, but in thy righteousness divine:
My pray'rs and alms, imperfect and defil'd,
Were but the feeble efforts of a child,
Howe'er perform'd, it was their brightest part,
That they proceeded from a grateful heart:
Cleans'd in thine own all-purifying blood,
Forgive their evil and accept their good;
I cast them at thy feet—my only plea
Is what it was, dependence upon thee;
While struggling in the vale of tears below,
That never fail'd, nor shall it fail me now.

    Angelic gratulations rend the skies,
Pride falls unpitied, never more to rise,
Humility is crown'd, and faith receives the prize.
(P, 1:295–96)

13

THE WORKINGS
OF AMBITION
May 1782–July 1785

During the first months after publication of *Poems by William Cowper, of the Inner Temple, Esq.*, the author experienced a lassitude, which he described to William Unwin. "I feel an invincible aversion to employment, which I am yet constrained to fly to as my only remedy against something worse. If I do nothing I am dejected, if I do any thing I am weary, and that weariness is best described by the word lassitude which is of all weariness in the world the most oppressive" (*L*, 2:51). He enjoyed the praise of his book as expressed by his friends. But he longed for more approval. There was some encouragement in magazine reviews. Nevertheless, Cowper felt that to please only friends and their connections did not speak to "the real value" of his book, but only to their partiality.

Then Cowper was overjoyed and energized by the comments of Benjamin Franklin, "one of the first Philosophers, one of the most eminent literary characters, as well as one of the most important in the political world, that the present age can boast of." Franklin had written to a friend who forwarded Franklin's letter to Cowper.

Sir   Passey. May 8. 1782.
I received the letter you did me the honor of writing to me, and am much obliged by your kind present of a book.–The relish for reading of

Poetry had long since left me, but there is something so new in the manner, so easy and yet so correct in the language, so clear in the expression yet concise, and so just in the sentiments, that I have read the whole with great pleasure, and some of the pieces more than once. I beg you to accept my thankfull acknowledgments, and to present my respects to the Author. (*L*, 2:49)

Franklin's praise helped dispel Cowper's lassitude, which was succeeded by "the workings of ambition" (*L*, 2:54).

In July and August 1782, Cowper wrote many letters to William Unwin with dramatic news about Lady Austen. They were reconciled. Lady Austen "seized the first opportunity to embrace your mother with tears of the tenderest affection" (*L*, 2:62). Lady Austen was "passionately desirous of consolidating all into one family" (*L*, 2:66). After proposing that William Cowper and Mary Unwin join with her in renting Mr. Small's house on Clifton Hill, Lady Austen decided on a better plan— to live in the vicarage at Olney. "She has now therefore no longer any connexion with the great City, she has none on earth whom she calls friends but us, and no Home but at Olney" (*L*, 2:69).

There has been much idle speculation about the "three-fold cord" of friendship between William Cowper and Mary Unwin in Orchard Side and Ann Austen next door in the vicarage. The reliable source is Cowper himself. He wrote continually about Mary after becoming her boarder in 1765 until her death in 1796. Andrew Brink understood that Cowper and Mary Unwin's special attachment was "good fortune for them both. . . . Their life together at Olney . . . was a model of devotion and mutual support."

Cowper's brief friendship with Ann Austen was refreshing and entertaining for them both. His life at Olney received so little stimulation from the outside world that he welcomed her facility for imagining objects for his poetry. That Lady Austen gave up her London home to live next-door was a strong indication that she was fascinated with Cowper and also headstrong.

His flirtatious ways and words with her were immature and could be misleading.

To a Lady
Who Wore a Lock of His Hair Set with Diamonds

The star that beams on Anna's breast
    Conceals her William's hair,
'Twas lately severed from the rest
    To be promoted there.
The heart that beats beneath that breast
    Is William's, well I know;
A nobler prize and richer far
    Than India could bestow.
She thus his favoured lock prefers,
    To make her William shine;
The ornament indeed is hers,
    But all the honour mine.

                (*P,* 2:24)

Lassitude was overcome in Lady Austen's company and Cowper resumed writing. William Bull planned to print Cowper's translations of some poems of Mme. Guion, whose work he admired. "The strain of simple and unaffected piety in the original, is sweet beyond expression. She sings like an Angel, and for that very reason has found but few Admirers" (*L,* 2:77). Jeanne de la Mothe Guion was a minor Christian poet who offended many by her embarrassing intensity and spiritual extravagance.

In addition to translations, Cowper was writing a poem about the fictitious John Gilpin, whose story had been told him by Lady Austen. Cowper's account of Gilpin's wild ride, first published in November 1782, was intended to make himself and "2 or 3 others laugh. . . . But now all the world laughs" (*L,* 2:91).

The author had ambiguous feelings about the success of "John Gilpin" and the inclusion of such light verse in his volume *The Task.* Cowper was "both flattered and grieved by the great celebrity of Gilpin's ride" (*L,* 2:342). "A serious poem is like a Swan, it flies heavily, and never far. But a Jest has the wings of a swallow that never tire and that carry it into every Nook and corner" (*L,* 2:370). Rather than writing translations or amusing verse, Cowper's core ambition was to publish another volume of serious original poetry. He explained himself to Mary Newton: "Having met with encouragement, I consequently wish to write again, but wishes are a very small part of the qualifications necessary for such a purpose. Many a man who has succeeded tolerably well in his first attempt has spoiled all by the second" (*L,* 2:92). Qualifications necessary for writing were explained for Joseph Hill when Cowper declined an invitation to visit his friend at Wargrove. Cowper was leading "the life I always wished for in country air and retirement . . . rooted where I am" and "having spirits that cannot bear a bustle" (*L,* 2:88–89).

The first four months of reconciliation with Lady Austen included notable examples of bustle. He told William Unwin of her tendency to bilious colic, which caused excruciating pains and anguish. A few days after one such attack, Lady Austen suffered "a frightfull Hysteric fit," one of the worse Cowper had ever seen (*L,* 2:74). After robbers had invaded the Jones's house in Clifton, Lady Austen's extreme excitability was evident. The family dined at Olney. Everyone else went back home, but "Lady Austen's Spirits having been too much disturbed to be capable of repose in a place where she had been so much terrified, she was left behind. She remains with us, till her lodgings at the Vicarage can be made ready for her reception" (*L,* 2:81).

After Lady Austen settled into the renovated vicarage, the bustle of these emergencies was replaced by a life of "constant engagement." In January '83 Cowper wrote to Unwin, "From a scene of the most uninterrupted Retirement we have passed at once into a *State of Constant Engagement. Not that our Society is much multiplied, the addition of an Individual has made all this difference.* Lady Austen and we pass our days alternately at each other's Château; in the morning I walk with one or other of the Ladies, and in the afternoon wind thread—thus did Hercules and thus probably did Sampson, and thus do I" (*L,* 2:98).

In February he wrote to Hill in the same vein of ascerbic self-mockery. "When I can, I walk—but always with a Lady under my arm; which again is amusing, and for the same reason, for to extricate the

Ladies out of all the Bogs into which I lead them, is no small proof of ingenuity and prowess. Thus I spend my mornings, and my Evenings in winding thread, Silk, and Cotton, or reading History to the aforesaid Ladies. Sigh now and say—happy creature! how I envy you" (*L*, 2:107).

Cowper wrote Hill in a different tone of voice to describe winter evenings in '82 and '83. This time was spent by

> a *domestic fireside,* in a retreat as silent as retirement can make it, where no noise is made but what we make for our own amusement. For instance, here are two Ladies and your humble Servant in company; one of the Ladies has been playing on the Harpsichord, while I with the other have been playing at Battledore and Shuttlecock. A little dog in the mean time howling under the chair of the former, performed in the Vocal way to admiration. This Entertainment over, I began my letter, and having nothing more important to communicate, have given you an account of it. (*L*, 2:96)
>
> I see the Winter approaching without much concern, though a passionate lover of fine weather, and the pleasanter scenes of Summer. But the long Evenings have their comforts too, and there is hardly to be found upon on earth, I suppose, so snug a creature as an Englishman by his fire-side in the Winter. I mean however an Englishman that lives in the country, for in London it is not very easy to avoid Intrusion. I have two Ladies to read to; sometimes more, but never less. At present we are circumnavigating the globe. (*L*, 2:172)

When spring arrived, Cowper wrote the first of many despairing letters to John Newton. In modern terminology Newton can be viewed as Cowper's spiritual adviser or confessor or psychiatrist. It was to Newton that Cowper bared his desperate heart. "We are tolerably well, but neither the Season nor the Wind which is East, are favorable to our spirits. They always sink in the Spring. Assure yourselves that we love you, and believe me" (*L*, 2:122).

In another letter Cowper elaborated on the place in scripture of divine wrath and also of "the broad and clear exhibition of Mercy." He disparaged those who meddle with the gospel, warning that "the word is a flaming sword, and he that touches it with unhallowed fingers, thinking to make a tool of it, will find that he has burnt them" (*L*, 2:125–26). As the month of April progressed, so did Cowper's depression. "My days are spent in vanity, and it is impossible for me to spend them otherwise. No man upon earth is more sensible of the unprofitableness of a life like mine, than I am, or groans more heavily under the burthen; but this too is vanity, because it is in vain; my groans will not bring the remedy, because there is no remedy for me. The time when I seem to be most rationally employed is when I am reading. My studies however are very much confined and of little use, because I have no books but what I borrow, and nobody will lend me a memory. My own is almost worn out" (*L*, 2:127).

By June Cowper could again write cheerfully to Newton that "we are glad to find that you still entertain the design of coming, and hope that you will bring Sunshine with you. We are well, and always mindfull of you. Be mindfull of us, and assured that we love you" (*L*, 2:146).

The period from the summer of 1783 to the summer of 1784 was a complex and all-important time for William Cowper. The central question was whether he could work out his ambition to become a serious poet while living in a state of depression and despair. The presence of Lady Austen at the Olney vicarage was, on the one hand, an antidote to despair and an inspiration to his writing. On the other hand, Lady Austen occupied so many hours in a day that Cowper had no time to write.

Cowper understood the importance to him of writing and was uniquely able, in the language of his heart, to explain how despair could be an impetus rather than an impediment to a poet. "Employment however, and with the pen, is through habit become essential to my well-being, and to produce always Original poems, especially of considerable length, is not so easy" (*L*, 2:411).

Of his story of John Gilpin, he told Unwin that these were "the most lucrative lines I ever wrote" and were written "in the saddest mood" (*L*, 2:91). He again used the image of himself as a mariner on board ship in a storm. He said that writing nonsense while suffering depression was like a seaman fiddling and dancing in a tempest.

Cowper came to understand that "verse was his favorite occupation." He had found a way to escape listening continually "to the language of a heart hopeless and deserted" (*L*, 2:225). The rhyme and rhythm of poetry, being difficult and therefore impossible to accomplish without concentration, provided escape from despair. He wrote again to Newton in the same vein after he had completed his poem "The Task." "Despair made amusement necessary, and I found poetry the most agreeable amusement. Had I not endeavor'd to perform my best, it would not have amused me at all" (*L*, 2:367).

Cowper believed that his writing was part of the providential goodness of God. He told Harriet of his identity as a poet. "Set me down therefore my Dear, for an industrious Rhimer so long as I shall have the ability, for in this only way it is possible for me, so far as I can see, either to honour God, or to serve man, or even to serve myself" (*L*, 2:544).

A few days later, Cowper continued his introspection, writing to Newton in a much more somber tone than he used with Harriet. Cowper reminded Newton of the thirteen years since he first descended into "the midnight of absolute despair." Distress drove him to writing. Or perhaps he was providentially led to it or compelled and scourged into it. However he came to be a writer, it must have been God's will because every other way of employing his time, "God continues to make impossible" (*L*, 2:548).

At the end of 1786, in a letter to Walter Churchey, a friend and Christian poet, Cowper asserted not only his identity as a writer, but particularly as a published writer: "But I know well that publication is necessary to give an edge to the poetical turn, and that what we produce in the closet is never a vigorous birth, if we intend that it should die there. For my own part, I could no more amuse myself with writing verse, if I did not print it when written" (*L*, 2:617).

Cowper's most important poem, "The Task," was inspired by a suggestion of Lady Austen's. Cowper said, "I began the 'Task'—for she was the lady who gave me the sofa for a subject" (*L*, 2:456). Bluntly put, to publish "The Task" eventually became for Cowper more important than the companionship of Lady Austen.

Cowper enjoyed Lady Austen's company as a reminder of the London life he had lost, when he associated with others who were well-born and educated, witty and flirtatious, and who enjoyed themselves in the city and at the seashore. Lady Austen was good company as well for Mary Unwin who had known a cosmopolitan life before her marriage. Cowper said that Lady Austen "had lived much in France, was very sensible, and had infinite vivacity. She took a great liking to us, and we to her" (*L*, 2:456).

The irony was that, by inspiring William Cowper to write "The Task," Lady Austen created conflict between Cowper's daily schedule with her and his imperative to write. "I was forced to neglect the Task to attend upon the Muse who had inspired the subject" (*L*, 2:457). Cowper and Mary Unwin's daily schedule with Lady Austen, as "Customs very soon became laws," included meetings at eleven in the morning, walking, dining, and reading until eleven at night.

The final break with Lady Austen in July 1784 was foreshadowed in Cowper's letter to Unwin eight months before. Here Cowper sounded relieved that she was absent. "An evening unexpectedly retired and which your mother and I spend without company (an occurrence far from frequent), affords me a favorable opportunity to write by to-morrow's post, which else I could not have found" (*L*, 2:184). The following week, Cowper made an even more revealing comment to Newton. "I have neither long visits to pay, nor to receive, nor ladies to spend hours in telling me that which might be told in 5 minutes" (*L*, 2:185).

When Cowper wrote to Unwin that Lady Austen had left Olney for good, he explained the break on the grounds of incompatibility: "A character with which we spend all our time should be made on purpose for us. Too much or too little of any single ingredient, spoils all. In the instance in question, the dissimilitude was too great not to be felt continually, and consequently made our intercourse unpleasant. We have reason however to believe that she has given up all thoughts of a Return to Olney" (*L*, 2:262).

It was in Cowper's letter to Hill four months later that the core truth about Lady Austen's departure was made clear: Cowper wanted fewer interruptions in his writing schedule. Even more, he wanted back his life of twenty years with Mary. In his final explanation, Cowper called Lady Austen "a Third." "We have, as you say, lost a lively and sensible neighbour in Lady Austen. But we have been long accustomed to a state of Retirement within one degree of solitude, and being naturally Lovers of still life, can relapse into our former duality without being unhappy at the change. To Me indeed a Third is not necessary while I have the companion I have had almost these 20 years" (L, 2:294).

Letters to William Bull and William Unwin during 1784 gave specific information about Cowper's use of "favorable opportunities to write." By diligent use of the pen, he was able to send his volume *The Task* to his publisher by the end of October.

In February Cowper told Bull that "The sofa . . . consists at present of four books and part of a fifth. When the sixth is finished the work is accomplished" (L, 2:217). In August he wrote that "The sofa is ended but not finish'd" because he was making changes. "I find it severe exercise to mould it and fashion it to my mind" (L, 2:269). The following month Cowper was transcribing his work and very concerned that when completed it would arrive safely at Johnson's on Leman Street, London. Cowper found transcribing to be "slavish work, and of all occupations that which I dislike most." He then made a confession about himself as a poet. He told William Unwin, "I would not write this freely on the subject of me or mine to any but yourself. Whatever I do, I confess that I most sincerely wish to do well, and when I have reason to hope that I have succeeded, am pleased indeed, but not proud; for He who has placed everything out of the reach of man, except what he freely gives him, has made it impossible for a reflecting mind that knows it, to indulge so silly a passion for a moment" (L, 2:277).

By October Unwin had received his long poem "The Task" with a letter revealing clearly the poet's purposes. Cowper wrote that the second book was "Satyrical. . . . I know that a reformation of such abuses as I have censured, is not to be expected from the efforts of a poet; but to contemplate the world, its follies, its vices, its indifference to duty and its strenuous attachment to what is evil, and not to reprehend were to approve it."

Cowper confessed that he had two reasons for placing the religious aspects of his book toward the end. "First that I might not revolt the Reader at his entrance, and secondly that my best impression might be made last. Were I to write as many Volumes as Lopez de Vega or Voltaire, not one of them all would be without this tincture. If the world like it not, so much the worse for them. I make all the concessions I can that I may please them, but I will not please them at the expense of conscience."

Without a regular plan for "The Task," the poet said that his reflections were "suggested always by the preceding passage." But Cowper did have one overriding aim, "to discountenance the modern enthusiasm after a London life, and to recommend rural ease and leisure as friendly to the cause of Piety and virtue." Cowper concluded, "if it pleases you, I shall be happy, and collect from your pleasure in it, an omen of its general acceptance" (*L*, 2:284–85).

Unwin was indeed pleased. Only ten days later, Cowper was able to write: "Your letter has relieved me from some anxiety, and given me a good deal of positive pleasure. I have faith in your judgment, and an implicit confidence in the Sincerity of your approbation. The writing of so long a poem is a serious business." Johnson had asked for more material to be published in the volume with "The Task." Cowper told Unwin that "Tirocinium," which he had begun two years ago, was resumed. "It turns on the question; whether an Education at school or Home be preferable. . . . My design is to Inscribe it to you; but you must see it first." Cowper concluded with comments about Unwin's corrections and various family messages. "I am tired of this endless scribblement. Adieu!" (*L*, 2:285–89).

In November Cowper told Joseph Hill that "Tirocinium" was finished. "You perceive that I have taken your advice and give the pen no rest" (*L*, 2:295). In writing two days later to William Bull, Cowper said he was transcribing "Tirocinium." "The business and purpose of it are to censure the want of discipline and the scandalous Inattention to Morals [in schools] especially in the largest, and to recommend private Tuition as a mode of Education preferable on all accounts. To call upon fathers to become the Tutors of their own sons, where that is practicable; to take home to them a domestic Tutor where it is not; and if neither can be done, to place them under the care of such a man as He to whom I am writing, some rural parson whose attention is limited to a few" (*L*, 2:295).

Cowper had a succinct message for Hill and Bull in November 1784: "I am gone to the Press again." As to Unwin, he had been told from the beginning about the progress of "The Task." Now it was Cowper's awkward responsibility and imperative to inform Newton:

> I am again at Johnson's; in the shape of a Poem in blank verse; consisting of Six books, and called the Task. I began it about this time Twelvemonth, and writing sometimes an hour in a day, sometimes half a one, and sometimes two hours, have lately finished it. I mentioned it not sooner, because almost to the last I was doubtfull whether I should ever bring it to a conclusion. Working often in such distress of mind as while it spurred me to the work, at the same time threat'ned to disqualify me for it. My Bookseller I suppose will be as tardy as before; I do not expect to be born into the world 'till the month of March, when I and the Crocuses shall peep together. (*L*, 2:291)

Two days later Cowper wrote to William Unwin on the subject of authorly secrets.

> I wrote to Mr. Newton by the last Post to inform him that I am gone to the Press again. He will be surprised and perhaps not pleased, but I think he cannot complain, for he keeps his own Authorly secrets without participating them with me. I do not think myself in the least degree injured by his reserve, neither should I, were he to publish a whole library without favoring me with any previous notice of his intentions. In those cases, it is no violation of the laws of friendship not to communicate, though there must be a friendship where the communication is made. But many reasons may concur in disposing a

writer to keep his work a secret, and none of them injurious to his friends. (*L*, 2:292)

The end of 1784 was a turning point for Cowper. He had completed "The Task" over the course of a year, complaining about "the writing of so long a poem" (*L*, 2:285). "Tirocinium" and "John Gilpin" were also ready to be included in his new volume. As 1784 came to an end, he used few but unambiguous words to express to Unwin the finality of his break with Lady Austen. "Lady A is neither returned nor returnable. She has hired a house at Bristol and furnished it" (*L*, 2:299).

In July 1785 the volume entitled *The Task and Other Poems, 1785* was published. Included were "The Task, A Poem in Six Books," an "Epistle to Joseph Hill, Esq.," "Tirocinium: Or, A Review of Schools," and "The Diverting History of John Gilpin."

14

DELINEATIONS OF THE HEART

1785

In 1785 William Cowper was in his midfifties. He and Mary Unwin were living out their seventeenth year at Orchard Side, Olney. In many respects, this year was one of great satisfaction for Cowper, satisfaction in his retired way of life, in his friendships, and most of all in his fulfillment as a poet. His despair remained, but sometimes "a glimpse of hope" broke in on him "like a flash in a dark night, during which the heavens seemed open'd only to shut again" (*L,* 2:357).

In the year 1785 Cowper expressed in his letters his deepest feelings, which he called the "delineations of the heart" (*L,* 2:285). He wrote to his friends about his life of rural retirement and about events leading up to the publication of *The Task.* Andrew Brink proposes that "the biography is fuller for Cowper than for almost any other English writer of the period; Cowper was a diligent and engaging correspondent who put as much of himself into letters as into poetry."[1] An early Cowper biographer, Robert Southey, said that "when letters are accessible, the writer may in great part be made his own biographer,—more fully, and perhaps more faithfully, than if he had composed his own memoirs, even with the most sincere intentions."[2]

Cowper understood the dimensions of his interior self and was able to reveal himself to others.

He that attends to his interior self,
That has a heart, and keeps it; has a mind
that hungers and supplies it.

(P, 2:172)

The winter of 1785 was severe, heavy with frost, cold, and dark. "Of all the Winters we have passed at Olney, and this is the 17th, the present has confined us most." Daily exercise had always been essential to the health of both Cowper and Mary Unwin. In the worst weather, they walked on a gravel path sixty yards long. For four months in 1785, they were able to walk into the fields only three times. Always concerned for the poor of Olney, Cowper decried their plight in such a bad winter. He told Newton about one woman in a mudwall cottage who suffered "the miseries of age, sickness, and the extremist penury" (*L,* 2:328).

Cowper had one disappointment when the walking season returned. "One of our most favorite walks is spoiled. The Spinney is cut down to the stumps. Even the lilacs and syringas to the stumps. Little did I think (though indeed I might have thought it) that the trees which screened me from the Sun last summer, would this Winter be employed in roasting potatoes and boiling tea-kettles for the poor of Olney" (*L,* 2:334–35).

Cowper's summer letters were enlivened with news of animals he loved. He told Unwin about his bulldog Mongo in a thunderstorm. "The moment that he heard the thunder, which was like the burst of a great gun, with a wrinkled forehead and with eyes divert'd to cieling whence the sound seemed to proceed, he barked. But he barked exactly in concert with the thunder. It thunder'd once, and he bark'd once, and so precisely in the very instant when the thunder happen'd that both sounds seemed to begin and end together." Near Orchard Side the lightning knocked down a chimney and split off the corner of the house "in which lay a fellow drunk and asleep upon his bed. It roused and terrified him, and he promises to be drunk no more; but I have seen a woefull end of many such conversions" (*L,* 2:364–65).

William Unwin and John Newton were the most significant of Cowper's friends during most of 1785. His letters to Unwin included many expressions of affection along with regular bulletins about progress toward publication of *The Task*. The first week in February, Cowper told Unwin that he had received and revisited and returned to Johnson the first two proof sheets. Two more were received a month later. Cowper felt that "the Press proceeds like a broad-wheeled wagon, slow and sure." He also compared it to the flight of a wild goose: "So the wild goose in the meadow flaps her wings and flaps them but yet she mounts not. She stands on tip-toe on the bands of Ouse, she meditates an ascent, she stretches her long neck, she flaps her wings again; the successful repetition of her efforts at last bears her above the ground, she mounts into the heav'nly regions exulting, and who then shall describe her song? To herself at least it makes ample recompense of her laborious exertions" (*L*, 2:332).

A month later, describing himself as an impatient author, Cowper asked Unwin to go by Johnson's and "just insinuate to him that were his remittances rather more frequent, that frequency would be no inconvenience to me" (*L*, 2:336). Unwin did, in fact, write to Johnson, as did Cowper. "The man Johnson is like unto some vicious horses that I have known. They would not budge 'till they were spurred and when they were spurred they would kick. So did He. His temper was somewhat disconcerted, but his pace was quicken'd and I was contented" (*L*, 2:345).

By May Cowper was much encouraged as he wrote what he called an author's letter to his friend. "In our printing business we now jog on merrily enough. The coming week will, I hope, bring me to an end of 'The Task,' and the next fortnight to an end of the whole" (*L*, 2:349). A month later Cowper had good news for Newton. "My book is at length printed, I returned the last proof to Johnson on Tuesday" (*L*, 2:353). But in late July, Cowper expressed sarcastic impatience. "I know not what Johnson is about, neither do I now inquire. It will be a month to-morrow since I returned to him the last proof. He might, I suppose, have published by this time without hurrying himself into a fever, or breaking his neck through the violence of his dispatch" (*L*, 2:358). The volume, *The Task*, was published in July of 1785.

That same month Cowper wrote to Unwin with deep feeling. "My heart tells me that in all my intercourse with my friends I wish to shine in nothing but esteeming and loving them as I ought" (*L*, 2:355). Such esteem and love was gradually restored between Cowper and Newton after their struggle over authorly secrets. In the end it proved true that theirs was "a friendship in which distance and time made no abatement" (*L*, 2:300).

Cowper understood that no matter how calmly Newton initially wrote about being kept in the dark on *The Task* and being superceded by Unwin in dealings with Johnson, in every line of his letters were "the soft murmers of something like mortification." Cowper tried to mollify Newton but could not go so far as to accede to his request to receive proof sheets as fast as they were printed. "I would no more show my poem piece-meal, than I would my house if I had one, the merits of the structure in either case being equally liable to suffer by such a partial view of it" (*L*, 2:305).

The low point in the friendship was just before Christmas when Cowper described Newton's last letter as "fretfull and peevish, and mine if not chargeable with exactly the same qualities, was however, dry and unsavory enough" (*L*, 2:312). A month later Cowper was more sanguine. "But we shall jumble together again, as people that have an affection for each other at bottom, notwithstanding now and then a slight disagreement, always do" (*L*, 2:317).

In April Newton wrote Cowper. "I am perfectly satisfied with the propriety of your proceedings as to the publication." Thus, Cowper was able to write, "Now therefore we are friends again" (*L*, 2:345). After *The Task* was published, Cowper said that Newton's "favorable sentiments" gave him more pleasure than those of anyone else" (*L*, 2:361).

John Newton was Cowper's unique and most significant spiritual companion. Cowper believed that their first meeting in Huntingdon was the work of God, and he never forgot the days when he was still secure in his faith and fortified by Newton's ministry at Olney. In mid-April of 1785, after the healing of their differences regarding *The Task*, Cowper addressed the subject that would dominate their friendship to the end, the possibility of his restoration to hope and spiritual wholeness.

> I am sensible of the tenderness and affectionate kindness with which
> you recollect our past intercourse, and express your hopes of my future

restoration. I too within the last eight months have had my hopes, though they have been of short duration, cut off like the foam upon the waters. Some previous adjustments indeed are necessary, before a lasting expectation of comfort can have place in me. There are those persuasions in my mind which either entirely forbid the entrance of hope or if it enter, immediately eject it. They are incompatible with any such inmate and must be turned out themselves, before so desireable a guest can possibly have secure possession. This, you say, will be done. It may be, but it is not done yet, nor has a Single step in the course of God's dealings with me, been taken towards it. If I mend, no creature ever mended so slowly that recover'd at last. I am like a slug or snail that has fallen into a deep well; slug as he is he performs his descent with an alacrity proportion'd to his weight, but he does not crawl up again quite so fast. Mine was a rapid plunge, but my return to day light, if I am indeed returning, is leisurely enough.

The conclusion of this letter, referring back to the early days in Huntington and Olney, is a poignant and sober confession of spiritual emptiness.

But I am alter'd since that time, and if your affection for me had ceased, you might very reasonably justify your change by mine. I can say nothing for myself at present, but This I can venture to foretell, that should the restoration of which my friends assure me, obtain, I shall undoubtedly love those who have continued to love me, even in a state of transformation from my former self, much more than ever . . . Yet from a Monarch to a beast is not so violent a transition, as from a spiritual man to such a man as I have been these many years. (*L*, 2:340–41)

In writing this long letter to Newton, Cowper summarized the delineations of a heart that felt separated from God. According to Andrew Brink, "writing verse was the best thing that Cowper ever did, a continuation on the deepest possible level of the self-revelation and accommodation to reality carried on in conversation and in letters."[3]

Cowper's clear understanding that his writing was a "weapon against despair" prefigured modern psychiatrists who propose that creativity is a technique for resolving internal conflicts. Andrew Brink's *Loss and Symbolic Repair* as well as Anthony Storr's *The Dynamics of Creation* are indispensable books for Cowper scholars, just as Cowper's insights about himself have been an essential component in the development of modern theories about creativity. Brink writes in his introduction that "poetry is a means of achieving strength from frailty, the ideal from the painfully limited sense of self."[4] Cowper stands apart from other poets in his uncommon insight into poetry's function "in striving for self-completion or at least in holding off despair."[5]

Possibly the most mistaken but often expressed view of Cowper is that he was a passive person. Lodwick Hartley's study of Cowper noted that "the tradition of 'Poor Cowper' and the 'stricken deer' has been so persistent and so fascinating that it is almost impossible for modern criticism to treat the poet without patronizing him."[6] In the midtwentieth century, *The Cambridge History of English Literature* was still referring to the poet's "tender, shrinking mind."

However, at the end of his life, Cowper was in reality striving mightily for wholeness as he wrote his last poem, "The Cast-away." Disparaging critics called this poem his "most pathetically personal" and "tragic final lyric." But Andrew Brink called "The Cast-away" his "most hauntingly truthful utterance," in which Cowper wrote of his lifelong, courageous struggle:

> But waged with death a lasting strife,
> Supported by despair of life.
>
> (*P*, 3:214)

Here are the delineations of a heart brave enough to fight to a bitter end. In conclusion, Brink writes, "Only the struggle fully to take his place in life, and to possess the strength to meet it face on, could engender creative efforts of the importance we find in Cowper's poetry."[7]

William Cowper's most sustained and successful creative work was his poem "The Task." In October 1784 Cowper sent William Unwin his new book, entitled *The Task,* which included the six-book poem "The Task" and some other writings.

Included with his book was a letter setting forth the poem's plan and purpose. In it, Cowper acknowledged that "The Task" did not have a clear, structured plan. "The reflections are naturally suggested always by the preceding passage" (*L,* 2:284–85). Cowper called this method "roving." In book 4 he ingenuously asks, "Roving as I rove, where shall I find an end, or how proceed?" (*P,* 2:193).

At this point in book 4 he has been criticizing evenings spent at the theatre or in playing cards or billiards. He then shifts his emphasis to praise of his own rural evenings—reading, enjoying music, winding silken threads for the ladies. At the conclusion of "The Task," the last lines of book 6, the poet again mentions his roving, which had been for fruit as well as merely for flowers. He had "rov'd far, and gathered much: some harsh, 'tis true."

Cowper also told Unwin about two consistent characteristics of all six books. "My descriptions are all from Nature. Not one of them the second-handed" (*L,* 2:285). In book 1 he tells Mary Unwin

> Thou know'st my praise of nature most sincere,
> And that my raptures are not conjured up
> To serve occasions of poetic pomp,
> But genuine, and art partner of them all.
>   (*P,* 2:121)

In a similar vein, he told Unwin, "My delineations of the heart are from my own experience" (*L,* 2:285). The *Oxford English Dictionary* quotes this sentence of Cowper's in order to define "delineation" as "the action of portraying in words."

Near the end of "The Task," Cowper portrays himself as a happy, obscure man, tranquil because he was

> Content indeed to sojourn while he must
> Below the skies, but having there his home.

His contemplation of the unseen heaven shows him "glories yet to be reveal'd." Cowper acknowledges that "his warfare is within," but lays claim to "triumphs o'er himself." He anticipates that his life will glide away,

> not vex'd with care
> Or stained with guilt, beneficent, approved,
> Of God and man, and peaceful in its end.
> (*P,* 2:260–62)

Here, interpreters of Cowper face a dilemma and the impossibility of its solution: Cowper's self-portrayal in words was not consistent with his life experience. He had not triumphed over inner battles. He was still vexed with care and stained with guilt. Little more than a year later, he would write to describe how during the previous thirteen years he had lived in "the midnight of absolute despair" (*L,* 2:548). Even before he wrote "The Task," he had told Newton, "There is no remedy for me" (*L,* 2:127). And tragically, Cowper's life was not "peaceful in its end."

Future interpretations in the work of scholars like Andrew Brink may give additional insight into the "pleasure in poetic pains" (*P,* 2:146). Does a depressive poet while at work actually feel optimistic and fully able to deny anxiety? At his desk with pen in hand, does he actually believe he has triumphed over his past and is awaiting a peaceful future? William Cowper himself asks these questions in "The Task."

> Are occupations of the poet's mind
> So pleasing, and that steal away the thought
> With one such address, from themes of sad import,
> That, lost in his own musings, happy man!
> He feels th' anxieties of life, denied
> Their wonted entertainment, all retire,
> Such joys has he that sings.
> (*P,* 2:146)

Cowper's letter to Unwin moved from general characteristics of the entire poem to specific purposes of certain chapters. The author asserted that book 2 of "The Task" has a specific purpose—to be "Satyrical" (*L*, 2:284). The *Oxford English Dictionary* provides a definition of "satirical" congruent with Cowper's usage: "The employment, in speaking or writing, of sarcasm, irony, ridicule, etc., in exposing, denouncing, deriding or ridiculing vice, folly, indecorum, abuses or evils of any kind."

The evil denounced at greatest length in book 2 (more than two hundred lines or a quarter of the whole) is corruption of the clergy. For this evil and all others, Cowper offers two general caveats. First, God's wrath and displeasure is expressed in natural disasters such as earthquakes, floods, and famine. Second, no matter how great various abuses are, Cowper still loves his native land. "England, with all thy faults, I love thee still—My country!" (*P*, 2:144).

Cowper lists the clergy's vices: peculation, sale of honor, perjury, corruption, forgery, and subterfuge of law. Cowper is scathing and bitter in describing clergymen he hates, especially affected preachers. "The di'mond on his lily hand . . . displaying his own beauty, starves his flock" (*P*, 2:149–50).

> The pastor, either vain
> By nature, or by flatt'ry made so, taught
> To gaze at his own splendour, and t'exalt
> Absurdly, not his office, but himself . . .
> Perverting often by the stress of lewd
> And loose example, whom he should instruct.
> (*P*, 2:152–53)

Cowper explains to Unwin the purpose of one other section of "The Task," that book 5 is "rather of a political aspect." Although roving over other topics, the primary subject of the fifth book is England's tradition of political freedom.

> Thee I account still happy, and the chief
> Among the nations, seeing thou art free:

My native nook of earth!
But th'age of virtuous politics is past. . . .
England's glory . . . is pale and sickly.
(P, 2:222–24)

In the concluding two hundred lines of book 5, Cowper roves widely over connections between freedom, God's grace, and God's self-revelation in nature.

Grace makes the slave a freeman. . . .
But transformation of apostate man
From fool to wise, from earthly to divine,
Is work for Him that made him.
(P, 2:228)

Cowper laments that few remember the purpose of a patriot's death,

And for a time insure, to his loved land,
The sweets of liberty and equal laws.
(P, 2:229)

Fewer still recall the martyrs, he continues, "and History, so warm on meaner themes, is cold on this" (*P*, 2:229).

A primary liberty, always available, is to enjoy the mountains, valleys, and rivers made by God's unwearied love,

that plann'd and built, and still upholds a world
So cloathed with beauty, for rebellious man.
(P, 2:230)

The man who "appropriates nature as his father's work . . . is indeed a freeman." The soul who knows the Maker sees in nature God's "unambiguous footsteps" (*P*, 2:230–31). When men become pure as God is pure,

Then we are free. Then liberty like day
Breaks on the soul, and by a flash from heav'n
Fires all the faculties with glorious joy.

(*P,* 2:233)

Cowper also told Unwin that the poet has a moral obligation to his readers. First Cowper pointed out that while "a reformation of such abuses as I have censured, is not to be expected from the efforts of a poet," still "to contemplate the world, its follies, its vices, its indifference to duty and its strenuous attachment to what is evil, not to reprehend, were to approve it" (*L,* 2:284). On cruelty to animals, Cowper writes with such feeling in "The Task" that his lines might well have brought about some reformation.

And I am recompensed, and deem the toils
Of poetry not lost, if verse of mine
May stand between an animal and woe,
And teach one tyrant pity for his drudge.

(*P,* 2:255)

Similarly, Cowper's lines in condemnation of human slavery are so intense he may well have been hopeful of being an agent of change. Cowper calls slavery "human nature's broadest, foulest blot,"

Chains him, and tasks him, and exacts his sweat
With stripes, that mercy with a bleeding heart
Weeps when she sees inflicted on a beast.

Cowper vows that he would not have a slave.

I had much rather be myself the slave
And wear the bonds, than fasten them on him.

(*P,* 2:139–40)

Another moral obligation Cowper felt to his readers, he told Unwin, was to include religious themes in his poems. While Cowper was willing to woo his readers by placing religious material at the end rather than the beginning of his poem, he was not willing to omit these subjects. "If the world like it or not, so much the worse for them." Cowper's tone in the letter was the authentic voice of a determined man. "I make all the concessions that I can that I may please them, but I will not please them at the expense of conscience."

Finally, Cowper concluded his letter to William Unwin by saying that "The Task" as a whole has one tendency, to discountenance the modern enthusiasm after a London life, and to recommend rural ease and leisure as friendly to the cause of piety and virtue (*L*, 2:284–85). Cowper's comments on London life in the poem are short and unflinching. But his belief that rural life promotes piety and virtue becomes throughout "The Task" a complex and compelling theology.

Cowper writes about London in books 1 and 2. London is the seat of the newest technologies and the center of the growing world of commerce. London is more the glory of the modern world than was Babylon of the ancient world. Cowper sees London as witty but not wise, as slack in discipline and uneven in justice. In a summary of all condemnations, Cowper states that London annuls and breaks the will of God. He feels wrath and pity when he thinks of London:

> Oh thou, resort and mart of all the earth,
> Chequer'd with all complexions of mankind,
> And spotted with all crimes; in whom I see
> Much that I love, and more than I admire,
> And all that I abhor.
>
> (*P*, 2:184)

Some fundamental concepts of Cowper's theology of nature are also established in book 1.

The air salubrious of her lofty hills,
The chearing fragrance of her dewy vales,
And music of her woods—no works of man
May rival these; these all bespeak a power
Peculiar and exclusively her own.
Beneath the open sky, she spreads the feast;
'Tis free to all—'tis ev'ry day renew'd.

(*P,* 2:128)

Cowper is especially intense and eloquent citing instances of man's refinements of God's creation such as a garden, greenhouse, or spinney. Cowper knows that the creation of a garden requires the hard work of digging up the soil and adding compost.

But elegance, chief grace the garden shows
And most attractive, is the fair result
Of thought, the creature of a polish'd mind.

(*P,* 2:179)

A garden provides "blest seclusion from a jarring world." The poet defends his retreat to the safety of his garden from a more public life.

What could I wish, that I possess not here?
Health, leisure, means t'improve it, friendship, peace,
No loose or wanton, though a wand'ring muse,
And constant occupation without care.

(*P,* 2:180)

The creation of a greenhouse, even more than of a garden, requires physical labor and understanding of horticulture. Cowper describes the building itself of wood and glass, the growth of seeds in pots, as well as transplantation and fertilization. He admonishes the rich not to begrudge the cost of a greenhouse.

Ye little know the cares,
The vigilance, the labor, and the skill
That day and night are exercised and hang
Upon the ticklish balance of suspense,
That ye may garnish your profuse regales
With summer fruits brought forth by wintry suns.
(*P,* 2:176–77)

He reminds the greenhouse owner of the ten thousand possible dangers from heat, cold, wind, and steam, even from mice, worms, and flies. Cowper enjoys the possibility of growing flowers that are "foreigners from many lands." The proper arrangement of such variety requires a "master's hand."

A spinney, like a garden or greenhouse, was to Cowper an "enclos'd demesne" where the hand of man refined the work of God.

So sportive is the light
Shot through the boughs, it dances as they dance,
Shadow and sunshine intermingling quick,
And dark'ning and enlight'ning, as the leaves
Play wanton, ev'ry moment, ev'ry spot.
(*P,* 2:126)

At the end of his letter to Unwin, Cowper said that the whole of "The Task," by enlarging on the love of rural life and nature, would promote piety and virtue. Regardless of how this theme would be received by the reading public, Cowper explored the connection between piety and nature in book 3, and to a greater extent in books 5 and 6.

I therefore recommend, though at the risk
Of popular disgust, yet boldly still,
The cause of piety and sacred truth
And virtue, and those scenes which God ordain'd

Should best secure them and promote them most;
Scenes that I love, and with regret perceive
Forsaken, or through folly not enjoyed.

(*P,* 2:180–81)

For Cowper any understanding of piety or nature, let alone their relationship, would be gained by wisdom, not knowledge.

Knowledge and wisdom, far from being one,
Have off-times no connexion.

Knowledge, built on the thoughts of other men, is seen as an unprofitable mass of materials. Wisdom is related to one's own thoughts and stems from acquaintance with God. Possessing wisdom, a man can see God in nature (*P,* 2:239).

The mind that has been touch'd from heav'n,
And in the school of sacred wisdom taught
To read his wonders, in whose thought the world,
Fair as it is, existed 'ere it was.

(*P,* 2:231)

Wisdom is associated with "the lamp of truth," "the mysterious word"—Christ himself.

So reads he nature whom the lamp of truth
Illuminates. Thy lamp, mysterious word!

(*P,* 2:232)

Thus, one side of Cowper's theology says that a man who becomes wise by knowing God will then be able to enjoy nature.

Acquaint thyself with God, if thou would'st taste
His works. Admitted once to his embrace,

Thou shalt perceive that thou wast blind before;
Thine eye shall be instructed, and thine heart,
Made pure, shall relish, with divine delight
'Till then unfelt, what hands divine have wrought.

(*P,* 2:231)

The obverse side of Cowper's theology of nature is the reverse of the first. Nature instructs man who is not yet acquainted with God. Nature "prompts with remembrance of a present God" (*P,* 2:243). Nature speaks in the seasons of the year, in the passage from summer to winter and to summer again.

From dearth to plenty, and from death to life,
Is Nature's progress when she lectures man
In heav'nly truth; evincing as she makes
The grand transition, that there lives and works
A soul in all things, and that soul is God.

(*P,* 2:241)

God not only created nature, but also sustains it.

Nature is but a name for an effect,
Whose cause is God. He feeds the secret fire
By which the mighty process is maintain'd,
Who sleeps not, is not weary.

This passage reaches its climax when Cowper declares that Christ rules all nature.

One spirit—His
Who wore the platted thorns with bleeding brows,
Rules universal nature.

(*P,* 2:242–43)

Finally, Cowper reconciles both sides of wisdom: that knowing God, man can appreciate nature; and, enlightened by nature, man can find God. Finally, nature's scenes of beauty are a foretaste of paradise restored.

> Thus heav'n-ward all things tend. For all were once
> Perfect, and all must be at length restored
> So God has greatly purposed.
>
> (*P*, 2:257)

15

A PRODIGIOUS WORK
1785–1786

The Task was an immediate success with critics and the reading public. Within two years of publication, a second and third edition were
released by Joseph Johnson. Particularly pleasing to William Cowper
were articles in three prominent publications, *Gentleman's Magazine,*
Critical Review, and *Monthly Review.* Lodwick Hartley summarized
how Cowper's work had been praised "for the simplicity and strength of
his style, the originality of his thought, the soundness and force of his
argument, and his ability as a satirist. Cowper's powers as a nature poet
and as a poet of humble life are, of course, highly praised."[1]

Ever since he had left London twenty years earlier, Cowper had
mourned the loss of his family and those connections formed at
Westminster School. After leaving St. Albans for Huntingdon, Cowper
had actually expected "to be abandoned by his family" and forgotten by
his friends (*L,* 2:443). He wrote a poem in the voice of Alexander
Selkirk, a Scottish sailor left on one of the Juan Fernandez Islands, who
was the model for *Robinson Crusoe.*

> My friends do they now and then send
> A wish or a thought after me?
> O tell me I yet have a friend,
> Though a friend I am never to see.
>> (*P,* 1:403–4)

He had become desperate because no relatives and few friends wrote to him. "A Wintry Kind of Indifference seems to have frozen up their Inkbottles. I wish for them a gentle thaw and I wait for it with Patience" (*L*, 1:130).

Now, two decades later, his bestseller *The Task* brought not only a thaw but also a flood of attention. So did the runaway popularity of his poem about the ride of John Gilpin, which was read aloud in London by the actor John Henderson. At the Free Mason's Tavern, a Mr. Phillips read "Poetical Extracts from the Works of William Cowper."

In a letter to her sister, Maria F. C. Cowper expressed the astonishment felt in the family about William's return from obscurity to fame. "That worthy Creature in so many years buried in shades, is now the *conversation* as well as *admiration* of the highest Ranks of people! All the wits and best writers of this age are eager to be introduc'd to him—but that cannot be. He shuns them all. 'Where does he live? Who is he? How can I come at him? Why will he not come amongst us?' etc. are perpetually ask'd—which not seldom leads those who are connected and related into some dilemma."[2]

The surviving members of his family most important to Cowper were Uncle Ashley and his daughters, Harriet Hesketh and Theadora, who had both loved their cousin William in the days of their youth. It was the popularity of "John Gilpin," first appearing anonymously in the *Public Advertiser* and then included in *The Task*, that inspired Harriet to write the author on October 12, 1785. Cowper's feelings about his poem "John Gilpin" had been ambivalent, but now as he wrote to Harriet, "I am indebted to him for a more valuable acquisition than all the laughter in the world amounts to, the recovery of my intercourse with you, which is to me inestimable" (*L*, 2:394).

William Cowper was soon writing to Ashley, not merely as his uncle but as a beloved father figure as well. "My dear Cousin [Harriet] who knew that I could laugh *once*, but who, not without reason, supposed that I had altogether renounced the practice, on the authority of honest John, takes heart, and writes to me again, after a silence of 15 years" (*L*, 2:502).

Eight months after her first letter to her cousin, Lady Hesketh went to Olney to visit him. The interval, from October 1785 to May 1786, was full of poetic and personal energy for William Cowper. At this time in his midfifties, he derived deep satisfaction from his translation of Homer, all the while perfecting the language of the heart in letters to his dearest "Coz."

He began translating Homer after he had finished *The Task* and sent the last corrected sheet off to Joseph Johnson. He had a pressing necessity of work to occupy his mind because as he told Newton, he "suffer'd not a little" in his spirits when he was idle. Unable to write original poetry as he wished and his friends expected, he turned to translating Homer. "One day being in such distress of mind as was hardly supportable, I took up the Iliad; and merely to divert attention . . . translated the 12 first lines of it" (*L*, 2:411).

Finding translation "a most agreeable amusement," Cowper soon calculated that the forty thousand verses of *The Iliad* and *The Odyssey* together would occupy him for a long time to come. He soon had a translation schedule of two hours in the morning and two in the evening.

In the early months of his work on Homer, Cowper displayed a confidence so sure that he took up a role new to him of encouraging Harriet Hesketh and even assuring his publisher that Homer would prosper. The basis of his confidence was his belief in Homer as "in point of purity, a most blameless writer" (*L*, 2:411). "Homer is the best Poet that ever lived for many reasons, but for none more than for the majestic plainness that distinguishes him from all others" (*L*, 2:483–84). Cowper was confident as well in his Westminster education in the classics and his long schooling in blank verse as he had labored over "The Task."

Cowper understood himself well and could laugh at his unexpected energy and self-assurance. To Harriet he wrote, "My Dear, I have been at the races. . . . I have been at Troy, where the principal heroes of the Iliad have been running for a prize" (*L*, 2:414). He acknowledged that he was "not by nature one of Homer's heroes." After sharing more of his publication plans with his cousin, he reminded her that he was "not naturally addicted to much rashness in making conclusions favorable to myself" (*L*, 2:417). He was even more straightforward in assuring his publisher that neither he himself nor Johnson would be dishonored. "Fear not, my friend!" (*L*, 2:473).

Cowper's arrangements with Joseph Johnson were settled without difficulty late in December 1785. "Johnson behaves very well" (*L*, 2:437). In regard to finances, Cowper said that Johnson was liberal and "behaves very handsomely" (*L*, 2:495). "I have reason to hope that I shall find myself sufficiently patronized and supported" (*L*, 2:434). The Homer was to be printed in two large quartos and paid for by subscription: three guineas on royal paper, two guineas on common paper. Five hundred subscribers would bring William Cowper £1000 clear.

Initially, Cowper found it hard to show his work to others or to accept the idea of an editor. He made a rare but facetious complaint to Harriet Hesketh about changes others might make in the text. "Poets, my dear, . . . are born to trouble, and of all poets, translators of Homer to the most" (*L*, 2:488–89). However, he became convinced that "other eyes than my own are necessary in order that so long and arduous a task may be finished as it ought" (*L*, 2:575).

In July Cowper's anxieties about editors lessened when Henri Fuseli, a Swiss friend of Johnson's, voluntarily offered his service. "He is an Historical Painter, and lives in St. Martin's Lane. . . . He's not only versed in Homer and accurate in his knowledge of the Greek . . . a perfect Master of our language . . . and has exquisite Taste in English poetry" (*L*, 2:574).

In a letter to Lady Hesketh, Cowper also comments on Fuseli's ability to inspire him. Speaking of the ninth book of *The Iliad*, Fuseli had observed that "to execute a translation of this book in particular, with felicity, appears to him a prodigious task. He considers it, and I think justly, as one of the most consummate efforts of genius handed down to us from antiquity, and calls upon me for my utmost exertions" (*L*, 2:614).

In this productive period of his life, William Cowper also gave his efforts to enlisting subscribers. He asked his friends to subscribe, even friends of his friends. An early list included his cousin Harriet, Walter Bagot, William Unwin, John Thornton, George Coleman, and Joseph Hill. He admitted that there was some embarrassment in asking former friends: "I have gulp'd and swallow'd" (*L*, 2:437). But he was "mustering all his forces" to fill what had been a profound need—to be back in touch with connections from the past (*L*, 2:434). He told Harriet Hesketh that his subscriber list "is likely to be splendid and numerous." Eventually the list included 498 subscribers, who had paid for 579 copies in all (*L*, 2:496).

In regaining indirectly a measure of life beyond the confines of Olney, Cowper was so exhilarated that his description of the local post office is freighted with pathos. "I am become the wonder of the Post Office in this town. They never sent so many letters to London in their lives. Then they read my directions and find that I write only to Lords and Ladys and Members of Parliament which has petrified them all with astonishment. How much more would they be amazed, could they but conjecture that it is even possible I may write to the King himself!" (*L*, 2:446).

William Cowper also wrote to two long-faithful friends and found a way to express his sense of completion. To William Unwin he said, "The Task has now succeeded beyond my utmost expectations; if Homer succeed as well,—and it shall not fail through any negligence of mine, I shall account my fortune, as a poet, made for ever" (*L*, 2:501).

To John Newton, he said, "Strange as it may seem to say it, and unwilling as I should be to say it to any person less candid than yourself, I will nevertheless say that I have not enter'd on this work, unconnected as it must needs appear with the interests of the Cause of God, without the direction of his Providence, nor altogether unassisted by him in the performance of it. Time will show to what it ultimately tends" (*L*, 2:480–81).

16

LETTERS FROM THE HEART

1785–1786

William Cowper's letters demonstrate both energy and optimism as he labored to translate Homer. He corresponded with his publisher, Joseph Johnson, with Walter Bagot and Joseph Hill about subscriptions and other matters related to his work. Cowper's letters to his most faithful correspondents, Unwin and Newton, were shorter and less frequent than was the norm.

But during these eight months, Cowper wrote letters to Harriet Hesketh different in insight and intensity than any he had previously composed. This burst of creativity began after Harriet's first letter of October 12, 1785, addressed to her "dear Cousin." (A misfortune of literary history is that few of her letters to Cowper survived because of his misguided habit of destroying correspondence.)

"Will you not be surpriz'd my dear Cousin," Harriet wrote, "at receiving a letter at this distant period from an old Correspondent, and still older Friend? one, who tho' she has long neglected to be the *former,* can never cease to be the *latter,* nor can ever forget the happy *hours &* *years* of friendly intercourse wch. she formerly enjoyed, with a valuable Friend, & Relation Wm. Cowper! 'tis in hopes of reviving a Correspondence wch. so many Years have Interrupted, that I now take up the pen, and if you my dear Cuz: have not quite forgot that such a person exists as Ld Hesketh, you may not perhaps be sorry, to be inform'd that she is still alive, & in perfect health" (*L*, 2:380).

This letter sounds not unlike Cowper himself. In his reply he praised Harriet's writing style and speculated that she would set aside any praise by saying "that is impossible, for I always write what comes uppermost, and never trouble myself either about method or expression" (*L*, 2:498). This was the best approach to writing letters, he wrote. "When I read your letters I hear you talk, and I love talking letters dearly, especially from you." He anticipated Harriet's June visit to Olney, when "I shall hear you and see you too" (*L*, 2:526).

Cowper's bedrock intent in writing to Harriet was to reveal his heart. "One letter from the heart is worth a thousand from the head, and if my heart does not dictate all that I write to you it deceives me indeed" (*L*, 2:428). One example of his intention to be candid was a letter in which he exposed his ambitions as a poet. "And now my precious Cousin, I have unfolded my heart to you in this particular, without one speck of dissimulation" (*L*, 2:543).

During this eight-month interval, Cowper elucidated for Harriet the basics of Mary Unwin's character as well as his relationship with her. "I live and have lived these 20 years with Mrs. Unwin, to whose affectionate care of me during the far greater part of that time, it is under Providence owing, that I live at all" (*L*, 2:382). Having written this two days after Harriet's first letter, he returned to the same theme eight months later as she was about to arrive in Olney. "Have I not reason to be thankful that, since Providence designed me to pass a part of my life, and no inconsiderable one neither, in a state of the deepest melancholy, he appointed me a friend in Mrs. Unwin, who should share all my sorrows with me, and watch over me in my helpless condition, night and day? What, and where had I been without her?" (*L*, 2:565).

Central to Cowper and Mary Unwin's relationship was her desire and ability to be a critic and guide for the poet. Cowper said that he would like to read his Homer book by book in the evenings to Harriet and Mary. "She has been my Touchstone always and without reference to her Taste and Judgment have I printed nothing" (*L*, 2:471).

Finally, before Harriet arrived in Olney, he wanted her to understand Mary Unwin's capacity for enduring friendship. "You are the first person for whom I have heard Mrs. U. express such feelings as she does for you, since I have known her. She is not profuse in professions, nor forward to enter into treaties of friendship with new faces, but when her friendship is once engaged it is inviolably secure and may be confided in even unto death. She loves you my Dear already, and how much more will she love you before this time twelvemonth" (*L*, 2:520).

One concept in Cowper's heart was the belief that a friendship could endure, though interrupted by time and distance. This belief acted forcefully against Cowper's dread of abandonment, which had grown in his heart after his mother died. In his first letter to Harriet, he wrote, "I can truely boast of an affection for you that neither years nor interrupted intercourse have at all abated" (*L*, 2:381). The following month he wrote again in the same vein. "It were a pity that, while the same world holds us, we, who were in a manner brought up together, should not love each other to the last. We do, however, and we do so in spite of a long separation; and although that separation should be for life, yet will we love each other" (*L*, 2:401).

Soon after the beginning of Harriet's correspondence with Cowper, she began to send him gifts. When she sent money, he gladly accepted what she "can spare without missing it" (*L*, 2:395). When she sent oysters, he wrote, "You may perceive that I . . . grow less and less coy in the matter of acceptance continually" (*L*, 2:409).

Enduring love, according to Cowper, grew out of thankfulness. He wrote to Harriet, "Your kindness reduces me to a necessity, (a pleasant one, indeed,) of writing all my letters in the same terms: always thanks,—thanks at the beginning and thanks at the end. . . . There is no person on earth whom I thank with so much affection as yourself" (*L*, 2:406).

In the language of the heart, Cowper wrote these words to Harriet four months before her arrival in Olney. "About three nights since I dreamed that, sitting in our summerhouse, I saw you coming towards me. With inexpressible pleasure I sprang to meet you, caught you in my arms, and said,—Oh my precious, precious cousin, may God make me thankful that I see thy face again!" (*L*, 2:487).

With the gift of a desk, someone named Anonymous became Cowper's new benefactor. The desk was no small gesture but "the most elegant, the compactest, the most commodious desk in the world, and of all the desks that ever were or ever shall be, the desk I love the most" (*L*, 2:418–19). It was made of cedar, "hinged, handled, and mounted with silver, inlaid with ivory . . . and stored with stationery ware" (*L*, 2:433).

Cowper knew that Harriet had *sent* the desk, but she assured him she was not the *giver*, who was to remain anonymous. Cowper wrote with strong emphasis and deep affection that he would never try to discover the identity of Anonymous. "I therefore know nothing of Anonymous, but that I love him heartily and with most abundant cause" (*L*, 2:461).

Because it was so painful not to be able to thank anyone for the desk, Cowper told Harriet that he would constitute her his "thank-receiver General." For the desk and whatever future gifts there might be, he would thank Harriet. Anonymous sent a snuffbox of tortoiseshell, on its lid a rural landscape complete with cottage, "The Peasant's Nest," and three pet hares of Cowper's—Puss, Tiney, and Bess. Cowper received a pocketbook, a purse, later elegant shoebuckles, and frequently money and letters, the climax being an annuity of fifty pounds.

There could be no doubt that "dear Anonymous," the profligate giver, was Theadora, Harriet's sister and William's sweetheart of long ago. In April he wrote Harriet in language that preserved the fiction that Anonymous was a man, but revealed otherwise in tone and content. "Who's there in the world that has, or can think that he has, reason to love me to the degree that he does? I believe you my Dear to be in full possession of all this mystery, you shall never know me while you live, either directly, or by hints of any sort, attempt to extort or to steal the secret from you. I should think myself as justly punishable as the Bethshemites for looking into the ark which they had not even a right to touch" (*L*, 2:521).

Cowper maintained all along that for Anonymous he would always be thankful. He wanted to inspire Harriet, the thank-receiver general.

THE PEASANT'S NEST.

Oft have I wish'd the peaceful covert mine.

Vide the Task, Book I.

Drawn & Engraved by Jn.º Greig.

FIGURE 6. *The Peasant's Nest*, from *Cowper Illustrated by a Series of views in, or near, the Park of Weston-Underwood, Bucks.* (London: Verner and Hood, 1803). Courtesy of the Library of Congress.

"Wonder with me, my beloved Cousin, at the goodness of God." He recalled Dr. Isaac Watts's redemptive words about sorrow turning to joy.

> —Can clear the darkest skies,
> Can give us day for night,
> Make drops of sacred sorrow rise
> To rivers of delight.
>
> (*L*, 2:462)

By February 1786 it was determined that Harriet Hesketh would visit William Cowper and Mary Unwin in Olney. The plan was to find separate quarters for Harriet and her servants for a June visit. "The whole affair is thus commodiously adjusted; and now I have nothing to do but to wish for June, and June my Cousin was never so wished for since June was made" (*L*, 2:483).

Rather than having nothing to do, Cowper and Mary Unwin worked tirelessly on the best housing for Harriet, choices in Olney being few. The solution was the vicarage, longtime home of the Newtons and briefly the residence of Lady Austen. Cowper wrote Harriet of his intense anticipation of her proposed visit. "We talk of nobody but you; what we will do with you when we get you, where you shall walk, where you shall sleep, in short everything that bears the remotest relation to your well-being at Olney occupies all our talking time, which is all the time that I do not spend at Troy" (*L*, 2:477).

Cowper's letters began to include detailed descriptions much praised by Bruce Redford in his book about eighteenth-century familiar letters, *The Converse of the Pen*. Redford demonstrates that "Cowper contrives genre scenes and landscapes whose pictorial syntax finds its closest equivalent in the work of two seventeenth-century Dutch masters, Vermeer and Pieter de Hooch."[1]

In one letter Cowper led Harriet through the vicarage garden and to the view from her bedroom windows. According to Redford, Cowper is here creating a space for Lady Hesketh to enable her to look through the house and travel through the garden.

It is square and well walled, but has neither arbour nor alcove nor other shade except the shadow of the house. But we have 2 gardens my Dear, and 3 Sitting places therein, besides a shady bench, all of which are yours. Between your mansion and ours is interposed nothing but an Orchard, into which a door opens out of our garden, and the same door which was made in the garden wall of the Vicarage when Lady Austen lodged there, being opened again (it is now walled up) will afford us the easiest communication imaginable; will save the round about by the town, and make both houses one. The house is not in the town, nor more than 40 yards out of it, and has the pleasantest situation that any house can boast in Olney. Your Chamber windows look over the river and over the meadows to a village called Emberton and command the whole length of a long bridge described by a certain poet, together with a view of the road at a distance. (*L*, 2:518–19)

Cowper often mentioned his favorite walks. His enjoyment of Lavendon was described in a letter, and the loss of its beauty lamented in a poem. "There was, indeed, sometime since, in a neighboring parish called Lavendon, a field, one side of which formed a terrace, and the other was planted with poplars, at whose foot ran the Ouse, that I used to account a little paradise: but the poplars have been felled and the scene suffered so much by the loss, that though still in point of prospect beautiful, it has not the charm sufficient to attract me now" (*L*, 2:531–32).

THE POPLAR-FIELD

The poplars are fell'd, farewell to the shade
And the whispering sound of the cool colonnade,
The winds play no longer, and sing in the leaves,
Nor Ouse on his bosom their image receives.

Twelve years have elaps'd since I first took a view
Of my favourite field and the bank where they grew,

And now in the grass behold they are laid,
And the tree is my seat that once lent me a shade.

The blackbird has fled to another retreat
Where the hazels afford him a screen from the heat,
And the scene where his melody charm'd me before,
Resounds with his sweet-flowing ditty no more.

My fugitive years are all hasting away,
And I must ere long lie as lowly as they,
With a turf on my breast, and a stone at my head,
Ere another such grove shall arise in its stead.

'Tis a sight to engage me, if any thing can,
To muse on the perishing pleasures of man;
Though his life be a dream, his enjoyments, I see,
Have a being less durable even than he.

(*P,* 2:25–26)

Redford observes that the reader of Cowper's letters is "invited to participate in a guided tour of the Olney microcosm." Cowper was eloquent in the simplicity with which he described his summerhouse or workshop. In the following invitation to Lady Hesketh, "Cowper insinuates a picture within a picture. When the gap in the existing scene has been filled up, his portrait of the solitary poet will be replaced by a vibrant conversation piece, framed in the 'old-fashioned' style."[2]

"I long to show you my workshop, and to see you sitting on the opposite side of my table. We shall be as close pack'd as two wax figures in an old fashioned picture frame. I am writing in it now. It is the place in which I fabricate all my verse in summer time. I rose an hour sooner than usual this morning that I might finish my sheet before breakfast, for I must write this day to the General. The grass under my windows is all over bespangled with dew-drops, and the birds are singing in the apple trees among the blossoms. Never Poet had a more commodious oratory in which to invoked his Muse" (*L*, 2:559).

Immediately after Harriet Hesketh arrived in Olney, Cowper wrote to John Newton about this summerhouse and his schedule of work on translating Homer. "As soon as breakfast is over, I retire to my nutshell of a summerhouse which is my verse-manufactory, and here I abide seldom less than three hours, and not often more. In the afternoon I return to it again, and all the day-light that follows, except what is devoted to a walk, is given to Homer. It is well for me, that a course which is now become necessary, is so much my choice. The regularity of it indeed has been, in the course of this last week a little interrupted, by the arrival of my dear Cousin Lady Hesketh, but with the new week I shall, as they say, turn over a new leaf, and put myself under the same rigorous discipline as before" (*L*, 2:569).

The vicarage was always associated with Newton, who had cared for Cowper there in the depths of his depression of 1773. "It is impossible that we should set our foot over the threshold of the Vicarage, without recollecting all of your Kindness" (*L*, 2:570).

There was much to stir deep emotion in the heart of William Cowper when he met Harriet face to face. His long-held conviction of abandonment by God included the belief that his connections with those he loved would not be continued into eternity. But now just before her arrival, he was able to conclude a letter to Harriet by saying: "Adieu my Beloved Cousin! God grant that our friendship which while we could see each other, never suffered a moment's interruption, and which so long a separation has not in the least abated, may glow in us to our last hour, and be renewed in a better world, there to be perpetuated for ever. For you must know that I should not Love you half so well if I did not believe that you will be my friend to Eternity. There is not room enough for friendship to unfold itself into full blow, in such a nook of a Life as this. Therefore I am and must and will be— Yours for ever—Wm Cowper" (*L*, 2:553).

When Harriet entered the vicarage on June 21, 1786, the church bells rang. "I am fond of the sound of Bells, but was never more pleased with

FIGURE 7. Cowper's summerhouse at Orchard Side, Olney, from *Cowper Illustrated by a Series of views in, or near, the Park of Weston-Underwood, Bucks.* (London: Verner and Hood, 1803). Courtesy of the Library of Congress.

those of Olney, than when they rang her into her new habitation." No wonder Harriet's arrival was overwhelming for William Cowper, whose spirits broke down "under the pressure of too much Joy" (*L*, 2:572).

In the first week of Harriet's visit, Cowper was as usual writing in his garden workshop, his "nutshell of a summerhouse." He told Earl Cowper about his cousin's arrival. "Lady Hesketh who is come to brighten the obscurest nook in the world with her presence, and to make me happy who have known and loved her from childhood, but who had not seen her 'till she arrived here last week, these twenty years" (*L*, 2:571).

Soon he wrote to William Unwin about his visitor at Orchard Side. "She pleases every body, and is pleased in her turn with every thing she finds at Olney; is always cheerful and sweet temper'd, and knows no pleasure equal to that of communicating pleasure to us and to all around her. This disposition in her, is the more comfortable, because it is not the humour of the day, a sudden flush of benevolence and good spirits occasion'd merely by a change of scene, but it is her natural turn and has govern'd all her conduct ever since I knew her first. We are consequently happy in her society, and shall be happier still to have you to partake with us in our joy" (*L*, 2:572).

A week later he wrote Hill in the same vein: "My dear Cousin's arrival, has, as it could not fail to do, made us happier than we ever were at Olney. Her great kindness in giving me her company is a cordial that I shall feel the effect of, not only while she is here, but while I live" (*L*, 2:578).

17

LIABLE TO DESERTION
1786

A plan with far-reaching consequences was foremost in the thoughts of Cowper and Mary Unwin. Without Harriet Hesketh, the plan would never have been imagined or realized. "She leaves nothing unsaid, nothing undone, that she thinks will be conducive to our well-being" (*L*, 2:582).

As early as the past April, Cowper had written Harriet about the possibility of leaving Olney "for Olney has no hold upon us in particular. Here we have no family connections, no neighbors with whom we can associate, no friendships. If the country is pleasant, so also are other countries" (*L*, 2:514).

Then in May there arose the concrete possibility of moving to Weston, where the Throckmortons owned a house, the Lodge, "at present empty. It is a very good one, infinitely superior to ours. When we drank chocolate with them, they both expressed their ardent desire that we would take it, wishing much to have us for nearer neighbors" (*L*, 2:539).

William Cowper, Mary, and Harriet were already thinking about the drawbacks of Olney but failing to imagine or foresee how difficult it would be for him to move. Cowper urged William Unwin to think about the disadvantages of Orchard Side and the advantages of Weston. "Here we have a bad air in the Winter impregnated with the fishy-smelling fumes of the Marsh Miasma, there, we shall breath in an atmosphere untainted. Here, we are confined from September to March, and some-times longer, there we shall be upon the very verge of pleasure grounds in which we can always ramble, and shall not wade through almost impos-sible dirt to get at them. Both your Mother's constitution and mine have suffer'd materially by such close and long confinement" (*L,* 2:573).

The "infinitely superior" house at Weston would cost more money. Cowper brought up this problem with Mary's son. "Within the twelve-month my income has received an addition of a clear £100 per annum" (*L,* 2:576). All of this had come at the initiative of Harriet and included the £50 annuity from Anonymous. Thus the purse had been replenished "of your once poor poet of Olney." The larger house at Weston would require furniture, "all which my kind Cousin will provide, and fit up a parlour and a Chamber for herself into the bargain" (*L,* 2:573). A month later Cowper wrote Unwin that "my Cousin is lavish . . . and sets no bounds to her kindness" (*L,* 2:583).

Cowper wrote a lighthearted tale of the summer of 1786 for Walter Bagot: "After having lived 20 years at Olney we are on the point of leav-ing it, but shall not migrate far. We have taken the house in the village of Weston belonging to Mr. Throckmorton . . . Lady Hesketh is our good angel by whose aid we are enabled to pass into a better air and a more walkable country. The imprisonment that we have suffer'd here for so many winters, has hurt us both. That we may suffer it no longer, she stoops to Olney, lifts us from our swamp and sets us down on the ele-vated grounds of Weston Underwood" (*L,* 2:587).

There was every reason to expect that John and Maria Throckmorton would be ideal landlords as well as friends. Earlier, they had given Cowper and Mary Unwin keys to their gardens and access to their many acres. Now the friendship would grow. Cowper anticipated winter evening con-versations. Mrs. Throckmorton had even promised to help transcribe Homer, to "be my Lady of the Ink Bottle" after Lady Hesketh had returned to London. Cowper looked forward as well to the companion-ship of the Chesters and Wrights, who also lived near Weston, "all of them good-natured agreeable people." Cowper told Unwin, "The more I see of the Throckmortons the more I like them. He is the most accomplished man of his years that I remember to have seen, is always sensible in Conversation and kind in his behavior, and conducts himself handsomely and unexceptionally in the business of Landlord and Tenant. She is cheerful and good-natured to the last degree" (*L*, 2:577).

Cowper and Mary and "the Throcks" shared many interests, especially in gardens and woodlands. When he showed them the garden and the greenhouse at Orchard Side, Cowper cut a bouquet of myrtle for Maria. Later, fearing that Mrs. Throckmorton could not make the slips strike root in water, Cowper sent his laborer to Weston with a wheelbarrow of myrtles and canary lavender. In telling this story to Harriet, he joked, "Dites moi, my chere, ne suis-je homme tout à fait poli?" (Tell me, my dear, am I not a very polite man?) (*L*, 2:533).

Another, earlier episode also involved the Throckmortons and their grounds: "A most unfortunate mistake is made by that gentleman's Bailiff in his absence. Just before he left Weston last year for the Winter, he gave him orders to cut short the tops of the flowering shrubs that lined a serpentine walk in a delightful grove celebrated by my poetship in a little piece that you remember, called the Shrubbery. The Dunce misapprehending the order, cut down and faggotted up the whole grove, leaving neither tree, bush, nor twig; nothing but stumps about as high as my ancle. Mrs. T——n told us that she never saw her husband so angry in his life" (*L*, 2:539). Cowper was prophetic when he wrote, "We are likely to be very happy in our connexion with the Throcks" (*L*, 2:585).

The five months of Harriet Hesketh's visit were coming to an end. She left Olney on November 14, 1786. William Cowper's heart was always vulnerable to feelings of desertion. He wrote Harriet at the time of his fifty-fifth birthday to say that the Lodge at Weston was neat, sunny, warm, and comfortable even in wintry weather. However, his central desire was to see his dear Harriet as soon as possible. "O for you my Cousin, to partake these comforts with us!" (*L*, 2:599). Perhaps she would be able to come in the spring to see that the house looked even better than when she saw it last, the parlor elegant, the study neat, warm, and silent, awaiting new chairs. In January he summarized his feelings. "May God bless thee and preserve us both to another happy meeting!" (*L*, 3:8).

William Cowper and Mary Unwin moved from Olney to the Throckmortons' Lodge in Weston on November 15, the day after saying good-bye to Harriet. After twenty years at Orchard Side, Cowper's feelings about moving were deeply complex. On the one hand, his new home was larger, more comfortable, and better furnished. Long walks were immediately accessible through the Throckmortons' elegant grounds. His cousin Harriet had her own quarters and had promised never to let a year pass without visiting.

Two days after moving, he commented to Walter Bagot that the life of a man could well be shortened by "frequent removals from place to place." It is not easy to ascertain the tone of his next comment: "The confusion which attends a transmigration of this kind is infinite, and has a terrible effect in deranging the intellects" (L, 2:596).

On the same day he wrote to William Unwin on the same theme: "When God speaks to a Chaos, it becomes a scene of order and harmony in a moment,—but when his creatures have thrown one house into confusion by leaving it, & another by tumbling themselves and their goods into it, not less than many days' labor and contrivance is necessary to give them their proper places" (L, 2:597).

Cowper invited the Newtons to visit. "You, I hope, My dear Friend and Mrs. Newton will want no assurances to convince you that you will always be received here with the sincerest welcome" (L, 2:598).

As had often been the case in writing to Newton, Cowper plunged into the depths and contradictions of his feelings. Orchard Side had been his prison, yet he "felt something like a heart-ach when I took my last leave of a scene that certainly in itself had nothing to engage affection. But I recollect that I had once been happy there, and could not without tears in my eyes bid adieu to a place in which God had so often found me" (L, 2:597).

A letter Cowper had written to Newton three years earlier had expressed ambivalent and contradictory feelings about Olney. "Thus I am both free and a Prisoner at the same time." He was not shut up in the Bastile, there were no moats around his castles, no locked gates without keys. If Cowper was a prisoner, he was also bound to Olney by

WESTON LODGE
The Residence of the late W.ᵐ Cowper Esq.ʳ

Drawn by Jn.ᵗ Greig & Engraved by J. Storer.

FIGURE 8. Weston Lodge, where Cowper lived for ten years, from *Cowper Illustrated by a Series of views in, or near, the Park of Weston-Underwood, Bucks.* (London: Verner and Hood, 1803). Courtesy of the Library of Congress.

attachment and love. "An invisible uncontrollable agency, a local attachment, an inclination more forcible than I ever felt even to the place of my Birth, serves me for Prison walls and for bounds which I cannot pass" (*L*, 2:150–51).

He gave expression to his love for Orchard Side by saying that "the very Stones in the garden walls are my intimate acquaintance" (*L*, 2:150–51). Later, in his letters to Harriet, he expressed even more powerfully his love of his summerhouse and garden. "There you shall sit, with a bed of mignonette at your side, and a hedge of honeysuckles, roses, and jasmine; and I will make you a bouquet of myrtle everyday" (*L*, 2:476).

When Cowper called himself a prisoner at Olney, he was often referring to weather so bad that he and Mary were prevented from the walking that was essential to their health. In the severe winter of 1785, he said that "a country rendered impassable by frost that had been at last resolved into rottenness, keeps me so close a prisoner" (*L*, 2:321). By March of that year, "clean roads and milder weather have once more released us, opening a way for our escape into our accustomed walks" (*L*, 2:334).

How then, was Cowper both a prisoner and free? The answer did not rest with the weather. If he had ever decided to leave his obscure nook for a period of time, "I should return to it again with rapture, and be transported with the sight of objects which to all the world beside would be at least indifferent; . . . But so it is—as it is so, because here is to be my abode, and because such is the appointment of Him that placed me in it. Here I spent 5 years in a state of warfare, and here I have spent almost 11 in a state of despair. . . . Nevertheless, it is the place of all the world I love the most, not for any happiness it affords me, but because here I can be miserable with the most convenience to myself, and with the least disturbance to others" (*L*, 2:151).

The most cogent reason that Cowper never left Olney—to visit Hill, to be reunited with the Unwins or the Newtons—was suggested in his poem "The Faithful Bird." The friends in the poem are two goldfinches. It was not unusual for Cowper to see parallels in the relationships of animals and the interactions of humans. The poem suggests that he was, by choice, a prisoner in Olney, choosing to remain confined with his friend Mary, preferring not to escape to the wider world.

THE FAITHFUL BIRD

The Green-house is my summer seat,
My shrubs displaced from that retreat
    Enjoy'd the open air,
Two Gold-finches whose sprightly song
Had been their mutual solace long
    Liv'd happy Pris'ners there.

They sang as blithe as finches sing
That flutter loose on golden wing
    And frolick where they list,
Strangers to liberty, 'tis true,
But that delight they never knew
    And therefore never mist.

But Nature works in ev'ry breast
With force not easily suppress'd
    And Dick felt some desires
That after many effort vain
Instructed him at length to gain
    A pass between his wires.

The open windows seem'd t'invite
The Free-man to a farewell flight
    But Tom was still confined;
And Dick, although his way was clear
Was much too generous and sincere
    To leave his friend behind.

For settling on his cage's roof,
By chirp and kiss he gave him proof
   That to escape alone
Was freedom little to his taste,
Nor would he move, 'till I at last,
   Return'd him to his own.

Oh ye who never knew the joys
Of Friendship! satisfied with noise
   Fandango, Ball and Rout,
Blush, when I tell you how a Bird
A prison with a friend preferr'd
   To liberty without.

               (*P,* 2:29–30)

Two weeks after William Cowper and Mary Unwin moved into their new home in Weston, they received news. Mary's son and Cowper's devoted friend William Unwin was dead.

Cowper's "Creed" included the concept that the intellect depends on God for energy, just as the heart depends on the Holy Spirit for grace (*L,* 3:10). Cowper and Mary Unwin would need strong minds and hearts to live, recently deprived of Harriet's companionship, and in a new home, under heavy burden of grief.

Cowper never forgot that, leaving St. Albans, William Unwin was his first friend in Huntingdon and his means of meeting Mary. In early May of 1783, while listening to Sunday morning church bells, he expressed his abiding love for William Unwin. "If I can tell you no News, I tell you at least that I esteem you highly, that my friendship with you and yours is the only balm of my life, a comfort sufficient to reconcile me to an Existence destitute of every other" (*L,* 2:132).

Later Cowper told Unwin, "I have no friend in the world with whom I communicate without the least reserve, yourself excepted" (*L,* 2:178). The first sign that Cowper's health might break down came in a letter to Harriet ten days after Unwin died. Cowper reported a forced interruption in his schedule with Homer. "I have not touched Homer to day. Yesterday was in one of my terrible seasons, and when I rose this morning I found that I had not sufficiently recover'd myself to engage in such an occupation. Having letters to write, I the more willingly gave myself a dispensation" (*L*, 2:610). But two days later he wrote, "The cloud that I mentioned to you, my cousin, has passed away, or perhaps the skirts of it may still hang over me. I feel myself, however, tolerably brisk, and tell you because I know you will be glad to hear it" (*L*, 2:616).

Thus Cowper continued with Homer. He wrote cheerfully to Joseph Hill with enthusiastic comments about the village of Weston, the walks in the neighborhood, and his new house, "in all respects commodious, and in some, elegant" (*L*, 2:610–11). He asked Hill to send money, saying that carpenters, masons, and smiths are expensive servants. As to money, he did not want Harriet Hesketh to worry. "Trouble not thyself my sweet Coz about money-matters. I have drawn upon my Banker Josephus, and shall be rich enough to hold out 'till you yourself shall be rich also" (*L*, 2:620).

Cowper and Mary Unwin were both sustained by the memory of William's goodness and the peace with which he had passed from this world. Cowper told Harriet that "Poor Mrs. Unwin you will suppose is in great affliction, but she bears her severe heart-aches with a resignation to the will of God. . . . She has spent her life in the practice of an habitual acquiescence in the dispensations of Providence" (*L*, 2:603).

On his part, Cowper was astonished by the mystery that God had brought Unwin to the prime of life and precisely then removed him. Cowper noted Unwin's devoted children and loving wife, his parish by which other clergy were inspired, and his value to his friend. "So farewell my friend Unwin! The first man for whom I conceived a friendship after my escape from St. Albans, and for whom I cannot but still continue to feel a friendship, though I shall see thee with these eyes no more" (*L*, 2:606–7).

It was to John Newton that Cowper wrote of the profound meaning for him of Unwin's death and the consequences already unfolding. After a visit one day to Orchard Side, Cowper likened the deserted house to a deserted person, his former home to himself.

> Once since we left Olney I had occasion to call at our old dwelling, and never did I see so forlorn and woeful a spectacle; deserted of its inhabitants it seemed as if it could never be dwelt in for ever. The coldness of it, the dreariness and the dirt, made me think it no unapt resemblance of a soul that God had forsaken. While he dwelt in it and manifested himself there, he could create his own accommodations and give it occasionally the appearance of a palace, but the moment he withdraws and takes with him all the furniture and embellishment of his graces, it becomes what it was before he enter'd it, the habitation of vermin and the image of desolation. Sometimes I envy the living, but not much or not long, for while they Live as we call it, they too are liable to desertion. But the Dead who have died in the Lord, I envy always, for they I take it for granted, can be no more forsaken. (*L*, 2:616–19)

A month later Cowper was on the edge of a breakdown. "The mind of a man is not a fountain, but a cistern, and mine, God knows, a broken one" (*L*, 3:10). Newton would, of course, be familiar with Cowper's biblical images from Jeremiah (2:13) and the Gospel of John (4:10). God is the fountain of living water. Those who forsake God make for themselves broken cisterns that can hold no water.

In his last words to Newton for many months, the poet used the image of a storm at sea that recurred in his letters and poems over the course of his writing life. In this letter of January 1787 he wrote that his mind has experienced tempests unknown to most others. His has been "the most turbulent voyage that ever Christian mariner made" (*L*, 3:11). He has tried to survive the gales under the shelter of Homer's mountains and forests.

William Cowper was without hope. He wrote that he would give up all the "fame and honor and glory that may be acquired by poetical feats of any sort," to enjoy a measure of hope. "God knows that if I could lay me down in the grave with Hope at my side, or sit with Hope at my side in a dungeon all the residue of my days," he would cheerfully forgo fame (*L*, 3:11).

Cowper's last letter until the end of July went to Harriet Hesketh. Unlike the theoretical and theological questions raised in letters to Newton, for his dear cousin he described his symptoms. His nights are almost sleepless, he wrote. He is unable to do any work on Homer, which he has had to abandon just when he needs it most.

He walked constantly with Mary Unwin. At times of extreme stress, "I keep her continually employ'd and never suffer her to be absent from me many minutes. She gives me all her time and all her attention and forgets there is another object in the world" (*L*, 3:12–13). At age sixty-three Mary Unwin was in a perilous sea along with fellow mariner William Cowper.

This final letter was written over a three-day period. On the last day Cowper gave Harriet an update on his health. "My fever is not yet gone, but sometimes seems to leave me. It is altogether of the nervous kind and attended now and then with much dejection." He signed his letter, "Adieu Dearest, Dearest Cousin. Yours Wm C" (*L*, 3:15).

18

A SEASON OF SATISFACTIONS
July 1787–December 1791

After his six-month-long depression ended, William Cowper enjoyed one of the most satisfying periods of his life, from July 1787 until December 1791. He was in his late fifties. Weston quickly became home. In letters to friends and family, he wrote of life in this delightful part of Buckinghamshire. "Here we have a good house in a most beautiful village, and for the greatest part of the year a most agreeable neighborhood" (*L,* 3:121). Weston had a special quality essential to Cowper, that of snugness as opposed to wildness.

Weston was an area in which there were many walks, "some in groves and some in fields and some by river's side" (*L,* 3:334). Cowper loved walking and in this respect could not be better situated than in a neighborhood where he was "daily finding out fresh scenes" (*L,* 3:56). After six years at Weston, Cowper told Lady Hesketh that "of all the earth" Weston is "the spot that delights me most" (*L,* 4:362).

During Cowper's years at Weston, he never spent a night away from home until the desperate circumstances of 1792. He always had warm invitations from friends like Mrs. King or his long-lost relatives in Norfolk. Joseph Hill often invited Cowper to Wargrove during the many years of their friendship. In a 1790 letter to Hill, Cowper said he hadn't slept away from home for nineteen years. "This is the effect of a cause with which I will not darken a letter that I have begun in good spirits" (*L*, 3:403).

The mutual devotion of William Cowper and Mary Unwin never wavered either in Olney or Weston. He could not even imagine life without her. "The day of separation, between those who have loved long and well, is an awful day. . . . I have one comfort and one only; bereft of that, I should have nothing left to lean on; for my spiritual props have long since been struck from under me" (*L*, 3:424).

He recognized the strain placed on Mary by his periodic depressions and almost chronic melancholy. "Never was the mind of man benighted to the degree that mine has been; the storms that have assailed me would have overset the Faith of every man that ever had any. . . . Mrs. Unwin's poor bark is still held together, though shatter'd by being toss'd and agitated so long at the side of mine" (*L*, 3:37).

The Weston house had ample room for visitors and servants. Lady Hesketh was the most frequent visitor. Mary Unwin's daughter and son-in-law came, as well as the Newtons and younger new friends such as Samuel Rose. In addition to visitors, Cowper enjoyed the companionship of the Throckmortons while walking through their elaborate grounds or enjoying dinners with them and their friends. Thus, one of the delights of Weston was that Cowper could avoid either oppressive solitude or any decree of activity that could impinge on his time for reading and writing.

After recovering in the summer of 1787 from his breakdown, Cowper resumed his correspondence with Samuel Rose, Joseph Hill, and most importantly, with Lady Hesketh, calling her "the kindest of my friends." At first his sentences were awkward and stiff. "I write but little because writing is become new to me; but I shall come on by degrees" (*L*, 3:20).

Indeed, by November and December he was sending a flood of weekly letters to his dearest Coz and waiting eagerly for her next visit. The letters of William Cowper to Harriet Hesketh in the late 1780s are written with freedom and joy because he knew that she was glad to read whatever he wanted to write. "Running over what I have written, I feel that I should blush to send it to any but thyself. Another would charge me with being impelled by a vanity from which my conscience sets me clear, to speak so much of myself and my verses as I do. But I thus speak to none but thee, nor to thee do I thus speak from any such motives. I egotize in my letters to thee, not because I am of much importance to myself, but because to thee, both *Ego* and all that *Ego* does, is interesting" (*L*, 3:292). He uses the language of the heart without guile or self-consciousness. After she had left Weston in the fall of 1789, he expressed great dissatisfaction with his recent letters. "I have mourn'd for the loss of you and they [the letters] have not said so" (*L*, 3:255).

The modest accomplishments of country life became in his letters high entertainment. Two days in a row, Cowper walked to Gayhurst, an hour each way. He felt his horizons expand and his spirits rise. His "ambulatory faculty" was "delectable" to him. His little spaniel, Beau, was his pupil "in the science of fetch and carry." One day Beau almost killed a pheasant. "Beau, the handsomest creature in the world were it not for the extreme brevity of his tail, observing the pheasant's felicity in that respect whose tail was of a length unexampled, conceived envy at the sight and would have slain him. Foolish creature, could he by killing him have made that tail his own, who would not have laughed at a dog's rump adorned with a pheasant tail! So little do we sometimes understand our own true advantage" (*L*, 3:160).

On another day Beau caught a water lily in the river, which he set down at Cowper's feet. This episode not only enlivened a letter to Lady Hesketh but also shortly became a poem, "The Dog and the Water-lily."

> I must tell you a feat of my Dog Beau. Walking by the River-side I observed some Water-Lilies floating at a little distance from the Bank. They are a large white flower with an Orange colour'd Eye, and extremely beautiful. I had a desire to gather one, and having your long Cane in my hand, by the help of it endeavor'd to bring one of them within my reach. But the attempt proved vain and I walked forward. Beau had all the while observed me very attentively. Retreating soon after toward the same place, I observed him plunge into the river while I was about 40 yards distant from him, and when I had nearly reached the spot, he swam to land with a Lily in his mouth, which he came and lay'd at my foot. (*L*, 3:189)

Between the fall of 1788 and the spring of 1792, Lady Hesketh made four visits to Weston, staying about four months each time, normally in the fall or winter. Cowper looked forward to each visit. "I have made in the Orchard the best Winter walk in all the parish, shelter'd from the East, and from the North East, and open to the Sun, except at his rising, all the day. Then we will have Homer and Don Quixote, and then we will have saunter and Chat, and one Laugh more before we die. Our Orchard is alive with creatures of all kinds, poultry of ev'ry denomination swarms in it, and pigs the drollest in the world" (*L*, 3:187).

When she arrived, Cowper delighted in her presence. "The winter is gliding merrily away while my Cousin is with us. She annihilates the difference between Cold and Heat, gloomy skies and cloudless." Over the years Harriet and Mary enjoyed each other, and Cowper joked about their nonstop conversations, even at breakfast. "Not having seen each other since they parted to go to bed, they have consequently a deal to communicate" (*L*, 3:232).

When Cowper was waiting for Lady Hesketh to arrive or watching for an overdue letter, he could become distraught. "Write, I beseech you, and do not forget that I am now a batter'd actor upon this turbulent stage, that what little vigour of mind I ever had, of the self-supporting kind I mean, has long since been broken, and that though I can bear nothing well, yet anything better than a state of ignorance concerning your welfare. I have spent hours in the night, leaning upon my elbow and wondering what your silence means" (*L*, 3:92).

Two days later he wrote of receiving her letter: "But my mind is now easy; your letter has made it so, and I feel myself as blithe as a bird in comparison. I love you my Cousin, and cannot suspect, either with or without cause, the least evil in which you may be concern'd, without being greatly troubled" (*L*, 3:93).

The death of Ashley Cowper on June 6, 1788, brought William, his nephew, and Harriet, his daughter, even closer together in their grief and shared memories. Harriet received powerful letters of condolence and incomparable letters of gratitude that Cowper wrote to her and to her sister Theadora. They had sent him various possessions of Ashley's, notably his watch and his snuffbox.

"To be the proprietor of any thing that was once my Uncle's will make me rich. A mere trifle acquires value by having been the property of such a man; but his watch will be a Vade mecum with which I shall hold a thousand conversations when I am in the woods alone; nor will his Snuff-box fall a whit short of it as a most desirable companion. The Love I bore him, and the honour I have for his memory will make them both inestimable to me" (*L*, 3:191).

Writing three letters about Ashley in the ten days after his death, Cowper demonstrated his recall of days long past. To Lady Hesketh he wrote, "Let it comfort us now that we have lost him only at a time when Nature could afford him to us no longer, that as his life was blameless so his death was without anguish, and that he is gone to heaven" (*L*, 3:175). To Hill he wrote, "Thus it is that I take my last leave of poor Ashley, whose heart toward me was ever truly parental, and to whose memory I owe a tenderness and respect that can never leave me" (*L*, 3:174). Cowper recalled Ashley's amiable and excellent character. Even more clearly, he remembered Ashley's face. As he wrote to Lady Hesketh, "My memory retains so perfect an impression of him that had I been painter instead of poet I could from these faithful traces have perpetuated his face and form with the most minute exactness" (*L*, 3:178).

A formal memorial for Ashley Cowper was composed by "his nephew William of Weston."

Farewell! Endued with all that could engage
All hearts to love thee, both in youth and age.
In prime of life, for sprightliness enroll'd
Among the Gay, yet virtuous as the Old;
In Life's last stage—Oh blessing rarely found!
Pleasant as youth with all its blossoms crown'd;
Through ev'ry period of this changeful state
Unchanged thyself—Wise, Good, affectionate
    Marble may flatter; and lest this should seem
O'ercharged with praises on so dear a theme,

Although thy worth be more than half suppress'd,
Love *shall* be satisfied, and veil the rest.

(P, 3:25)

At the end of this series of letters, Cowper paid Harriet the finest of all his tributes. He anticipated her own death and urged her "not to be hasty to accomplish her journey, . . . for of all that live thou art one whom I can least spare, for thou also art one who shall not leave thy equal behind thee" (*L,* 3:177).

William Cowper and John Newton had been corresponding for almost twenty years, since the prominent evangelical clergyman had taken up his duties at St. Mary Woolnoth in London. Newton always remained faithful to his deeply troubled friend, never condemning his religious despair but encouraging hope of better days on earth and a future in heaven. On his part, Cowper never forgot John and Mary Newton's care for him, day and night, in the Olney vicarage.

After his recovery of 1787, Cowper resumed his correspondence with Newton in his accustomed vein of hopelessness but with a shade of apology. He didn't intend to write about his remoteness from God's presence, "but the pen once in my hand, I am no longer master of my own intentions" (*L,* 3:107). After Cowper learned of Mary Newton's many illnesses, he apologized to Newton. "I ought not to have written in this dismal strain to you in your present trying situation, nor did I intend it" (*L,* 3:426).

During 1790 Cowper became increasingly preoccupied with the brevity of life and especially with his few remaining years on earth. Autumn leaves were one illustration. "A yellow shower of leaves is falling continually from all the trees in the country. A few moments only seem to have pass'd since they were buds, and in few moments they will have disappeared. It is one advantage of a rural situation that it affords many hints of the rapidity with which life flies, that do not occur in towns and cities. It is impossible to a man conversant with such scenes as surround me, not to advert daily to the shortness of his existence here, admonished of it as he must be by ten thousand objects." Flowers spoke of

161

hopelessness "and thus to me is Hope itself become like a withered flower that has lost both its hue and its fragrance" (*L*, 3:425–26).

On December 15, 1790, Mary Newton died. William Cowper's condolence letters to John Newton were as deeply personal as were those of 1788 to Lady Hesketh on the death of her father. As Mary Newton was dying, Cowper was already praising her husband for his strength "and joy on your account, who are enabled to bear with so much resignation and cheerful acquiescence in the will of God, the prospects of a loss which even they who knew you best, apprehended might prove too much for you" (*L*, 3:441).

Several months later, Cowper again mentioned Newton's "serenity of mind" after great loss. Unlike less insightful friends, Cowper understood how best to embrace Newton by joining with him in the vivid remembrances of the past with Mary. Cowper had a profound grasp of the realities of grief, with which he had first become acquainted as a small boy. "No day passes," he wrote, "in which I do not look back to the days that are fled, and consequently none in which I do not feel myself affectionately reminded of you and of Her who you have lost for a season. I cannot even see Olney spire from any of the fields even in the neighborhood, much less can I enter the town, and still less the vicarage, without experiencing the force of those mementos."

The remembrance of the past was not a passing dream. "Our actual experiences make a lasting impression; we review those which interested us much when they occurred, with hardly less interest than in the first instance, and whether few years or many have intervened, our sensibility makes them still present; such a mere nullity is time to a creature to whom God gives a feeling heart and the faculty of recollection" (*L*, 3:491).

Finally, six months after Mary Newton's death, Cowper was prescient enough to understand how regrets could undermine the recovery of the widower. Credit might rightly go to William Cowper for any serenity of mind that Newton could establish.

> You speak of your late loss in a manner that affected me much, and when I read that part of your letter I mourn'd with you and for you; But surely, I said to myself, no man had ever less reason to charge his con-

duct to a wife with anything blameworthy. Thoughts of that complexion, however, are no doubt extremely natural on the occasion of such a loss, and a man seems not to have valued sufficiently, when he possesses it no longer, what, while he possess'd it, he valued more than life. I am mistaken too, or you can recollect a time when you had fears, and such as became a Christian, of loving too much, and it is likely that you have even pray'd to be preserved from doing so. I suggest this to you as a plea against those self-accusations which I am satisfied that you do not deserve, and as an effectual answer to them all. You may do well to consider that had the Deceased been the Survivor, she would have charged herself in the same manner, and I am sure you will acknowledge without any sufficient reason. The truth is that you both loved at least as much as you ought, and, I dare say, had not a friend in the world who did not frequently observe it." (*L*, 3:532–33)

One of the most surprising aspects of Cowper's return to emotional health in 1787 was the discipline and excitement with which he resumed work on Homer. "I'm still at the old sport; Homer all the morning and Homer all the evening" (*L*, 3:374). So had he worked for six years, excepting the first six months of 1787. Translating Homer, he told Lady Hesketh, was "the delight of my heart" (*L*, 3:68). To Robert Glynn he expressed the same enthusiasm. Homer had been "a perpetual source of amusement" (*L*, 3:448).

But he wanted Joseph Hill to understand that he was fatigued by avocations that were merely amusements but didn't require attention. Homer engaged him much and attached him closely. Cowper believed that he was working on literature of unparalleled beauty. "The original surpasses every thing, it is of immense length, is composed of the best language ever used on earth and deserves, indeed demands, all the labor that any Translator, be he who he may, can possibly bestow on it" (*L*, 3:448). To translate such language deserved every effort.

The work that lies before me engages unavoidably my whole attention. The length of it, the Spirit of it, and the exactness that is requisite to its due performance, are so many most interesting subjects of consideration to me, who find that my best attempts are only introductory to others, and that what to-day I suppose finished, to-morrow I must begin again. Thus it fares with a Translator of Homer. To exhibit the Majesty of such a Poet in a modern language is a task that no man can estimate the difficulty of' 'till he attempts it. To paraphrase him loosely, to hang him with trappings that do not belong to him, all this is compartively easy. But to represent him with only his own ornaments and still to preserve his dignity, is a labour that if I hope in any measure to atchieve it, I am sensible can only be atchieved by the most assiduous and unremitting attention. (*L*, 3:70)

For John Newton Cowper chose to emphasize the spiritual values to be discovered in Homer. "I know not where we can find more striking exemplars of pride, the arrogance, and the insignificance of man, at the same time that by ascribing all events to a divine interposition, he inculcates constantly the belief of a Providence, insists much on the duty of Charity toward the Poor and the Stranger, on the respect that is due to superiors and to our Seniors in particular, and on the expedience and necessity of Prayer and piety toward the Gods" (*L*, 3:533).

William Cowper's final years of Homer involved much more than translation. In a busy ten months from September 1790 to July 1791, Cowper dealt with revisions, subscriptions, and an important financial agreement with his publisher Joseph Johnson. He had essential practical help from Joseph Hill and Samuel Rose; Johnny Johnson, his young relative from Norfolk, would prove to be especially helpful.

Throughout, Cowper maintained his energy and optimism. "Instead of finding myself the more at leisure because my long labour draws to a close, I find myself the more occupied. As when a horse approaches the goal, he does not, unless he be jaded, slacken his pace, but quicken it, even so it fares with me. The end is in view; I seem almost to have reached the mark; and the nearness of it inspires me with fresh alacrity . . . It is still necessary that waking, I should be all absorpt in Homer, and that, sleeping I should dream of nothing else" (*L*, 3:306–7).

On September 8, 1790, Cowper wrote, "I am particularly frisky, having this very day sent all Homer to London (*L,* 3:412). Johnny Johnson delivered the manuscript to Joseph Johnson, publisher. A year later Cowper had completed revisions, as he told Mrs. King. "I have actually revised the whole work and have made a thousand alterations in it, since it has been in the press. I have now, however, tolerably well satisfied myself at heart, and trust that the printer and I shall trundle along merrily to the conclusion" (*L,* 3:473).

Subscriptions to his Homer were of ongoing concern to Cowper. He particularly hoped that his friends from London days would want to buy his volumes. He explained himself to Rowley: "I cannot help considering my subscription as a sort of test of their constancy who formerly professed a kindness for me. They in whom a spark of that kindness survives will hardly fail to discover it on such an occasion, and seeing the affair in this light, I feel myself a little grieved and hurt that some names which old friendship gave me a right to expect, are not to be found in my catalogue. The Lord Chancellor, however, has done handsomely, having twice honoured me with his name, once by solicitation, and in the second instance voluntarily. He is, like yourself, a man whose attachments are made of stuff that is proof against time and absence" (*L,* 3:417).

Johnny Johnson was tireless in garnering subscriptions at Cambridge. "A thousand thanks for your splendid assemblage of Cambridge luminaries, Cowper wrote him. "I am highly satisfied and even delighted with it" (*L,* 3:495). Cowper told Rose all about Johnny. "My cousin Johnson has done great things for me at Cambridge. He is such another friend as you, active and warm in my interest to a degree that suits me exactly; me, who never could do myself any good, and had therefore always great need of such as would do it for me" (*L,* 3:497).

On the subject of subscription money, Cowper wrote with a somewhat acid pen to Mrs. Throckmorton. Someone had suggested that Cowper might be offended by the receipt of subscription money. "Now I wish him to know that my delicacy is never offended by the receipt of money. On the contrary, I esteem the want of money, commonly called poverty, the most indelicate thing in the world, and so did the ancient Romans" (*L,* 3:467).

All his life long, Cowper had been asking Joseph Hill for money, both for portions of his own meager capital and for gifts from the successful lawyer's own purse. In March 1791 the poet had to ask again. "The old theme recurs, I want money, fifty pounds of good and lawful money of Great Britain. . . . After all this plowing and sowing on the plains of Troy, once fruitful, such at least to my translating predecessor [Pope], some harvest, I hope, will arise for me also, which will enable me to restore what I have spent of yours, and to replace some of my own annihilated hundreds" (L, 3:474).

While Cowper has sometimes been accused of a cavalier attitude about accepting handouts from friends and relatives, he habitually called himself, in a self-depreciating way, "a poor poet." No matter what tone of voice he adopted, it was of great importance to Cowper that his Homer be a financial success. "I have heard vulgar people say—No butter will stick upon my bread—An adage which, when I review the Past, Vulgar as it is, I feel myself ready to adopt; but I will not at present adopt it, in hopes that Homer may yet butter a crust or two for me before I die" (L, 3:496).

At the end of May 1791, Cowper told Mrs. King that his work on Homer was at an end. "I rejoice to be able to say that my release is at hand, for the last line of the Odyssey will be printed this day. There remain the Preface, the List of Subscribers, and 2 or 3 odd matters beside, and then I shall once more be at liberty" (L, 3:516–17).

The first week in July was a very difficult time for Cowper as he struggled to come to financial terms with his publisher. Joseph Johnson at first made an offer disadvantageous to Cowper, but his second offer was better. Several months later Cowper summed up what had occurred, adopting a philosophical attitude in a letter to Bagot: "I know not how it happen'd that Johnson disgraced himself by making me a paltry offer in the first instance, for in the second he proposed handsome terms and such as could not be objected to. We are all compounded of Good and Evil, and our behavior is according to the preponderancy of either at the moment. In him, the Daemon of avarice prevail'd at first, and, at last, the spirit of Liberality" (L, 3:569).

Cowper had two experienced advocates to argue his position with Joseph Johnson. Both Rose and Hill were deeply attached to Cowper and trained in the law as well. Cowper had no doubts about his inexperience with finances, calling himself "a perfect fool" and "non compos." "Awkwardness and extreme incompetence in all business is my misfortune, but avarice I believe is not my fault" (*L*, 3:539).

Graciousness and gratitude were among Cowper's finest attributes. He wrote to Rose: "On your management for me I shall rely with the most perfect tranquility, and heartily acquiesce in the result of your negotiation. . . . What appears to you to be reasonable will be perfectly content with me" (*L*, 3:538–39). To Hill Cowper said: "I have great cause therefore to be thankful both to you and to the Rose who have relieved me from so great a part of my burthen, and have brought this affair to an issue honorable, and therefore perfectly satisfactory to me" (*L*, 3:545).

There was a great void ahead for the erstwhile translator of Homer, who always relied on work at his desk to keep his demons at bay. But for the moment he was content. "I have nothing to do now but to wait as quietly as I can for the opinion of my readers, and have the better hope of success being conscious of having neglected nothing that might insure it" (*L*, 3:545). With Lady Hesketh, Cowper could always laugh at himself, even on a subject as serious as the publication of his six years of work: "I shall at last reap the reward of my labours, and be immortal probably for many years" (*L*, 3:391).

In the 1790s no one was more helpful to Cowper than his young cousin Johnny Johnson. Cowper was sensing a void—the empty block of time long occupied by Homer. He was referring frequently in his letters to his sixtieth birthday. Then came "one of the most favorable occurrences that in the evening of my days could possibly have befallen me" (*L*, 3:498). In January 1790 William Cowper received a hand-delivered letter from a member of his mother's family, Johnny Johnson, for whom he "immediately conceived a great affection" (*L*, 3:334). Cowper's mother had had three nieces, Harriet Balls, Anne (Rose) Bodham, and Catharine Johnson, the mother of Johnny. Cowper was thrilled to be back in touch with members of his mother's family with whom he had always felt "the bond of nature." "I was thought in the days of my childhood much to resemble my mother" (*L*, 3:349–50).

Cowper's childhood memories included happy days playing at Catfield with Harriet Balls, now "an unaffected, plain-dressing, good-temper'd, cheerful, motherly sort of a lady" (*L*, 3:530). When Mrs. Balls, with Johnny and Catharine his sister, visited Weston, they filled the void left by the conclusion of Cowper's work on Homer. "I am well contented to resign to them the place in my attention, so lately occupied by the Chiefs of Greece and Troy" (*L*, 3:524). He repeated the same thought in another letter. "With these my kindred I console myself for the loss of the fine old Grecian, and with these I could unbend my mind which may not fare the worse for a little relaxation after such long and constant exercise" (*L*, 3:528).

Johnny's letter and visit the next day had been more than "a fortunate occurrence." The result was that Cowper gained the child he never had. He immediately loved Johnny like a son and believed the young man "not unwilling to serve me in that capacity" (*L*, 3:431). Whether in delivering Cowper's Homer to the publisher or in serving as Cowper's caregiver during his appalling last illness, Johnny never failed in filial devotion.

When Cowper first met Johnny, he was twenty-one, a divinity student at Cambridge, his face already expressing sweetness of temper and "a mind much given to reflection and an understanding that in due time will know how to show itself to advantage" (*L*, 3:337).

Cowper was soon giving Johnny parental advice about leaving Mathematics for the study of Greek so that when the young man became a parson he could "look well to your flock when you shall get one" (*L*, 3:367). The older man continued, "Let your Divinity, if I may advise, be the Divinity of the glorious Reformation" (*L*, 3:385). Cowper, like a proud father, even teased Johnny about his way of walking. "Continue to take your walks, if walks they may be called, exactly in their present fashion, 'till you have taken Orders. Then indeed, forasmuch as a skipping, curvetting, bounding Divine might be a spectacle not altogether seemly, I shall consent to your adoption of a more grave demeanor" (*L*, 3:454).

The first letter from Johnny brought not only a son into Cowper's life, but also a picture of his mother, which Johnny had prompted Rose Bodham to send. Cowper wrote to Harriet Hesketh that "he would rather possess it than the richest jewel in the British crown." He remembered his mother's face perfectly and the picture was a "very exact resemblance" (*L*, 3:348). He wrote to Mrs. Bodham that his mother was the delight of his heart and he remembered perfectly "a multitude of the maternal tendernesses which I received from her" (*L*, 3:349).

The receipt of his mother's picture prompted him to recognize that he loved her as much now as fifty-two years before. "I kissed it and hung it where it is the last object that I see at night, and, of course, the first on which I open my eyes in the morning" (*L*, 3:349). The picture had become his mother.

> And while that face renews my filial grief
> Fancy shall weave a charm for my relief,
> Shall steep me in Elysian reverie,
> A momentary dream, that Thou are She.
>
> And while the wings of Fancy still are free,
> And I can view this mimic show of thee,
> Time has but half succeeded in his theft,
> Thyself removed, thy pow'r to sooth me left.
> (*P,* 3:56–60)

The season of satisfaction in Weston was coming to an end. Cowper had never been far from his home, even in an emotional sense, as he regained his life after the six-month breakdown of 1787. He had become closer than ever to Harriet Hesketh, kept in touch with John Newton, and welcomed Samuel Rose and Johnny Johnson into the center of his life. He had completed the monumental task of translating Homer.

During these satisfying years, Mary Unwin remained the person whom Cowper loved most fully and depended on most completely. In midsummer of 1791, just after Homer had been sent to the publisher, Cowper wrote to Mrs. King about Mary's physician, Dr. Raitt, and his expectations for his patient.

Of Dr. Raitt we may say in the words of Milton—

His long experience did attain
To something like prophetic strain.

The doctor foretold that "though her disorders might not much threaten life, they would yet cleave to her to the last, and she and perfect health must ever be strangers to each other" (*L*, 3:350–51). Mary was in her late sixties.

Her many disorders were commonly headaches, pains in her side, and loss of sleep. In January 1789 she had a bad fall on ice-covered gravel, from which she was very slow to recover. For a month she was confined upstairs and could walk only with a cane and a helper. After she had ventured downstairs and been taken for a brief walk in the orchard, Cowper told Mrs. King that "she recovers though even more slowly than she walks" (*L*, 3:270). In May he wrote that "no person ever recover'd more imperceptibly" (*L*, 3:288).

Cowper wrote to Rose Bodham about Mary's health, which was "the only subject on which she practises any dissimulation at all; the consequence is that when she is much indisposed I never believe myself in possession of the whole truth, live in constant expectation of hearing something worse, and at the long run am rarely disappointed" (*L*, 3:356).

Mary Unwin's failing health caused an agitation in Cowper's spirits, but he lived on as well as could be expected, with the highs and lows to which he was accustomed. In the summer of 1790, he wrote to Lady Hesketh, "I am I thank God at the present writing as well and in as good spirits as at any time these many years" (*L*, 3:384). But in the next winter he described to Mrs. King his nervous fever, "a disorder to which I am subject, and which I dread above all others because it comes attended by a melancholy perfectly insupportable" (*L*, 3:449).

In 1791 Cowper was struggling to find occupation. Different plans were suggested to him including original poetry and new translations. Then Joseph Johnson offered him the opportunity to be an editor of a new edition of Milton's works. "Thus I shall have pass'd through the three gradations of authorship, Poet, Translator, and Editor" (*L*, 3:570). The proposed volumes were to be elaborate, well illustrated by Fuseli. Cowper's responsibilities were "to select notes from others, and to write original notes, to translate the Latin and Italian poems, and to give a correct text. I shall have years allowed me to do it in" (*L*, 3:572).

Meanwhile, the first edition of Homer was selling well. In the *Gentleman's Magazine*, the reviewer treated Cowper with "both Compliments and censure" (*L*, 3:590–91). Cowper wrote to James Hurdis, "The Reviewer in the *Gentleman's Magazine* grows more and more civil. Should he continue to sweeten at this rate, as he proceeds, I know not what will become of the little modesty I have left. I have availed myself of some of his strictures, for I wish to learn from every body" (*L*, 3:597).

A letter of December 21, 1791, marked the end of Cowper's season of satisfactions. During a visit that had begun in October, Lady Hesketh had been sick. "Her disorder was at first the rheumatism. She applied a blister, which having only half its effect, had occasioned her much trouble" (*L*, 3:592). Three weeks later Rose heard again from Cowper: "Lady Hesketh is far from well. She has ventur'd these last two days to dine in the study, else she has kept her chamber above this fortnight. She has suffered however by this first sally and has taken cold as I fear'd she would" (*L*, 3:599).

But on December 21 there was far worse news than Lady Hesketh's poor health. Cowper wrote Samuel Rose a vivid description of Mary Unwin's first stroke: "On Saturday last, while I was at my desk near the window, and Mrs. Unwin at the fire-side opposite to it, I heard her suddenly exclaim—Oh Mr. Cowper, don't let me fall—I turn'd and saw her actually falling together with her chair, and started to her side just in time to prevent her. She was seized with a violent giddiness which lasted, though with some abatement, the whole day, and was attended too with some other most alarming symptoms. At present however she is relieved from the vertigo, and seems in all respects better, except that she is so enfeebled as to be unable to quit her bed for more than an hour in a day" (*L*, 3:598–99).

William Cowper saw the stark reality of his own situation. Mary Unwin had been his nurse. Harriet Hesketh had been his inspiration. Now Cowper was called to give both women all his attention, yet himself the victim of recurring and sometimes insupportable melancholy. He caught Mary in his arms as she was falling to the ground. At that moment, he wrote, he knew he was living in "a house of Invalids" (*L*, 3:598–99).

FIGURE 9. Portrait of William Cowper by George Romney, 1792. Courtesy of the National Portrait Gallery, London.

PART THREE

LOSING HOME AND HEALTH

19

ZEALOUS AND CONSTANT ENDEAVORS

1792

As the new year of 1792 began in the Weston household of William Cowper, Mary Unwin, and Harriet Hesketh, a letter arrived for Cowper from Eartham in Sussex. The writer, William Hayley, was to forge with Cowper a friendship so significant that its effects would extend past the poet's death in 1800 and culminate in Hayley's collection of Cowper's writings and the publication of the first biography of Cowper.

Hayley was also writing a book on Milton, but in his letter he dismissed the idea that there was any basis for antagonism or jealousy between the two men in regard to their scholarly work. Hayley was writing a biography, he explained, whereas Cowper was writing notes on Milton's works. There was certainly a market, in Milton's "expanding glory," for both expensive publications. Hayley began the letter by stating his "affectionate admiration" for Cowper's poetry and concluded, "your very cordial admirer." Enclosed was a poem.

> Cowper! delight of all who justly prize
> The splendid magic of a strain divine, . . .
> Let us meet with kind fraternal aim,
> Where Milton's shrine invites a votive throng
> With thee I share a passion for his fame.[1]

Soon a friendship flourished between the two writers. "He is now," said Cowper, "convinced that I love him, the chief acquisition that my own verse has ever procured me" (*L,* 4:39). Hayley's education, not unlike Cowper's, was gained at Eton, Cambridge, and the Middle Temple. Hayley became an accomplished linguist, fluent in Hebrew, Latin, and Greek, as well as French, Spanish, and Italian. Hayley was married in 1769 to Eliza Ball. She was older than her husband and mentally unstable, and the couple often lived separately. Miss Betts, a housemaid, gave birth to Hayley's only child, Thomas Alphonso.

Unlike Cowper, Hayley was a man of property and the squire of the Suffolk village of Eartham. Hayley's personality and character were complex and highly individualistic. He was uniquely equipped both to admire Cowper's writings and to help Cowper in times of deepest depression. In his memoirs Hayley wrote about himself in the third person with considerable insight: "As the Hermit of Felpham put it in his autobiography, he possessed a 'restless desire to subserve the intent of his friends, even when those friends were as unpardonably indolent in persecuting their own concerns.'"[2]

Of Hayley, Evelyn Bishop wrote, "The chief occupation and delight of Hayley seems to have consisted in zealous and constant endeavors to serve his friends, while they lived, and to celebrate their talents and virtues after their decease."[3]

Although many writers of the time tried to characterize the life and work of the complex, flamboyant William Hayley, it was Cowper, in his language of the heart, who wrote with special understanding about him even before Hayley's 1792 visit to Weston. To Lady Hesketh, Cowper mentioned Hayley's "candour, liberality, and generosity" (*L,* 4:39). When Cowper was planning Hayley's visit to Weston, he wrote again to Harriet. "His letters are in truth so affectionate, his desires to assist me so earnest, and there is even such a tenderness in his whole manner toward me, that terrified as I always am at the thought of a stranger, and terrified as I doubtless shall be even at the sight of Him, I yet long to see him" (*L,* 4:48).

After the visit, Cowper wrote to Samuel Rose that Hayley was "learned without the least ostentation, warm-hearted, interesting in his manners, and humane and friendly to a decree of which there are few examples" (*L*, 4:133).

In the spring of 1792, the Weston household was, in Cowper's phrase, "a veriable scene." Always unnerved by change, Cowper spoke with deep regret of the Throckmortons' departure to live in Bucklands. As he wrote to Newton, "I feel the loss of them, and shall feel it, since kinder or more friendly treatment I never can receive, at any hands, and I have always found at theirs" (*L*, 4:22).

Later during the same week in March, Lady Hesketh returned to London. Rose came for a brief visit, but soon Cowper remarked that he and Mary Unwin were "reduced to their dual state." Cowper was able to resume his correspondence and live a somewhat normal life, but by May he and Mary were focused on Hayley's upcoming visit. "Mary can vouch for me, and I can vouch for Mary, that we think of nothing else, as is sufficiently proved by our conversing on that theme only. Hayley will like this wilderness we say as we walk, and Hayley will be prodigiously pleased with that prospect, and they are so near at hand that it will not fatigue him to reach them, and thus we make you the burden of our song upon all occasions" (*L*, 4:75).

From May 15 to June 1, Hayley was a guest in Weston. Cowper wrote, "Everybody here has fallen in love with him, and wherever he goes everybody must."[4] Hayley's own pleasure "under this very kind, poetical roof" was expressed in a letter to his intimate friend, the painter George Romney. "My brother bard is one of the most interesting creatures in the world, from the powerful united influence of rare genius and singular misfortunes, with the additional charm of mild and engaging manners."[5]

Hayley was sensitive to the unusual relationship between Cowper and Mary Unwin. "It seemed hardly possible to survey human nature in a more touching and more satisfactory point of view—Their tender attention to each other, their simple, devout gratitude for the mercies which they had experienced together, and their constant, but unaffected propensity to impress on the mind and heart of a new friend the deep sense which they incessantly felt of their mutual obligations to each other, afforded me very singular gratification."[6]

Hayley's visit to Weston came, as Cowper said, at "a propitious time." On May 22 Mary had another, more severe paralytic stroke, which left her with unintelligible speech, a useless right arm, and the inability to walk. At the first shock William Cowper could do little more than cry out in agony, "There is a wall of separation between me and my God."

But William Hayley immediately began to organize a series of practical aids to the stroke victim. Here was the writer of florid prose and effusive letters, the sometime instigator of unwanted meddling, able to step up selflessly to take charge. Immediately appreciating Hayley's role, Cowper wrote to Lady Hesketh, "It has happen'd well, that of all men living the man most qualified to assist and comfort me, is here" (*L*, 4:79).

Hayley used a primitive electrical machine to encourage blood circulation. He wrote to Dr. Austin in London. Thus began a long and arduous time in which Mary improved literally by inches. Mary helped herself by a level of courage and faith deeply admired by Cowper. "It is a great blessing to us both that, poor, feeble thing as she is, she has a most invincible courage, and a trust in God's goodness that nothing can shake" (*L*, 4:105–6).

Cowper again wrote to Lady Hesketh about Hayley's role: "Where could I have found a man, except himself, who could have made himself so necessary to me in so short a time, that I absolutely know not how to live without him?" (*L*, 4:82).

When Hayley left to return to Eartham in June, William Cowper and Mary Unwin had to manage without him. The very day after William Hayley's departure, he wrote bluntly to Rose that if Mary was not restored to him, "Actum esset de me" ("It is all over for me") (*L*, 4:86).

He continued to express his "perpetual apprehensions" of Mary's relapse (*L*, 4:121) and his fears of losing his "faithful, long-tried, and only Intimate" (*L*, 4:159). The most striking image Cowper used for a life lived in fear of Mary's death was written for Charlotte Smith. "I live," he said, "under the point of a sword suspended by a hair" (*L*, 4:419).

In the sonnet Cowper wrote for William Hayley on his departure, however, there was a vein of underlying optimism.

Hayley—thy tenderness fraternal shown
    In our first interview, delightful guest!
    To Mary and me for her dear sake distress'd,
Such as it has made my heart thy own
Though heedless now of new engagements grown;
    For threescore winters make a wintry breast,
    And I had purpos'd ne'er to go in quest
Of Friendship more, except with God alone.
    But Thou has won me. Nor is God my Foe,
Who e're this last afflictive scene began
    Sent Thee to mitigate the dreadful blow
    My Brother, by whose sympathy I know
Infallibly thy true deserts to scan,
No more t'admire the Bard, than love the Man.
                    (*P,* 3:184)

No matter the occasional brilliance of Cowper's writing, during the months of June and July he was frustrated by the impossibility of working at his desk or making progress on Milton. His exasperations spilled out in a letter to his publisher. "I am the Electrician, I am the Escort into the Garden, I am wanted in short on a hundred little occasions that occur every day in Mrs. Unwin's present state of infirmity" (*L,* 4:144).

Cowper wrote in the same vein to Lady Hesketh: "I am crazed with having much to do and doing nothing. Every thing with me has fallen into arrears to such a decree that I almost despair of being able by the utmost industry to redeem the time that I have lost" (*L,* 4:151). A letter to Samuel Teedon described Cowper's dreams: "My nocturnal experiences are all of the most terrible kind. Death, Church yards and carcases, or else thunder storms and lightenings, God angry, and myself wishing that I had never been born" (*L,* 4:93).

Johnny Johnson paid a brief visit to Weston in June, providing moral support and practical help. Cowper wrote to Hayley about how they managed to take Mary for walks in the orchard. Two poles under a chair-bottom were manned by two servants. Cowper and Johnny supported

Mary's elbows. Thus she was carried to the orchard path. Taken out of the chair carriage, Mary walked, propped up on either side, again by her elbows (*L*, 4:117).

After Johnny left, Newton arrived. This visit was a great encouragement. Cowper said that some spiritual feelings had been awakened because the Lord came with Newton. "The comforts that I received under your ministry in better days all rush'd upon my recollection, and, during two or three transient moments seem'd to be in a decree renew'd" (*L*, 4:162).

The most interesting event of July was the arrival of the artist Lemuel Abbott. At the request of Mrs. Bodham and as arranged by Johnny, her nephew, Abbott came to Weston to paint Cowper's portrait in sittings between July 12 and 23.

In Abbott's work Cowper is dressed in a green archery coat, buff waistcoat, and breeches. He has a pen in hand and a large book open on the handsome desk given him by Theadora. Cowper was delighted by the experience of sitting and by the results. He wrote some doggerel for Hayley.

> Abbott is painting me so true
> > That, trust me, you would stare
> And hardly know at the first view
> > If I were here or there.
> > > (*L*, 4:148)

Cowper's letter to Lady Hesketh joked about his own charming lineaments and proportions. "I verily think the Pourtrait, exclusive of the likeness which is the closest imaginable, one of the best I ever saw" (*L*, 4:153).

When Abbott's work was completed, Cowper wrote a vivacious letter to William Bull. "The likeness is so strong that when my friends enter the room where the picture is they start, astonish'd to see me where they know I am not. Miserable man that you are to be at Brighton instead of being here to contemplate this prodigy of art, which therefore you can never see. For it goes to London next Monday to be suspended awhile at Abbot's, and then proceeds to Norfolk where it will be suspended for ever" (*L,* 4:156).

In the final letter about Abbott's work, Cowper was not only jocular but also both proud and pleased. "Well! this picture is at last finished, and well finished, I can assure you. Every creature that has seen it has been astonished at the resemblance. Sam's boy bowed to it, and Beau walked up to it, wagging his tail as he went, and evidently showing that he acknowledged its likeness to his master. It is a half-length, as it is technically, but absurdly called; that is to say, it gives all but the foot and ankle. To-morrow it goes to town, and will hang some months at Abbot's, when it will be sent to its due destination in Norfolk" (*L,* 4:160).

Astonishingly, from August 1 to September 17 William Cowper and Mary Unwin went away from Weston to visit William Hayley in Eartham. Hayley had first proposed the journey five months previously. Cowper had explained that it could not be.

> But how should I who have not journey'd 20 miles from home these 20 years, how should I possibly reach your country? You will wonder perhaps, after hearing me boast of my freedom from disease, wherein the impossibility can consist. But consider what habit is, and consider how every year that is spent entirely at home, adds terrours to the thought of quitting it. To this consideration add another, of which at present you are not apprized, that though I labour under no bodily disability properly so call'd, I have sad spirits, a mind continually subject to melancholy, and sometimes cover'd with the darkest shade of it. Your state of body therefore, not more than my state of mind, seems to lour on the hope of our meeting till we shall meet in a long hereafter. (*L,* 4:37)

A month later, in April, Cowper made his point more succinctly. "As to any migrations of mine, they must I fear, notwithstanding the joy I should feel in being a guest of yours, be still considered in the light of Impossibles" (*L,* 4:51).

By the end of June he was considering this "formidable but pleasing enterprise" (*L,* 4:134). To make the trip Mary should be able to walk alone, cut her own food, feed herself, and wear her own shoes, not his. Not having been in a carriage for seven years, how would Mary tolerate the motion? A week before setting off on this 120-mile journey with Mary, Cowper asked for prayers from William Bull, who had introduced Cowper to the poems of Madame Guion. "It is a tremendous exploit that I feel a thousand anxieties when I think of it. . . . The journey and the change of air together with the novelty to us of the scene to which we are going, may, I hope, be useful to us both, especially to Mrs. Unwin who has the most need of restoration" (*L*, 4:157). The last letter to Hayley before leaving Weston told about Cowper's dejection of spirits: "I am hunted by spiritual hounds in the night season." But he was ready to set forth in hopes that he would recover his habit of study. "Soon I, my Mary, my Johnny, and my dog, shall be skipping with delight at Eartham" (*L*, 4:160).

Southey's biography of Cowper included many details about Eartham. Hayley's father had bought in 1743 a small estate in the village, which was about six miles from Chichester. After his father died and was buried in the village churchyard, William Hayley grew to love Eartham more and more, moving there in 1774. Although he could be imprudent in making expensive improvements, he said he had inherited from his father "a passion also for building and gardening, for pictures and for books; and a contempt for money, romantic and imprudent."[7]

Cowper, Mary, Johnny, the servants, and the dog Beau left Weston on August 1, spent the first night in Barnet where Samuel Rose met them and traveled the next day with them as far as London. They met General Cowper briefly in Kingston and spent the next night in Ripley, arriving at Eartham on April 3. Three days later Cowper wrote to Greatheed about Eartham, "almost a paradise." "Here we are, in the most elegant mansion, and surrounded by the most delightful pleasure grounds . . . They occupy three sides of a hill, which, in Buckinghamshire, might well pass for a mountain, and from the summit of which is beheld a most magnificent landscape, bounded by the sea, and in one part of it by the Isle of Wight." He told Greatheed that their reception had been "the kindest that it was possible for friendship and hospitality to contrive" (*L*, 4:164–65).

Cowper began to write to Rose and Lady Hesketh of Mrs. Unwin's increasing cheerfulness and ability to sleep twice as much as she had in Weston. After two weeks passed, he wrote to Newton. "Thus it has pleased God to answer our prayers for a safe conveyance hither, and I have a hope that he will further answer them by making the air of this place and the beautiful scenery of it conducive to the renewal both of her health and spirits, and of mine" (*L*, 4:173).

The most important event during the Weston visitors' six weeks at Eartham was the arrival of George Romney and his execution of William Cowper's portrait. Hayley had long been a generous and extravagant host at Eartham, inviting over the years men of prominence in the literary and artistic worlds. Hayley was drawn not only to talent of striking originality but also to those whose talents were affected for good and ill by melancholic temperaments.

George Romney had visited Eartham many times before he met Cowper there in August 1792. Hayley was sympathetic to Romney's family history of depression. The two men had similar marital sorrows. Hayley had long lived apart from his wife. Romney had left his wife and two children behind when he went to London. After thirty-seven years of desertion, he returned to his wife as a famous painter but broken down in body and mind.

When Romney met Cowper, both men were intensely aware of their own "singular infirmity of mind" and tendencies to "tremble at phantoms."[8] Both could be eloquent in conversation. Both the artist and his subject were deeply satisfied by the Cowper portrait that Romney was able to create at Eartham.

Romney worked in pastels, a medium unusual for him. He considered Cowper's portrait one of his best. As to Cowper himself, he said the likeness was my "exact counterpart." As David Cross wrote, "the portrait is indeed a superb late head and one of Romney's finest works."[9]

This portrait was soon a subject of debate as to the degree that it revealed Cowper's melancholy and incipient madness. The first opinion was given by Cowper himself. In his sonnet to Romney, he said that no symptoms of woe could be observed in the portrait.

To George Romney, Esq.

Romney, expert infallibly to trace
    On chart or canvas, not the form alone
    And semblance, but, however faintly shown,
The mind's impression too on ev'ry face—
With strokes that time ought never to erase
    Thou hast so pencill'd mine, that though I own
    The Subject worthless, I have never known
The Artist shining with superior grace.

Yet This I mark—that symptoms none of woe
    In thy incomparable work appear.
Well—I am satisfied it should be so,
    Since, on maturer thought, the cause is clear;
For in my looks what sorrow could'st thou see
While I was Hayley's guest and sat to Thee?
                         (*P,* 3:189)

Hayley wrote that Romney "wished to express what he often saw in studying the features of Cowper—'the poet's eye in a fine frenzy rolling.'" Hayley himself felt that the portrait grew out of the deep affection "*con amore*" between painter and subject and was "one of the most masterly and most faithful resemblances that I ever beheld." Southey quoted Leigh Hunt's comment that Romney's portrait showed "a fire fiercer than that either of intellect or fancy, gleaming from the raised and protruded eye."[10]

The best-known debate about the portrait came about through Hayley's determination to preserve Romney's work in Cowper's biography. Hayley cleverly deflected the hysterical objections of Lady Hesketh to Blake's miniature and engraving from Romney's pastel original. She thought her beloved cousin had a frenzied, and thus unacceptable, appearance.

There can be no doubt of the understanding between Romney and Cowper and their mutual experiences of mental deterioration. In 1794

Romney wrote, "And if there is a situation more deplorable than any other in nature it is the horrible decline of reason and the derangement of the power we have been blessed with."[11]

Images of the power of the sea were brilliantly used both with Romney's brush and Cowper's pen in two of the best works created by either man. Cowper wrote "The Cast-away" and Romney painted *Boys Dancing on a Seashore*. As David Cross has said, "Though ostensibly this is a nostalgic portrait of the joys of childhood, one of the boys is dramatically lit against a forbidding black breaker, a metaphor of the abyss, in a work described as one of the most remarkable paintings produced in Britain in the 1790s."[12]

September 17 approached none too soon, this being the date long determined for Cowper's departure from Eartham. The visit could not have been longer sustained. Cowper and Mary were both distressed that she was still so disabled. Hayley perceived that Cowper wanted to go home.

Cowper told Lady Hesketh the week before the departure that the scenery was becoming oppressive, as beautiful as it may have been. His heart's home was in Weston. "The genius of the place suits me better; it has an air of snug concealment, in which a disposition like mine feels peculiarly gratified; whereas, here, I see, from every window, woods like forests, and hills like mountains,—a wilderness, in short, that rather increases my natural melancholy, and which, were it not for the agreeables I find within, would soon convince me that mere change of place can avail me little" (*L*, 4:189).

Hayley knew that Mary Unwin, however she may have benefited from the vacation, was infirm. The coming of fall and winter made it essential "for them to reach their own fireside by the time they had proposed." Hayley said that "their departure was a scene of affectionate anxiety, and a perfect contrast to the gayety of their arrival at Eartham."[13]

The night of the seventeenth Cowper wrote to Hayley from Kingston with especially tender messages for his son Tom: "I left you with a heavy heart, and with a heavy heart took leave of our dear Tom at the bottom of the chalk-hill. But soon after this last separation, my troubles gushed from my eyes, and then I was better. . . . Prayers that God may bless you and yours, and reward you a hundred fold for all your kindness. Tell Tom I shall always hold him dear for his affectionate attentions to Mrs. Unwin. From her heart the memory of him can never be erased" (*L*, 4:194–95).

The travelers visited General Cowper in Ham and Samuel Rose in London although Cowper was scarcely able to speak, overcome with the anxieties of travel and his fears for Mary. "In the dark, and in a storm, at eight at night they found themselves at their own backdoor" (*L*, 4:196).

20

A CHRONICLE OF ACTIONS JUST AND RIGHT

1793–1795

When William Cowper returned home to Weston in September 1792, he was overwhelmed by the realities of his life with Mary Unwin. He wrote to Samuel Teedon, an Olney schoolmaster of intense religious fervor, "My frame of mind continues such as it was before I went to Eartham; almost always low, and often inexpressibly dejected" (*L*, 4:197). A month later he wrote Joseph Hill that in spite of breathing the purest air of the magnificent Eartham countryside, neither he nor Mrs. Unwin were improved. She was still unable to walk without assistance, and he came back "the same miserable thing" who went away (*L*, 4:246).

In Weston he was unable to write. One day, as he told William Hayley, he was set to write but from many causes, he gave up. In another letter he described himself "bound in magic chains of sloth." Especially in regard to working on Milton, Cowper said that "the consciousness that there is so much to do and nothing done, is a burden that I am not able to bear" (*L*, 4:225). His most poignant self-analysis was written for Teedon. A dagger in Cowper's heart was the fear of Mary Unwin's death. The old terrors of abandonment, of being an outcast, returned in full force. "In one moment all may be undone again and I left desolate" (*L*, 4:208).

He wrote to John Newton in November. Cowper tried without success to realize his old friend's expectations. Newton believed that Cowper could be delivered from a concept of God as enemy, "a foe omnipotent to destroy." But for Cowper, "The Future appears as gloomy as ever, and I seem to myself to be scrambling always in the Dark among rocks and precipices without a guide, but with an enemy ever at my heels prepared to push me headlong" (*L*, 4:234–35).

The first week in December, Cowper seemed to break free, writing a series of more hopeful letters. He told Joseph Hill, "My spirits however have improved within the last week or ten days, quite contrary to my expectation" (*L*, 4:246).

Cowper was still unable to sound crisp and amusing as was normally the case in his letters to Harriet Hesketh, his dearest Coz. His letter of December 1 cited his sixty-first birthday as a propitious turning point toward better spirits. "I think of bestirring myself soon and of putting on my Miltonic trammels" (*L*, 4:248). Writing to Samuel Rose, Cowper anticipated his friend's visit and that of Johnny as well.

Cowper's letter to Hayley at this time was filled with expressions of pleasure at having received Romney's portrait of the squire of Eartham. "The picture is arrived safe. . . . There is no fear now that I shall not often think of you, seeing that you are always before my eyes." Cowper enclosed a poem.

> In language warm as could be breathed or penn'd
> Thy portrait speaks th' Original my friend—
> Not by those looks that indicate thy mind,
> They only speak, thee Friend of all Mankind;
> Expression here more soothing still I see!
> That Friend of All a partial Friend to Me.
>
> (*L*, 4:251–52)

Some encouragement notwithstanding, William Cowper was once more overcome by thoughts of the month of January. He reminded Newton of "the same season in the dreadful 73 and in the more dreadful 86. I cannot help terrifying myself with doleful misgivings. . . . God only knows where this will end" (*L*, 4:254–55).

Even Cowper's letter of thanks to Romney for Hayley's portrait was colored with a melancholy for which the only cure would be the arrival of spring. "I have been a poor creature ever since I saw you; dispirited to the greatest degree and incapable of all mental exertion; a state from which I do not expect deliverance till the buds shall peep and less sullen skies revive me" (*L*, 4:245).

January and February of 1793 were dominated by what Cowper told Johnny were two evils. The first was the condition of Cowper's "poor invalid." Mary was "not at all advanced in her powers of helping herself" (*L*, 4:283). The second evil was Cowper's inability to write. He attempted to make a joke of this plight for his dearest Coz.

> My pens are all split, and my ink-glass is dry,
> Neither wit, common-sense, nor ideas have I.
>   (*L*, 4:289)

The overriding evil of this desperate winter was the theme of numerous letters to Teedon. In various ways Cowper expressed his conviction that, having offended God, he would be deserted and abandoned. "For though all things are possible to God, it is not possible that he should save whom he has declared he will destroy" (*L*, 4:289).

Nine months of 1793, from March to November, serve as a representative portion of the entirety of William Cowper's years at home in Olney and Weston. Against all odds and with unsurpassed courage, he was able to fashion for the last time a life that included those elements essential to his mind, heart, and soul.

First, he had no intention of spending even one night away from home. In spite of Mary's physical disabilities and Cowper's mental infirmities, they had many invitations to visit devoted friends who competed jealously to entertain them. Hayley urged their return to Eartham, the Throckmortons wanted them to enjoy Bucklands, and Johnny assured them of a warm family embrace in Norfolk. Joseph Hill and Samuel Rose reiterated long-standing invitations. Lady Hesketh often recommended a change of scene. Cowper's replies were always the same. Any

Drawn & Engrav'd by J.Storer.

VIEW FROM THE ALCOVE.
—————————— *Now roves the eye ;*
And, posted on this speculative height,
Exults in its command. ——————
Vide the Task, Book I.

FIGURE 10. *View from the Alcove,* from *Cowper Illustrated by a Series of views in, or near, the Park of Weston-Underwood, Bucks.* (London: Verner and Hood, 1803). Courtesy of the Library of Congress.

advice that he leave Weston was useless. "It is in vain that thou Counsellest me to leave Weston. . . . This is moreover of all the earth the spot that delights me most" (*L*, 4:362).

Few human beings have ever had William Cowper's powerful capacity for friendship. His letters to friends were his language of love. Now in 1793 he fought to maintain his correspondence. Because of his busy days, he wrote Hayley, "you ought to account it an instance of marvelous grace and favour that I condescend to write even to you" (*L*, 4:307–8). When a letter from Hayley seemed overdue because he had been silent longer than usual, enquiries were made to Rose. Cowper said that he was anxious about Hayley, "having been possess'd by a thousand fears about you lest you had relapsed and were incapable of writing, or perhaps dead" (*L*, 4:438).

Cowper always depended on Harriet's letters when she was away and lived in expectation of her next visit. Since his dearest Coz had first visited him in Olney, he had never before 1793 waited so long to see her. Asking on the first of June when she would arrive, he urged for himself and Mary, "Give us a hope, and a determinate point for that hope to fix on and we will endeavor to be satisfied" (*L*, 4:344).

William Cowper knew beyond any doubt that he had to write to exist in any meaningful sense, to prevent becoming "a wither'd tree, fruitless and leafless" (*L*, 4:307). He accepted the fact that in the middle of 1793, he could not write poetry because his mind was not free. He told Hayley that for original verse he had to be alone and undisturbed. Cowper discovered, as well, that he was unable to make headway with notes on Milton. Therefore he went back to a second edition of Homer as a sure refuge from the storm of his present life (*L*, 4:359–60).

To advance with corrections and transcriptions of Homer required that Cowper write by morning candlelight. He continued at his desk for three hours before he had any breakfast, taking advantage of his only opportunity to be uninterrupted "stalking and strutting in Homeric stilts." Cowper said he was always tired, which he attributed to old age (*L*, 4:307–8).

Another essential, which Cowper struggled to include in his busy days, was enjoyment of his house and garden. Crumbling house beams had necessitated a complete overhaul of his study. "Not a stick of the old room remains, but everything is completely new, and when finish'd it will be far the smartest room in the neighborhood" (*L,* 4:335). With materials from the old study, Cowper himself built a summerhouse (*L,* 4:361).

Two other garden additions were an unmitigated delight, both gifts from Johnny and "constant mementos" of his kindness. After Johnny's August visit, Cowper "walked into the garden with Mary in the afternoon, and to my inexpressible surprize, saw there a smart sun-dial mounted smartly on a stone pedestal. Having order'd no such thing I enquired of course how it came there" (*L,* 4:391). Sam Roberts, who had been Cowper's servant for many years, told Cowper it came from Johnny Johnson.

The second gift was a bust of Homer. Even if it was not authenticated as such, in Cowper's eyes the bust was always that of "my dear old Greecian." Cowper hired a stone cutter to make a pedestal for the bust on which were carved Cowper's own words.

> The Sculptor? nameless though once dear to Fame.
> But this Man bears an everlasting name.
>
> (*L,* 4:371)

To express his appreciation, Cowper dedicated a poem to Johnny.

To John Johnson Esq.
on His Presenting Me with an Antique Bust
of Homer

Kinsman belov'd, and as a son by me!
    When I behold this fruit of thy regard
    The scuptur'd form of my old fav'rite bard,
I rev'rence feel for him, and love for thee.
Joy too and grief. Much joy that there should be
    Wise men and learn'd, who grudge not to reward

With some applause my bold attempt and hard,
Which others scorn. Critics by courtesy.

The grief is this, that sunk in Homer's mine
    I lose my precious years, now soon to fail,
Handling his gold, which, howsoere it shine,
    Proves dross, when balanced in the Christian scale.

Be wiser thou—Like our forefather Donne,
Seek heav'nly wealth, and work for God alone.

                        (*P,* 3:194)

William Cowper's life in Weston from March to November 1793 can be called courageous because of the way in which he adjusted to the condition of his beloved Mary. He was at his desk before dawn because letters were the only writing he could do after Mary got up for the day. "While I write, my poor invalide, who is still unable to amuse herself either with book or needle, sits silent by my side, which makes me in all my letters hasten to a conclusion" (*L,* 4:325).

Mary's daily walk in the orchard was undertaken supported by Cowper and another helper. Mary needed assistance at meals. She had, in fact, no capacity for independent living. But in June Cowper told the Newtons that "she is cheerful, seldom in much pain, and has always strong confidence in the mercy and faithfulness of God" (*L,* 4:350). Cowper said that while Mary was not better, he had to be satisfied if she were not worse. Soon he would no longer have that satisfaction.

Halfway through this interval in 1793, during which Cowper for the last time was able to enjoy his house and garden, correspond with friends, and work on Homer, all the while taking care of Mary, he picked up his pen and gave the world two examples of his creative genius. The first, in May, was a sonnet for Mary.

Mary! I want a lyre with other strings,
    Such aid from heav'n as some have feign'd they drew,

An eloquence scarce giv'n to mortals, new
And undebased by praise of meaner things,
That 'ere through age or woe I shed my wings,
   I may record thy worth with honor due,
   In verse as musical as thou art true,
And that immortalizes whom its sings.
But thou hast little need. There is a book
   By seraphs writ with beams of heav'nly light,
On which the eyes of God not rarely look,
   A chronicle of actions just and right.
There, all thy deeds, my faithful Mary, shine,
And, since thou own'st that praise, I spare thee mine.
                  (*P,* 3:194–95)

The second example of his power as a writer was a paraphrase of lines from *Paradise Lost.*

Seasons return, but not to me returns
God, or the sweet approach of heav'nly day,
Or sight of cheering truth or pardon seal'd,
Or joy or hope, or Jesus' face divine.
                (*L,* 4:351)

In November 1793, six months after his sonnet about Mary's "actions just and right," William Cowper said good-bye to her in another poem. In the first two lines of the sonnet for Mary he had implored help from heaven. He needed "a lyre with other strings" to write verse as musical and true as Mary's deeds had been. When he wrote "To Mary," he played on his new lyre.

Cowper was prescient about what lay ahead. He had foreseen two years earlier a house of three invalids. Now he understood more fully what that house would be like. Mary's mind was fading as well. Harriet Hesketh lacked the health and toughness required to be in charge of such a household. So he said good-bye, although Mary would not die and be buried in East Dereham until 1796.

Over the years of their long friendship, Cowper had written many tributes to Mary. From his first meeting with the Unwins in 1765, Cowper had spoken forcefully about his new friends: Mrs. Unwin had "a very uncommon Understanding" (*L*, 1:121–22). Two months later, he elaborated. "I assure you I have never conversed with any body that kept my Mind in better Training or more constant Exercise than Mrs. Unwin does" (*L*, 1:128).

In Cowper's long poem, "The Task," two miniature portraits of Mary stand out. In book 1 she is the companion of his walks. She understands and shares his love of nature, doubling his joy. Her arm, "fast lock'd in mine," is a pleasure such as could be inspired only by love (*P*, 2:120). In book 3, at home in the morning he enjoys "sweet converse . . . with her who shares his pleasures and his heart" (*P*, 2:172).

While over the years Cowper and Mary Unwin continued to view their love as one of mutual support, many times it was she who took care of *him*. In 1792 when she was a stroke victim, Cowper looked back over the thirty years of Mary's care. "The utmost attention that I can bestow upon her is not more than she is well entitled to by that which she has for thirty years bestow'd upon me, during which time she has more than once watch'd over me day and night for months together, taking a share in my afflictions that has been fatal to her own constitution, and has largely contributed to the illness by which she suffers now" (*L*, 4:115).

The reciprocity of their thirty-year relationship was clearly explained by Cowper in a letter he wrote to his publisher Joseph Johnson to tell him not to expect any progress in Cowper's work on Milton. "We have lived together thirty years and now become so necessary to each other that our respective indispositions affect us both equally, and if she is too ill to use her knitting-needles, my pen is of course idle" (*L*, 4:177).

Among Cowper's most affecting words about his love for Mary were those written in one sentence to Harriet Hesketh. "Mary has been my Touch-stone always" (*L*, 2:471).

When Cowper was preparing to write a valedictory poem for Mary, he first wrote "A Tale" about a husband and wife in the animal kingdom who taught humans how to love (*P,* 3:195). A "Chaff-finch" and his mate, finding no nesting place in Scotland's forlorn, bare land, built their nest in the mast of a ship. With the law "of never-failing love," the male bird went to sea with the female sitting on her eggs and he cheering her with song. In spite of the billows and blasts, "nothing could divide them," "their union undefil'd."

Then he wrote the poem "To Mary" with his new lyre, the strings of which were simple words in three-line stanzas, each with a single one-syllable rhyme. Cowper's dominant image was golden light, a sun that shines through the overcast skies of declining health and wintry age.

After each of the fourteen stanzas, Cowper wrote "My Mary!" As the Cowper scholar and psychiatrist Andrew Brink asked, "Is there any poem of profounder appreciation of another person than this?"[1] In spite of Mary's unused knitting needles, blurred speech, and feeble limbs, at the least touch of her hand on his, the "golden beams of oriental light" shone to illuminate their love.

To Mary

The twentieth year is well-nigh past
Since first our skie was overcast,
Ah would that this might be the last
       My Mary!

Thy spirits have a fainter flow,
I see thee daily weaker grow—
'Twas my distress that brought thee low
       My Mary!

Thy needles once a shining store
For my sake restless heretofore
Now rust disused and shine no more
       My Mary!

For though thou gladly wouldst fulfill
The same kind office for me still
Thy sight now seconds not thy will
      My Mary!

But well thou played'st the houswife's part
And all thy threads with magic art
Have wound themselves around this heart
      My Mary!

Thy indistinct expressions seem
Like language utter'd in a dream,
Yet me they charm whate'er the theme
      My Mary!

Thy silver locks once auburn bright
Are still more lovely in my sight
Than golden beams of orient light
      My Mary!

For could I view nor them nor thee,
What sight worth seeing could I see?
The Sun would rise in vain for me
      My Mary!

Partakers of the sad decline
Thy hands their little force resign,
Yet gently prest press gently mine
      My Mary!

And then I feel that still I hold
A richer store ten-thousand fold
Than misers fancy in their gold
      My Mary!

Such feebleness of limbs thou prov'st
That now, at ev'ry step, thou mov'st
Upheld by two, yet still thou lov'st
      My Mary!

And still to love though prest with ill,
In wintry age to feel no chill
With me is to be lovely still
      My Mary!

But ah by constant heed I know
How oft the sadness that I show
Transforms thy smiles to looks of woe
      My Mary!

And should my future lot be cast
With much resemblance of the past,
Thy worn-out heart will break at last
      My Mary!
          (*P,* 3:206)

William Cowper could, at crucial times, acutely observe the present and clearly imagine the future. In December 1791 he had first described his Weston home with Mary Unwin, Harriet Hesketh, and himself as "a house of three invalids." Now, two years later, Harriet arrived for her final visit, which was to last from November 1793 to July 1795. She came to attempt to manage a household in which all three principals were invalids in far worse condition than before.

Mary Unwin had never recovered from her stroke. Now there were new symptoms. Cowper told Hayley that "poor Mary sleeps but ill, and has been frequently tortured with a pain in her face" (*L,* 4:373). Cowper wrote to Johnny that "Mrs. Unwin suffers sadly half starved by a most painful disorder of her tongue" (*L,* 4:409). More serious still, even before Harriet's arrival, Mary had been sinking into a state of second childhood.

As Hayley was to write, "Mary Unwin's cheerful and beneficent spirit could hardly resist her own accumulated maladies. Gradually imbecility of body and mind were beginning to be painfully visible." The shape of imbecility was "eagerly grasping for dominance."[2]

As to William Cowper, he had effectively said good-bye to Mary in his remarkable poem. No matter in what ways she declined, no matter the difficulty of her care, Cowper would never part from her. Johnny wrote that Cowper's own health was damaged by his constant care of Mary. "There can be no doubt that an arrangement of this sort was highly prejudicial to the health of Cowper, and that it hastened the approach of the last calamitous attack with which the interesting sufferer was yet to be visited."[3]

After Harriet had been with them one month, Cowper wrote to Hayley, "We are much as usual. Mrs. U not worse, Lady H always cheerful. I, sometimes smother'd in melancholy" (L, 4:442). Then the month of January began. He told Rose that he carried the load of dejection not uncommon for that month, and he told Teedon that with the New Year always came "added shades of Misery and despair." After writing a long letter to Hayley on January 5, 1794, William Cowper did not again write a single letter until a year and a half later, at the end of August 1795.

Hayley wrote that January 1794 was the beginning of "a long season of darkest depression in which the best medical advice, and the influence of time, appeared equally unable to lighten the afflictive burthen which pressed incessantly on his spirits."[4] Johnny observed that January 1794 was the beginning of Cowper's "descent into those depths of affliction from which his spirit was only to emerge by departing from the earth."[5]

Harriet Hesketh was in a hopeless situation, trying to live with and have some means of managing the daily lives of Mary Unwin and William Cowper. Harriet herself had not been well the year before when at Cheltenham she had had gallstones causing "excruciating anguish" (L, 4:201). Cowper had written to her his concern that she would "hide from me the worst half of your malady let it be what it may. God preserve thee, restore thy health and give us a comfortable meeting once more in the winter" (L, 4:152).

Harriet went briefly to see the renowned Dr. Willis, who subsequently visited Cowper at Weston. Hayley's biography of Cowper revealed that "there was something indescribable in his appearance." A friend told Hayley that Cowper would not eat. "Now and then a very small piece of toasted bread, dipped generally in water, sometimes mixed with a little wine."[6] The patient refused to take the medicines prescribed by Dr. Willis.

Hayley, normally received by Cowper "with the most lively expressions of affectionate delight," was now ignored. The only human contact Cowper seemed to tolerate was Hayley's son Tom who spoke with the gentle voice of childhood. There was "no glimmering of joy" when Cowper was told of a pension from the King, an annuity of three hundred pounds a year payable to Rose as trustee. Hayley had worked tirelessly to have this pension granted.

When Hayley left Weston in the spring of 1794, Cowper seemed to awaken from his stupor to express "extreme reluctance" to let his friend depart. Hayley said, "I hardly ever endured an hour more dreadfully disturbing than the hour in which I left him."[7] The friends were never to see each other again.

Harriet Hesketh was certainly to be pitied and could not continue in a house of three such invalids. Antagonism grew between her and Mary Unwin, whom she called "the old Enchantress." It was impossible for Harriet to accept Mary's mental decline and to understand that nothing would ever alter the bond between Mary and William Cowper. As Hayley put it, to separate them "was a measure so pregnant with complicated distraction, that it could not be advised or attempted."[8]

On July 27, 1795, Harriet saw that she would have to go her separate way. It must have been unbearable for Harriet to suffer the loss, while Cowper still lived, of her animated, beloved friend of the heart who had always called her his dearest Coz.

The day had come for Johnny Johnson to undertake an amazing feat of devotion. He took William Cowper and Mary Unwin to Norfolk on a pilgrimage that would end only in first Mary's, then William's death. While some speculated about a return to Weston, William Cowper knew better. He wrote his precise, desperate thoughts on his window shutter.

Farwell dear Scenes—for ever clos'd to me,
Oh for what sorrows must I now exchange you.

Me Miserable—How could I escape
Infinite Wrath, and Infinite Despair,
Whom Death, Earth, Heaven, and all combin'd to ruin,
Whose friend was God, but God swore not to aid me.

(P, 3:208)

21

NO LIGHT
PROPITIOUS SHONE
1795–1800

Villiam Cowper lived for almost five years after leaving Weston. Cowper's letters have given us a remarkably detailed picture of this interval, which was dominated by Cowper's overwhelming depression. Some views are small snapshots: Norfolk villages, horses and carriages, family groups. Other impressions are of the full sweep of the human condition, especially the triumph of the human spirit over extreme adversity.

One month after he left Weston, Cowper wrote his first letter in more than a year and a half. He wrote to Lady Hesketh that he had no expectation of ever seeing her or Weston again.

In early September 1795 he wrote his second letter, this time to John Buchanan, who lived near Olney and Weston. Here the depth of Cowper's homesickness, his longing for his beloved Weston was revealed: "I beg Sir, if you favour me with any answer to this, that you will not waste ink and paper in attempting to console me. . . . Tell me if my poor birds are living. I never see the herbs I would give them without a recollection of them, and sometime am ready to gather them, forgetting that I am not at home" (*L*, 4:451–53).

When Cowper used the word "taken" in reference to his departure from Weston, it is the very word he often used about his childhood when he was taken from home and sent away to school. After his father died and Cowper left Berkhamsted forever, he had written to Samuel Rose, "I sighed a long adieu to fields and woods from which I once thought I should never be parted, and was at no time so sensible of their beauties as just when I left them all behind me to return no more" (*L*, 3:42–43).

This poignant expression of homesickness could apply as well to Cowper's departure from Weston. Two months after being taken from his Weston home, he told Lady Hesketh, "I shall never see Weston more. I have been tossed like a ball into a far country, from which there is to be no rebound for me." He acknowledged that he would be experiencing infinite despair whether in Norfolk or Weston "but to have passed the little time that remained to me there, was the desire of my heart" (*L*, 4:456).

No matter how severely depressed he was, Cowper could still conjure up images that made him his own interpreter. His thoughts, he wrote, were like "loose and dry sand, which the closer it is grasped slips the sooner away" (*L*, 4:457). His mind wandered in a shattered mode of thinking. From a cliff rising above the shore at Mundesley, he saw a solitary pillar of rock. "I have visited it twice, and have found it an emblem of myself. Torn from my natural connexions, I stand alone and expect the storm that shall displace me" (*L*, 4:450). In another letter to Lady Hesketh, he imagined drowning in a storm. "The night contradicts the day, and I go down the torrent of time into the gulf that I have expected to plunge into so long" (*L*, 4:458–59).

In the penultimate letter he would ever write to Harriet, Cowper told of his dire sensations on the Norfolk coast. Nature had become for him "an universal blank." Whether mountains or hills, rivers or the magnificent ocean, every scene had become "an insipid wilderness" (*L*, 4:463–64).

The interval between July 1795 and April 1800, that is, between Cowper's departure from Weston and his death in East Dereham, must have been devastating for Harriet. She had watched two carriages pull away from the home at Weston, carrying William Cowper, Mary Unwin, and Johnny Johnson, together with servants and helpers. Her health declined. Johnny wrote that soon after the departure of Cowper, Harriet Hesketh had become sick because of "her protracted and painful confinement with her revered relative during the early stage of his calamitous depression."[1]

Unlike the joy of receiving Cowper's lively, brilliant, and very affectionate letters over so many years, recently the correspondence had been heartbreaking. When Cowper was dying, Harriet was too ill to visit him or even, subsequently, to attend the burial. But hers was a story of revitalization in the cause of protecting the reputation of Britain's most loved poet. On the marble tablet honoring Cowper, which she commissioned for the East Dereham church where his ashes were buried, an inscription included the admonition that England could well exult "in his spotless fame."

> His highest honours to the heart belong;
> His virtues form'd the magic of his song.

William Cowper had a deep capacity for friendship. In the Olney-Weston years when he never left home, some friends were able to visit him. But the cultivation of his friendships was accomplished primarily through his letters. His ability to express affection and empathy, and his genius in the use of words, make his letters among the best in the history of literature.

The contacts Cowper had in the five years of his wanderings in Norfolk give some impression of the different types of people to whom he was especially close. John Newton he had met when he first lived with Mary Unwin and her family. A churchman of deep faith, Newton along with his devoted wife, took care of Cowper during a serious breakdown and tried to nurture Cowper's faith. In all the subsequent years of Cowper's spiritual turmoil and imagined loss of God's salvation, Newton never gave up trying to help.

Cowper wrote to Newton in the summer of 1798, thanking him for having written a letter containing "many kind expressions, which would have encouraged, perhaps, and consoled any other than myself, but I was, even then, out of the reach of all such favorable impressions" (*L*, 4:462).

The last letter Cowper ever wrote, on April 11, 1799, was again to Newton to thank him for a book that Johnny had been reading aloud. "If it afforded me any amusement, or suggested to me any reflections, they were only such as served to imbitter, if possible, still more the present moment, by a sad retrospect to those days when I thought myself secure of an eternity to be spent with the Spirits of such men as He whose life afforded the subject of it. But I was little aware of what I had to expect, and that a storm was at hand which in one terrible moment would darken, and another still more terrible, blot out that prospect for ever—Adieu Dear Sir, whom in those days I call'd Dear friend, with feelings that justified the appellation—" (*L*, 4:466).

One of Cowper's more recent friendships was with William Hayley. They instantly became close. Hayley was well acquainted with grief, familiar with depression. Some critics in Hayley's lifetime, others in the present day, have been disparaging of his florid, effusive writing style. But he was an insightful man, as demonstrated by his understanding of how to persuade Cowper to leave Weston and visit Eartham. At the end of Cowper's life, Hayley was unable to visit him because his beloved son, Thomas Alphonso, was on his deathbed just as Cowper was breathing his last. While some of Cowper's friends were jealously disparaging of each other, Hayley understood how Cowper benefited from Johnny's devotion, calling him "a man with rare union of tenderness, intelligence, and fortitude."[2]

Three other friends traveled considerable distances to pay Cowper farewell visits. In the summer of 1798 the dowager Lady Spencer and Sir John Throckmorton saw Cowper when he could scarcely rouse himself to speak to them. The Throckmortons' warm relationship with William Cowper had developed, not in letters, but in neighborliness. Cowper's beloved Weston home, the Lodge, was on their extensive property. The final visitor in March 1800 was Samuel Rose, who at age twenty had met Cowper in 1787. A smart lawyer and devoted family man, Rose died very young only four years after Cowper's passing.

Finally, there was Cowper's friendship with the unique and irreplaceable Johnny Johnson who wrote a detailed, almost day-by-day account of their travels in Norfolk. Cowper had been overjoyed by his initial contacts with Johnny, who represented a renewal of ties with Cowper's long-lamented mother. Johnny arranged for Cowper to receive her portrait. Johnny appreciated Cowper's interest in his studies, treating the young man exactly as a much-loved son.

Cowper wrote to Lady Hesketh with enthusiasm about the progress toward Johnny's theological degree at Cambridge. Johnny in turn received every encouragement. "Lay aside your anxiety; I have little doubt of your success. At any rate remember that you will be admitted into your sacred office exactly at the time, and by the means that God's Providence has appointed" (*L*, 4:347).

In June 1793 there was great distress about a delay in Johnny's ordination because of inattention by the bishop of Bristol. Then the bishop of Norwich agreed to proceed as had been planned. Cowper wrote joyfully to Johnny, "Nothing in short seems wanting in the whole affair, to make it the happiest event that could be, and may God but give you grace, as I trust he will, to exercise your new functions as becomes a Minister of his Gospel, your lot will be indeed a good one. Your entrance into the Church, your condition in it, and your performance of the duties it imposes on you, will be all honorable and such as will afford constant matter of thankfulness to yourself and to all who love you" (*L*, 4:357).

Only five years later, Johnny set forth from Weston with William Cowper and Mary Unwin on a journey fraught with difficulty and distress. They spent a fortnight in the parsonage at North Tuddenham, three weeks in a rented house in Mundesley, and then had lengthy stays at Denham Lodge near Swaffham, and finally at Johnny's own home in East Dereham. There Mary Unwin died on December 15, 1796. The last place where Cowper lived was a larger house nearby.

During this pilgrimage of compassion, Johnny never waivered in trying to rouse William Cowper from the depth of his despair. Johnny initiated long walks, read aloud for hours, and cajoled Cowper into working on his translation of Homer. Johnny had a clear sense from the beginning of what lay ahead and that he would need "the necessary fortitude for sustaining so long a journey with so helpless a charge."[3]

At the beginning of the journey, as Johnny later wrote, Cowper talked easily one night in a churchyard by moonlight. "The gleam of cheerfulness with which it pleased God to visit the afflicted poet, at the commencement of his journey, though nothing that may at all be compared with it was ever again exhibited in his conversation, is yet a subject of grateful remembrance to the writer of this sketch; for though it vanished from the breast of Cowper, like the dew of the morning, it preserved the sunshine of hope in his own mind, as to the final recovery of his revered relative, and that cheering hope never forsook him till the object of his incessant care was sinking into the valley of the shadow of death."[4]

Johnny had necessary support from Margaret Perowne, a nurse who was talented by nature in helping the afflicted. She was "vigilant in providing for the wants of sickness, and resolutely firm in administering such relief as the most intelligent compassion can supply." During the last years of his life, Cowper preferred "her personal assistance to that of every individual around him."[5]

While the good weather continued, Johnny accompanied Cowper on long walks, often on the beach. When winter came on, Johnny began to read aloud. Cowper would listen for hours at a time to lengthy works of fiction and later to the reading of his own poetry.

Johnny was grasping for any new opportunity to distract Cowper from his miseries. In June 1796 a copy of Wakefield's edition of Pope's Homer came to hand. Johnny made it clear to Cowper that his own translations of Homer were discussed in Wakefield's book. After Cowper's regular morning visit to Mary Unwin's room, he usually walked around a large room nearby. There Johnny put out in clear view the twelve volumes of Wakefield. To his surprise, the next day he discovered that Cowper had found Wakefield's notes on his own translation, which he began to rework. Soon Cowper was revising the whole translation, daily producing almost sixty new lines. However, this occupation was interrupted by the move to Johnny's Dereham house and then by Mary Unwin's death. It wasn't completed until March of 1799.

The summer of 1797 was healthy for Cowper, with walks in the fields in back of Johnny's house and rides in an open carriage. Cowper, thanks to a better diet, gained back some weight and again had a ruddy complexion.

The faithful, inexhaustible Johnny saw his beloved patient through the last days of gradual decline and the last hours that marked the approach of death. "From this mournful period," he wrote, "till the features of his deceased friend were closed from his view, the expression which the kinsman of Cowper observed in them, and which he was affectionately delighted to suppose an index of the last thoughts and enjoyments of his soul in its gradual escape from the depths of despondence, was that of calmness and composure, mingled as it were, with holy surprise."[6]

A fitting conclusion to a study of William Cowper is to consider his exquisite precision of language at the death of Mary Unwin and at his own impending passing from this world. Sunk in a period of emotional darkness, Cowper could suddenly speak and write with brilliance.

In Johnny's account of the final pilgrimage through Norfolk, he described Mary Unwin's last moments. Johnny took Cowper upstairs to Mary's bedroom a half-hour before she died. Downstairs again, Johnny started to read aloud as a means of "composing the spirit of Cowper." Soon Cowper was told that Mary had died. In the dim light of dusk, Johnny took him upstairs to view the body. Cowper stared suddenly away "with a vehement but unfinished sentence of passionate sorrow," exclaiming, "Oh God, was it for this?"[7]

These words are precise, yet they call for interpretation. He was saying, could all the years of love and devotion to his Mary end with her death while Cowper still lived? His fear of abandonment began with his mother's death, and now he was abandoned once more.

At the end of the trip with Johnny through Norfolk, again and again Cowper spoke with dread of being left alone in a solitary mansion. He "clung exceedingly to those about him." On Sundays Johnny had to leave to fulfill his church duties. "On these occasions, it was the constant practice of the dejected poet to listen frequently on the steps of the hall door for the barking of dogs at a farm house which, in the stillness of the night, though at nearly the distance of two miles, invariably announced the approach of his companion."[8] Cowper was terrified of dying alone. The concluding stanza of "The Cast-away" includes the lines,

No light propitious shone,
When, snatched from all effectual aid,
We perish'd, each, alone.

(P, 3:214-16)

Cowper's own death came three years and four months after Mary's. Over a period of five days, Cowper passed slowly and quietly away. Margaret Perowne continued to care for him. Johnny continued to stand at the bedside, silently commending Cowper's soul to the Savior.[9]

At the last, Miss Perowne offered Cowper some cordial, which he rejected asking, "What can it signify?"[10] Cowper's brief, final question has many possible meanings: The cordial would do no good because death was upon him. Or, he was ready to die because he would never discover the meaning of his life. Certainly Cowper never understood that his life, more than any other, gave witness to courage in adversity.

For then, by toil subdued, he drank
The stifling wave, and then he sank.

(P, 3:214-16)

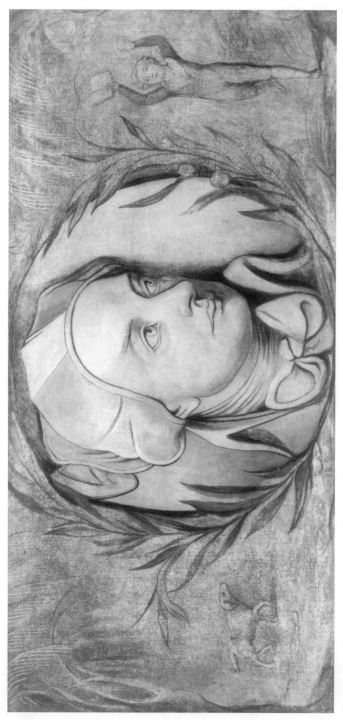

FIGURE 11. *William Cowper* by William Blake. Tempura. Courtesy of City Art Gallery, Manchester.

PART FOUR
POSTLUDE

22

A LITTLE MARINE HERMITAGE

1800–1803

At the seaside village of Felpham, a drama played out in the early days of the nineteenth century. The leading actor was William Hayley. With determination and dedication, he was able in early 1803 to publish the first biography of William Cowper.

Felpham was on the seashore only a mile from Bognor, seven miles from Chichester, and seven more from Eartham. The small village of a few dozen houses and a few hundred people was surrounded by large farm estates. Farm animals roamed the streets and farm laborers frequented the pub.[1]

William Hayley had written to Johnny Johnson on August 21, 1797, about his intention to live in Felpham. He was building "a Little marine hermitage" in his "favorite village of Felpham. I mean to reside in it seven or eight months in a year."[2] He would rent his Eartham home to friends who would take care of his books and papers there. He even hoped Cowper might recover his health by visiting Felpham.

Hayley called his home Turret House because of its tower, which contained his library and study.[3] The house and garden were shielded by high pebbled walls. In the library of Turret House, he intended to display busts by Blake of Hayley's literary heroes, including Homer, Dante, Chaucer, Tasso, Milton, Spenser, Shakespeare, Otway, Dryden, and

Cowper. A portrait by Blake of Thomas Alphonso Hayley was to hang prominently in the library.

Three years after Hayley decided to build a home in Felpham, his world changed. Within twenty-three days he suffered the deaths of his beloved son Tom and his greatly loved friend William Cowper. Soon Hayley's life was consumed by a fierce determination to write a biography of Cowper. Turret House in Felpham was to be Hayley's workplace.

Hayley's purpose in the biography was clear. He wrote, "I have regarded my own intimacy with him [Cowper] as a blessing to myself, and the remembrance of it is now endeared to me by the hope that it may enable me to delineate the man and the poet, with such fidelity and truth, as may render his remote, and even his future, admirers minutely acquainted with an exemplary being, most worthy to be intimately known, and universally beloved."[4]

There was never any question of Hayley's scholarship and extraordinary energy. But he was criticized by his contemporaries for his tendency to be manipulative and to mold others' lives to fit his wishes. These traits helped Hayley in the confounding work of writing Cowper's biography. The basic task was to create an accurate outline of Cowper's life and to assemble Cowper's poems and letters. There was not a moment to waste. Cowper's letters and poems were scattered among his friends. The protective Lady Hesketh was reluctant to release any papers in her possession.

The outline of Cowper's life was elusive because of his mental derangements and depressions, together with the reluctance of others to examine the facts. Hayley's collecting of letters and poems was hampered by Cowper's attachment to privacy. In the 1780s he had even written to Mary's son-in-law Matthew Powley, "Keep no letters."

Some of Hayley's most striking personal characteristics helped him accomplish his task as a biographer of Cowper. As G. E. Bentley wrote, "Hayley was a generally good and generous man." Essential to Hayley's work was the immediate cooperation of Lady Hesketh and Johnny Johnson. Even while he cajoled and goaded them, his warmth and affection for them modified his complaints.

Bentley described Hayley's own autobiography as "written in an ornate and convoluted prose."[5] However, this style, so distasteful to modern ears, became an asset in Hayley's letters as he marshalled his formidable energies to the task of prying information and manuscripts from Harriet Hesketh, Johnny Johnson, and others. Hayley wrote of himself in the third person. Of the years 1800–1803 he wrote, "Hayley's chief labor, indeed almost his obsession was his biography of William Cowper."[6]

In this undertaking a first challenge was the cooperation of Harriet, Cowper's "redoubtable cousin." She controlled Cowper's papers and the family interest. She was said to "almost adore her cousin the poet and thought him all perfection . . . Most significantly Lady Hesketh was determined that no hint should appear in print of Cowper's manifest madness. . . . No biography of value could be written without her help, and no honest biography could be written with it."[7]

Hayley's letters to Lady Hesketh were often masterpieces of cajolery. He was suave and complimentary while at the same time unbending. As early as December 24, 1800, he praised Lady Hesketh for the "olive branch" she offered in her "pacific letter."[8] Hayley developed a fine talent for calming the excitable Harriet.

Samuel Greatheed in letters and conversations disclosed some details of Cowper's depressions and instability, which Lady Hesketh had wished to "shield from the Publick Eye." She wrote to Hayley in a near frenzy. "Oh dear—can you Sir really suppose that I feel no enmity against the man who has destroy'd my peace of mind for ever!—who has injured a whole family in its tenderest point!—has cruelly and *inhumanly* revealed Secrets disclosed to Him, under the sacred seal of Friendship! And broke ev'ry tye that binds man to man."[9]

The "tenderest point" of her family was indeed mental illness, not only of the poet but also of other family members. Lady Hesketh had tirelessly taken care of her father, Ashley, when he had been depressed. William Cowper himself had written a memorial for his Uncle Ashley that concluded with the couplet

Although thy worth be more than half supprest,
Love shall be satisfied, and veil the rest.

(*P,* 3:25)

At the time of Cowper's death, Lady Hesketh was still caring for her sister Theodora who spent under Harriet's roof a twilight life of seclusion, inactivity, and breakdowns. E. M. Bishop points out Hayley's remarkable success in gaining Lady Hesketh's trust. In the letter to Hayley that included her tirade against Greatheed, for example, she concluded, "In your hands, Sir, I know he [Cowper] will be safe."[10]

Only two months after Cowper's death, Hayley was beginning to contact Rose, Hill, Newton, Edward Thurlow, and others who might have information or poems or letters. Soon both Hayley and Lady Hesketh realized Johnny Johnson's importance to the Cowper biography. Lady Hesketh complimented Johnson on his eagerness to help with Cowper's biography. Hayley urged him to send an outline of Cowper's life.

In early 1801 Hayley dispatched the first of the many letters written to quicken the pace of Johnny's efforts: "Let me entreat you to supply me speedily with all the intelligence that you know I must want. I have already written the intended Introduction to my biographical work; and I want immediately all the particulars that I expected from you; parentage, birth, education, etc., etc. in the form of abridged annals."[11]

Four months later, acknowledging that he as well as Johnny had distractions and other things to do, Hayley wrote: "I hope in a little time to proceed with regularity and spirit in my biographical work; and I beg you to recollect, that I can not proceed properly till you supply me with the documents you have kindly promised . . . for I depend on your accuracy as to the dates, etc., of all the material incidents in the life of our friend."[12]

At the end of July, Hayley cried out in a letter, "Neglect not your Hermit!" The biographer had come to a chasm in the collection of materials. The problem was the decade of the 1770s, especially Cowper's breakdown in 1773. "I am in darkness in regard to these ten years . . . Send all the light you can, speedily."[13]

By September Hayley had his heart set on persuading Johnny to come and work with him at Felpham. "I hope you mean to devote a part of your autumn to the Turret, where I shall be happy to have you as my fellow student, my guide, and my critic in all the concluding part of my arduous task. . . . Let us cherish a cheerful expectation that you and I may write the blessed word *finis* together in the turret."[14]

Throughout October Hayley's pleas to Johnny became more urgent. "I have so many questions to ask you, my dear Johnny, that it will be impossible for me to finish without you. . . . Write instantly to your anxious and affectionate Hermit."[15] The strain on Hayley, understandable since he had embarked on the Cowper biography very soon after the deaths of Cowper and Tom, was becoming apparent. Hayley could not bear to leave the Turret even to visit Eartham. He had to live as a hermit because "My heart and soul are so full of these two dear affectionate angels, Cowper and Tom! that I seem to converse with them on my pillow before the dawn of day." He wrote that he was asking the angel Tom to inspire him with ideas about Cowper.[16]

As 1802 began, both sides of Hayley's nature, the affectionate and the persistent, were apparent in one letter. Addressing "the tardy Johnny of Norfolk," he said, "I love thee with all thy faults." He concluded, "And now my dear Johnny, as you are a special good fellow in the main, though too fond of your pillow and procrastination."[17]

William Hayley's biography of William Cowper was published in early 1803. The product of one man's persistence against all odds, the book was an immediate and overwhelming success.[18] Lady Hesketh received a presentation copy and immediately wrote a rave review. Her words were the first notes in a chorus of congratulations. After reading the first volume late into the night, she wrote on December 28, 1802, "I can go no further, till I have expressed to you some part of the admiration I feel on the Life. Its merit more than answered all the expectations I had formed. . . . You will not think I mean to flatter you, when I say that you have . . . executed it con amore e con spirito . . . The elegance and animation of the style can only be equalled by the extreme tenderness and delicacy with which you touch on particular subjects, too affecting in their nature not to be seen with real pain by me, and which would indeed have been insupportable, had they been drawn by a rougher pencil."[19]

Hayley relished the praise and the considerable financial rewards from brisk sales. He continued to receive much new material, which led to a third volume and soon a third edition. Lady Hesketh was motivated to search further and sent Hayley a new "cargo of manuscript."[20] Included was the handwritten copy of "Yardley Oak." The next edition published for the first time another of Cowper's most important poems, "The Cast-away."

During the first decade of the nineteenth century, William Cowper's fame grew. As the Hayley biography was being read, so too was Cowper's poetry. He became England's best loved and most enjoyed poet.

When Hayley decided to move to Felpham in 1797, he did not foresee that the Turret would become his workshop for the greatest success of his life. Nor could he have known that a coworker would be the genius William Blake. Just as modern scholarship has advanced the knowledge of Cowper's life and work, so too modern Blake studies have elucidated his years in Felpham and his connections to William Cowper. Although Blake never met Cowper during the poet's lifetime, yet he loved Cowper and provided profound interpretations of Cowper's melancholy and madness.

Hayley met Blake in 1784, and the two men first worked together as Thomas Alphonso Hayley was dying. Blake received Hayley's commissions to engrave some of Tom's drawings as well as a portrait medallion of the boy. At first Hayley was not pleased with Blake's work. But after Tom died, Blake wrote an extraordinary condolence letter. He urged Hayley to think of Tom as an "Angel or Spirit" with whom he could communicate as Blake did with his deceased brother. These Angels were for Blake "the powers of memory and the imagination that create art."[21]

Hayley became closer to Blake, who shortly "succumbed to a profound depression."[22] Hayley had been supportive of Cowper in his worst times and now wanted nothing more than to help Blake. Agreeing with Hayley's plan, Blake left London and went to Felpham to work on another portrait of Tom.

The earliest months of Blake's stay in Felpham were happy. Both he and his wife, Catherine, enjoyed a cottage rented from a Mr. Grinder for £20 a year. Blake wrote, "Our Cottage . . . is more beautiful than I thought it, and more convenient. It is a perfect model for cottages . . . Nothing can be more Grand in its Simplicity and Usefulness . . . No other formed House can ever please me so well nor shall I ever be persuaded I believe that it can be improved either in Beauty or Use."[23]

Blake's cottage had three rooms, including a kitchen, and staircases at both ends leading to the bedrooms upstairs. The cottage looked out on a garden and fields, the beach, and the shimmering sea only a quarter mile distant. There was "the scent of wild purple thyme and the sound of larks." Writing about their little thatched house, Blake said, "We are very Happy sitting by a wood fire in our Cottage, the wind singing above our roof and the sea roaring at a distance."[24]

One of Blake's most important commissions from Hayley was to create engravings from portraits of William Cowper to be included in the biography. The frontispiece of volume 1 was to be Blake's engraving of a *Portrait in Crayons Drawn from the Life by Romney* in 1792. Hayley had confidence in this commission because "it will be executed con amore, as he [Blake] idolized the Poet, and will have as fine a portrait to work from as pencil ever produced."[25]

Blake's miniature from Romney's portrait of Cowper incurred a more hysterical reaction from Lady Hesketh than had any part of the text of the biography. She wrote Hayley on March 19, 1801,

[On one subject] I am determin'd—absolutely determined!—I mean this subject of the picture, which I have this moment receiv'd and for which I do indeed thank you; tho' the Sight of it has in real truth inspired me with a degree of horror, which I shall not recover from in haste! . . . I cannot restrain my Pen from declaring that I think it dreadful! Shocking! and that I intreat you on my Knees not to suffer so horrible a representation of our angelic friend to be presented to the publick and to disgrace and disfigure a work I long so much to see. . . .

I cannot bear to have it in my possession nor wou'd I for worlds, shew it to any one. . . . I must observe that I have no doubt that the Original from which this fatal Miniature is taken is a very fine Picture, considered as a Picture, & I even believe the miniature is very well executed . . . [but I must intreat] that you will not be so cruel as to multiply this fatal resemblance, by having the picture engrav'd[!][26]

Hayley was as always skillful and suave in pacifying the volatile Harriet. He never used direct rebuttal, but gracefully changed the subject to praise Blake's character and to express affectionate concern for the lady's feelings. While exercising his arts of diplomacy, he never even considered not including Blake's engraving from Romney's portrait in the published biography.

Another picture that Hayley intended for his book about Cowper was the portrait by Thomas Lawrence. Lady Hesketh agreed to send the original for engraving by Blake after Hayley's reassurances on November 22, 1801: "Fear not for your celestial drawings:—it shall not be taken out of the Frame, if it arrives to gratify my worthy artist who works constantly in my study. . . —for He is in Truth an excellent Creature with admirable Talents."[27]

A year later, on December 1802, Lady Hesketh was about to receive her presentation copy of the Cowper biography. Hayley was skillfully cosseting Harriet: "I know your tender Humanity will spare my good zealous Coadjutor the Engraver, if you think He has failed in one Portrait, as I am confident You must think he has succeeded delightfully in the second."[28]

Lady Hesketh immediately replied that though she would prefer the Romney portrait not to be published, yet she forgave Blake from her heart beforehand. Having received the biography, in a postscript to Hayley she wrote, "I must tell you that I admire Romney's head of all things!" She said it was "softened." Blake wrote at the end of January 1803 an astonished and exuberant letter to his brother James. "My Heads of Cowper for Mr H's life of Cowper have pleased his Relations exceedingly & in Particular Lady Hesketh & Lord Cowper . . . to please

Lady H. was a doubtful chance who almost adord her Cousin the poet & thought him all perfection & she writes that she is quite satisfied with the portraits & charmed by the great Head in particular tho she never could bear the original Picture."[29]

While Blake lived in Felpham, enjoying the cottage, joyously observing the natural world and working hard side by side with Hayley in the Turret, he also produced a very great amount of work not related to Cowper. He wrote ballads and made engravings intended to accompany them in a published volume. He wrote an "immense number of verses."[30]

All the while Blake was torn between two worlds. While he worked for money—doing miniature portraits and engravings—he suffered from neglect of his own visions. "I cannot live without doing my duty to lay up treasures in heaven . . . I find on all hands great objections to my doing anything but the mere drudgery of business & intimations that if I do not confine myself to this I shall not live."[31] Finally, Blake understood that he had to return to London. "I can alone carry on my visionary studies in London unannoyed & that I may converse with my friends in Eternity, See Visions, Dream Dreams & prophecy and speak Parables unobserv'd & at liberty from the Doubts of other Mortals—perhaps Doubts from Kindness but Doubts are always pernicious Especially when we Doubt our Friends."[32]

Blake had to distance himself from his friend Hayley's good intentions and sometimes overbearing personality. Because of Hayley's innate goodness, "his loyalty to Blake persisted even in the most trying circumstances."[33] And Hayley continued to love Blake "for his simplicity of character and his religious fervour, for his unworldliness and his vulnerability."[34]

23

PERILOUS POWERS
OF IMAGINATION
1800–1803

In Felpham, from September 1800 to September 1803, William Blake was a man with boundless visions living in a miniature world. His home was with his wife, Catherine, in a small cottage near the sea. His work was in William Hayley's Turret House, where Hayley had a comprehensive library and print collection as well as a study. There, every day, the two men "worked industriously side by side."[1]

Hayley's work on the Cowper biography was "indeed almost his obsession."[2] His goal was "to delineate the man and the poet" with "fidelity and truth." While Blake's work included poems and pictures unrelated to Cowper, he was, like Hayley, immersed in Cowper's life and thought.

Blake created many renditions of Cowper's face. From Romney's penetrating portrait with its hint of frenzy in the eyes, Blake made first a miniature portrait and then an engraving. Right there in the Turret, Blake kept his plates and tools, acid and wax, pens and brushes. As Bentley has written, Blake retouched the plates for a new edition of Hayley's biography, engraved new plates for an octavo edition, and worked on plates for Cowper's translation of Milton's Latin and Italian poems.[3]

Blake met others besides Hayley who had been close to William Cowper. Johnny Johnson was particularly devoted to Cowper's memory and visited Felpham in 1801 and 1802. Johnny's conversation must have ranged over family memories of Cowper in early days and on his constant care of Cowper after leaving Weston and to the end.

Blake developed an intimacy with Cowper, a man he had never known in life. Blake said that Cowper's letters were "perhaps or rather certainly the very best letters that were ever published."[4] Central to their posthumous intimacy were the "perilous powers of imagination" they shared. In a poem entitled "William Cowper Esqre" Blake wrote, "You see him spend his Soul in Prophecy."[5]

Blake experienced in Felpham a spiritual schism between his money-making work as an engraver commissioned by others and his prophetic soul. Thus he wrote to Thomas Butts: "I labored incessantly & accomplished not one-half of what I intend because my Assistant folly hurries me often away while I am at work, carrying me over Mountains and Valleys, which are not real, in a land of Abstraction where spectres of the dead wander. . . . I endeavor to . . . chain my feet to the world of Duty & Reality; but in vain!"[6]

A year later Blake wrote to Butts again: "That thing I have most at Heart . . . is the Interest of True Religion and Science . . . I am under the direction of Messengers from Heaven, Daily & Nightly."[7]

Like Blake, William Cowper's life was divided, but in a different pattern. Cowper had good years, when he studied at Westminster School and later when he enjoyed the rural pleasures in Olney and Weston of his summerhouse and pet hares, gardening, and walking. He had satisfying hours at his desk in early mornings, writing with wit and affection to friends and relatives who understood his language of the heart. Contrariwise, Cowper had years of overwhelming despair and other times when he sank and drowned entirely in hopelessness and even madness.

William Hayley, a man free of the demons that haunted both Blake and Cowper, was of such a sympathetic nature that he could see the similarity between the artistic genius from London and the poet and correspondent from the countryside. "My diligent & grateful artist [Blake] resembles our beloved bard [Cowper] in the tenderness of his heart and in the perilous powers of an imagination utterly unfit to take care of himself."[8]

Of course the easily stirred-up Lady Hesketh did not appreciate Hayley's opinion that Blake's pictures were "almost as excellent and original as Cowper's poetry." Blake was far beyond the comprehension of Harriet, who had, in fact, always been in love with Cowper and considered him flawless.

Unlike Cowper, Blake eventually unified his divided life. Blake left behind not only his genius as an artist and writer, but also, in letters, his remarkable self-understanding. On December 4, 1804, he wrote, "I have lost my confusion of Thought while at work & . . . now no longer Divided nor at war with myself I shall travel on in the strength of the Lord God as Poor Pilgrim says."[9] Blake's recovery of his center began while he was still at Felpham. "Tho' I have been very unhappy, I am so no longer. I am again Emerged into the light of day. I still & shall to Eternity Embrace Christianity and Adore him who is the Express 'image of God.'"[10]

Blake went back to London, his spiritual home. There one day he went to an exhibition of the old masters' paintings, works by Albrecht Dürer, Michelangelo, and Leonardo da Vinci. Blake was inspired. "Excuse my enthusiasm or rather madness, for I am really drunk with intellectual vision whenever I take a pencil or graver into my hand."[11]

Blake died on August 12, 1827, at age sixty-nine. He saw his last vision on his deathbed: "He said he was going to that country he had all his life worked to see and expressed himself happy, hoping for salvation through Jesus Christ—just before he died his countenance became fair. His eyes brightened and he burst out into singing of the things he saw in heaven. In truth he died like a saint."[12]

William Cowper's last years, in contrast, were his most tragic and his last poem a masterpiece of despair and abandonment. Having met Cowper only after his death, Blake nonetheless understood that Cowper's powers of imagination were so perilous because, while the world of words and friends was fading away, his self-understanding became more vivid. Cowper came to see that he was divided and would never be unified. He would never recover from Mary Unwin's death, from the loss of Weston, from God's abandonment.

As Cowper lay dying in his bed at Johnny's house, he had no vision such as had been vouchsafed to William Blake. Cowper died wordless, almost imperceptibly, stilled and finally free.

Seventeen years after Cowper died, Blake wrote a note that was later found in J. G. Spurzheim's book, *Observations on the Deranged Manifestations of the Mind, or Insanity* (London, 1817). This work was focused on insanity caused by religion. Blake's note said that he had had a vision: "Cowper came to me and said, 'O that I were insane, always. I will never rest. Cannot you make me truly insane? I will never rest till I am so.'"[13] This vision illustrated Blake's comprehension of Cowper's suffering.

Blake's final tribute to Cowper was embedded in the creation of Spectre, a supernatural creature introduced in Blake's *Milton* and central to his masterpiece *Jerusalem*.[14] Blake began work on *Milton* in Felpham. The epic told of Milton's return to earth after he had been dead for a hundred years. Milton confronts his Spectre, who was his negation or reasoning power, and says that his purpose is to destroy it and to free his power of imagination.

Two centuries after Cowper's death, Morton D. Paley has provided illuminating analyses of Blake's *Jerusalem* and especially of the Spectre, plate 10. Paley's central insight is that "the Spectre's speech of *10* is an almost unbearably moving expression of the conviction of damnation . . . There is a model for the speech in the tragic life of William Cowper."[15]

In addition to being exposed in Felpham to Hayley and Johnny's extensive experiences with Cowper, Blake also had gained a knowledge of Cowper's writings while working in the Turret with Hayley. *Jerusalem* shows the influence of Cowper's work, for example in this passage from plate 10.

> I said: now is my grief at worst: incapable of being
> Surpassed: but every moment it accumulates more & more
> It continues accumulating to eternity! the joys of God advance
> For he is Righteous: he is not a Being of Pity & Compassion
> He cannot feel Distress: he feeds on Sacrifice and Offering:
> Delighting in cries & tears & clothed in holiness & solitude

But my griefs advance also, for ever & ever without end
O that I could cease to be! Despair! I am Despair
Created to be the great example of horror & agony: also my
Prayer is vain I called for compassion: compassion mockd[,]
Mercy & pity threw the grave stone over me & with lead
And iron, bound it over me for ever: Life lives on my
Consuming:& the Almighty hath made me his Contrary
To be all evil, all reversed & for ever dead: knowing
And seeing life, yet living not; how can I then behold
And not tremble; how can I be beheld & not abhorrd.[16]

The Spectre cries out, "O that I could cease to be! Despair!" Just as Cowper wrote of his despair on his window shutter when he left Weston for the last time in 1795, he wrote of the God not capable of pity or compassion. One of Cowper's most terrible images of despair is that he was buried alive. In his poem "Hatred and Vengeance, My Eternal Portion," Cowper says that both heaven and hell are closed to him. "I, fed with judgment in a fleshly tomb, am Buried alive above ground" (*P,* 1:209). The Spectre echoes this image. "Mercy & pity threw the grave stone over me. And iron, bound it over me for ever." In the same way, the Spectre concludes that this is "knowing and seeing life, yet living not."

Thus Blake had created in *Jerusalem* an unforgettable portrait of the Cowper who never found, as did Blake, a unification of the "World of Duty and Reality" with the Land of "Abstraction." However, Cowper's last poem did unify the tragic aspects of his entire life.

THE CAST-AWAY

Obscurest night involved the sky,
    Th' Atlantic billows roar'd,
When such a destin'd wretch as I
    Wash'd headlong from on board
Of friends, of hope, of all bereft,
His floating home for ever left.

No braver Chief could Albion boast
    Than He with whom he went,
Nor ever ship left Albion's coast
    With warmer wishes sent,
He loved them both, but both in vain,
Nor Him beheld, nor Her again.

Not long beneath the whelming brine
    Expert to swim, he lay,
Nor soon he felt his strength decline
    Or courage die away;
But waged with Death a lasting strife
Supported by despair of life.

He shouted, nor his friends had fail'd
    To check the vessels' course,
But so the furious blast prevail'd.
    That, pitiless perforce,
They left their outcast mate behind,
And scudded still before the wind.

Some succour yet they could afford,
    And, such as storms allow,
The cask, the coop, the flooded cord
    Delay'd not to bestow;
But He, they knew, nor ship nor shore,
Whate'er they gave, should visit more.

Nor, cruel as it seem'd, could He
    Their haste, himself, condemn,
Aware that flight, in such a sea
    Alone could rescue them;
Yet bitter felt it still to die
Deserted, and his friends so nigh.

He long survives who lives an hour
    In ocean, self-upheld,
And so long he, with unspent pow'r,
    His destiny repell'd,
And ever, as the minutes flew,
Entreated help, or cried, Adieu!

At length, his transient respite past,
    His comrades, who before
Had heard his voice in ev'ry blast,
    Could catch the sound no more;
For then, by toil subdued, he drank
The stifling wave, and then he sank.

No poet wept him, but the page
    Of narrative sincere
That tells his name, his worth, his age,
    Is wet with Anson's tear,
And tears by bards or heroes shed
Alike immortalize the Dead.

I, therefore, purpose not or dream,
    Descanting on his fate,
To give the melancholy theme
    A more enduring date,
But Mis'ry still delights to trace
Its semblance in another's case.

No voice divine the storm allay'd,
    No light propitious shone,
When, snatch'd from all effectual aid,
    We perish'd, each, alone;
But I, beneath a rougher sea,
And whelm'd in deeper gulphs than he.
                (*P,* 3:214)

Once again, Cowper used his most consistent and longest-lasting image, that of a shipwreck at sea culminating either in the voyager drowning or being condemned to wander alone on a barren coast. As early as the 1750s, he was affected by the drowning of his friend Sir William Russell. He wrote a poem to remember Russell and his lost sweetheart Theadora as well. The poem begins "Doom'd as I am in solitude to waste." The poet continues by lamenting his friend and paying an affectionate tribute to Theadora. Then Cowper turns to consider himself.

> See me—ere yet my destined course half done,
> Cast forth a wand'rer on a wild unknown!
> See me neglected on the world's rude coast,
> Each dear companion of my voyage lost!
> (P, 1:62)

Later, in one of his Olney Hymns, "Lovest Thou Me?," Cowper describes the intense but brief period when he was convinced of his salvation. Christ spoke and told him:

> I deliver'd thee when bound,
> And, when wounded, heal'd the wound;
> Sought thee wand'ring, set thee right,
> Turn'd thy darkness into light.
> (P, 1:157)

But only a decade later he wrote a poem to John Newton contrasting the state of their souls. Newton had just returned from a trip to the seashore:

> Your Sea of Troubles you have pass'd,
>   And found the peacefull Shore;
> I, Tempest-toss'd and wreck'd at last,
>   Come Home to Port no more.
> (P, 1:224)

In "The Cast-away" Cowper is doubly abandoned. His shipmates are forced to continue on by the furious blast of the wind, leaving "their outcast mate behind." The Cast-away understands their situation and does not condemn them.

> Yet bitter felt it still to die
> Deserted, and his friends so nigh.

After heroic efforts to continue swimming and repeated cries for help,

> For then, by toil subdued, he drank
> The stifling wave, and then he sank.

The last stanza applies the fate of the Cast-away directly to Cowper's fate:

> No voice divine the storm allay'd,
>   No light propitious shone
> When, snatch'd from all effectual aid,
>   We perish'd, each, alone;
> But I, beneath a rougher sea
> And whelm'd in deeper gulphs than he.

Cowper had been abandoned not only by human companions but also by God. Unlike Blake, Cowper was quiet in death. Unlike Blake, Cowper did not see a vision of heaven. There had once years ago been for Cowper a God who could have saved him. Of this God Cowper had written:

> God moves in a mysterious way,
> His wonders to perform
> He plants his footsteps in the Sea,
> And rides upon the Storm.
>   (*P,* 1:174)

The title of this poem is "Light Shining Out of Darkness." One can only hope that in some world after death, Cowper came to enjoy quiet seas and redemptive light.

Notes

PREFACE

1. Quotations from William Cowper's works are cited in the text with the following abbreviations: *L: The Letters and Prose Writings of William Cowper*, 5 vols., ed. James King and Charles Ryskamp (Oxford: Clarendon Press, 1976–86). *P: The Poems of William Cowper*, 3 vols., ed. John D. Baird and Charles Ryskamp (Oxford: Clarendon Press, 1980–95).
2. Herbert J. C. Grierson and J. C. Smith, *A Critical History of English Poetry* (London: Chatto & Windus, 1944), 237, 239.
3. Preface to *Memoir of the Early Life of William Cowper, Esq. with Introduction*, by William Cowper (London: R. Edwards, 1816).
4. Ibid.
5. *Critical History*, 242.
6. Ibid., 243.
7. *Monthly Review*, N.S., 79 (1816): 296.
8. David Faiver and Christine Gerrard, ed. *Eighteenth-Century Poetry: An Annotated Anthology* (Oxford: Blackwell, 1999), 486.

CHAPTER 1: ATTACHMENT AND LOSS

1. Lawrence Stone, *The Family, Sex, and Marriage in England 1500–1800* (New York: Harper Torchbooks, 1979), 55.
2. Ibid., 59.
3. Ibid., 261.
4. Ibid., 262.
5. William Hayley, *The Life and Posthumous Writings of Cowper, Esq.*, 4 vols. (London: Joseph Johnson, 1806), 1:H5.
6. Stone, *Family, Sex, and Marriage*, 273.
7. Roger L. Hiatt, Sr., M.D. "The Spectrum of Child and Parent Response to Eye Disease," *Annals of Opthalmology* 21 (1989): 325–30.
8. James Wardrop, *Essays on the Morbid Anatomy of the Human Eye*, vol. 1 (Edinburgh: Constable, 1808), chap. 11.
9. Robert Southey, *Southey's Life of Cowper*, 2 vols. (Boston: Otis, Broaders, & Co., 1839) 1:7 n.

CHAPTER 2: A SEASON OF CLEAR SHINING

1. Andrew W. Brink, *Loss and Symbolic Repair: A Psychological Study of Some Poets* (Hamilton, Ontario: Cromlech Press, 1977), 51.

2. James King, *William Cowper: A Biography* (Durham: Duke University Press, 1986), 5.
3. David Aberbach, *Surviving Trauma: Loss, Literature and Psychoanalysis* (New Haven and London: Yale University Press, 1989), 148.
4. Charles Ryskamp, *William Cowper of the Inner Temple, Esq.: A Study of His Life and Works to the Year 1768* (Cambridge: Cambridge University Press, 1959), 15.
5. Lawrence E. Tanner, *Westminster School: A History* (London: Country Life, 1934), 26.
6. Stone, *Family, Sex, and Marriage*, 178.
7. Ibid., 280.
8. Donald R. Hopkins, *Princes and Peasants: Smallpox in History* (Chicago and London: University of Chicago Press, 1983), 10, 11, 42.
9. Ryskamp, *Cowper*, 42.
10. J. C. D. Clark, *English Society 1688-1832* (Cambridge: Cambridge University Press, 1985), 93.
11. Ibid., 82.
12. Ibid., 103.
13. Ibid., 102.
14. Ibid., 103.

CHAPTER 3: O, ASK NOT WHERE CONTENTMENT MAY ABIDE

1. King, *Cowper*, 38.
2. Ibid., 21.
3. Ibid., 165.
4. Ibid., 26.
5. Ibid., 21–22.
6. Ryskamp, *Cowper*, 126–27.
7. King, *Cowper*, 24.

CHAPTER 4: A FIERCE BANDITTI

1. King, *Cowper*, 37.
2. Ryskamp, *Cowper*, 148–53.
3. David Cecil, *The Stricken Deer, or the Life of William Cowper* (London: Constable, 1929–30), 57.

CHAPTER 5: A SONG OF MERCY AND JUDGMENT

1. Max Byrd, *Visits to Bedlam: Madness and Literature in the Eighteenth Century* (Columbia: University of South Carolina Press, 1974), 156.
2. Ibid., 155.
3. Falconer Madan, *The Madan Family* (Oxford: Oxford University Press, 1933), chap. 8.
4. Richard Hunter and J. B. Wood, "Nathaniel Cotton, M.D., Poet and Physician," *Kings College Hospital Gazette* 36 (1957): 120-29.

5. Nathaniel Cotton, "Visions in Verse for the Entertainment and Instruction of Young Minds," in *The Poetical Works of Nathaniel Cotton* (London: Dodsley, 1751), 1.

CHAPTER 6: FAR FROM THE WORLD
1. Southey, *Life of Cowper*, 1:123.
2. Ryskamp, *Cowper*, 164–65.

CHAPTER 7: A TRANSIENT, HALF-SPENT LIFE
1. D. Bruce Hindmarsh, *John Newton and the English Evangelical Tradition* (Oxford: Clarendon Press, 1996), 16.
2. Ibid., 13.
3. Ibid., 188.
4. Ibid., 189.
5. Ibid., 200.
6. Ibid., 327.
7. John Johnson, *Poems by William Cowper, Esq. together with his Posthumous Poetry and A Sketch of His Life* (Boston: Phillips, Sampson & Co., 1849), 26.

CHAPTER 8: I HAD A BROTHER ONCE
1. Ryskamp, *Cowper*, 9.

CHAPTER 9: A HEART HOPELESS AND DESERTED
1. King, *Cowper*, 87.
2. Ibid., 88.

CHAPTER 10: STUDENT OF MANY ARTS
1. Brink, *Loss and Symbolic Repair*, 79.
2. Ibid., 77.
3. Anthony Storr, *The Dynamics of Creation* (New York: Ballantine Books, 1993), 198–99.

CHAPTER 11: THE INTERIOR SELF
1. Brink, *Loss and Symbolic Repair*, 78.
2. Ibid., 68.
3. Obituary of Anthony Storr, *New York Times*, March 28, 2001, C21.
4. Anthony Storr, *Solitude* (New York: Ballantine Books, 1988), 143.
5. Anthony Storr, *Dynamics of Creation*, 107.
6. Brink, *Loss and Symbolic Repair*, 53.
7. Roderick Huang, *William Cowper: Nature Poet* (London: Oxford University Press, 1957).

CHAPTER 12: THE WRITER WITH BUSINESS
1. Brink, *Loss and Symbolic Repair,* 304.
2. Storr, *Dynamics of Creation,* 304.

CHAPTER 14: DELINEATIONS OF THE HEART
1. Brink, *Loss and Symbolic Repair,* 46.
2. Southey, *Life of Cowper,* 2:102.
3. Brink, *Loss and Symbolic Repair,* 78.
4. Ibid., 4.
5. Ibid., 50.
6. Lodwick Hartley, "The Stricken Deer and His Contemporary Reputation," *Review of English Studies,* n.s. 9 (1958): 650.
7. Brink, *Loss and Symbolic Repair,* 78–79.

CHAPTER 15: A PRODIGIOUS WORK
1. Hartley, "The Stricken Deer," 644.
2. Madan, *Madan Family,* chap. 8.

CHAPTER 16: LETTERS FROM THE HEART
1. Bruce Redford, *The Converse of the Pen: Acts of Intimacy in the Eighteenth-Century Familiar Letter* (Chicago: University of Chicago Press, 1986), 80.
2. Ibid., 86–87.

CHAPTER 19: ZEALOUS AND CONSTANT ENDEAVORS
1. Southey, *Life of Cowper,* 2:190.
2. William Hayley, *Memoirs of the Life and Writings of William Hayley, Esq.,* ed. John Johnson, 2 vols. (London: Henry Colburn and Co., 1823), 2:155.
3. Evelyn M. Bishop, *Blake's Hayley* (London: Gollanez, 1951), 291.
4. Southey, *Life of Cowper,* 2:193.
5. Ibid., 2:193.
6. Ibid., 2:194.
7. Ibid., 2:222.
8. David A. Cross, *A Striking Likeness: The Life of George Romney* (Aldershot; Brookfield, VT: Ashgate, 2000), 3.
9. Ibid., 174–75.
10. Southey, *Life of Cowper,* 2:237–38.
11. Cross, *A Striking Likeness,* 175.
12. Ibid., 185.
13. Southey, *Life of Cowper,* 2:242.

CHAPTER 20: A CHRONICLE OF ACTIONS JUST AND RIGHT

1. Brink, *Loss and Symbolic Repair*, 61.
2. Hayley, *Life and Posthumous Writings of Cowper*, 4:115.
3. Johnson, *Poems by William Cowper*, 39.
4. Hayley, *Life and Posthumous Writings of Cowper*, 4:156.
5. Johnson, *Poems by William Cowper*, 41.
6. Hayley, *Life and Posthumous Writings of Cowper*, 4:146.
7. Ibid., 155.
8. Ibid., 150.

CHAPTER 21: NO LIGHT PROPITIOUS SHONE

1. Johnson, *Poems by William Cowper*, 59.
2. Hayley, *Life and Posthumous Writings of Cowper*, 4:174.
3. Johnson, *Poems by William Cowper*, 43.
4. Ibid., 44.
5. Ibid.
6. Ibid., 61.
7. Ibid., 52–53.
8. Ibid., 48.
9. Ibid., 60.
10. Ibid.

CHAPTER 22: A LITTLE MARINE HERMITAGE

1. G. E. Bentley, Jr., *The Stranger from Paradise: A Biography of William Blake* (New Haven: Yale University Press, 2001), 213–14.
2. Hayley, *Memoirs*, 2:85.
3. Peter Ackroyd, *Blake: A Biography* (New York: Ballantine Books, 1977), 220.
4. Hayley, *Life and Posthumous Writings of Cowper*, 4:190.
5. Ackroyd, *Blake*, 215.
6. Bentley, *Stranger from Paradise*, 237.
7. Ibid., 225.
8. Bishop, *Blake's Hayley*, 268.
9. Ibid., 269.
10. Ibid., 269.
11. Hayley, *Memoirs*, 2:117.
12. Ibid., 121.
13. Ibid., 125–26.
14. Ibid., 126.
15. Ibid., 127–28.

16. Ibid., 130.
17. Ibid., 134–36.
18. Bishop, *Blake's Hayley,* 284 ff.
19. Ibid., 285.
20. Ibid., 299.
21. Ackroyd, *Blake,* 213–14.
22. Ibid., 215.
23. Bentley, *Stranger from Paradise,* 213.
24. Ibid., 231.
25. G. E. Bentley, Jr., *Blake Records* (Oxford: Clarendon Press, 1969), 79.
26. Ibid., 79–80.
27. Ibid., 87.
28. Ibid., 112–13.
29. Ibid., 113.
30. Bentley, *Stranger from Paradise,* 243.
31. Ibid., 207, 223.
32. Ibid., 232–33.
33. Ibid., 234.
34. Ibid., 207.

CHAPTER 23: PERILOUS POWERS OF IMAGINATION
1. Bentley, *Stranger from Paradise,* 242.
2. Ibid., 237.
3. Ibid., 242.
4. Bishop, 272.
5. Bentley, *Stranger from Paradise,* 238.
6. Michael Davis, *William Blake: A New Kind of Man* (Berkeley and Los Angeles: University of California Press, 1977), 94.
7. Ibid., 97.
8. Ibid., 98.
9. Ibid., 115.
10. Bishop, *Blake's Hayley,* 281.
11. Davis, *William Blake,* 114.
12. Ibid., 163.
13. Ibid., 99.
14. Ibid., 98.
15. Morton D. Paley, "Cowper as Blake's Spectre," *Eighteenth Century Studies* 1 (Spring 1968): 245–46.
16. William Blake, "Jerusalem," Plate 10, lines 44–59. *William Blake, The Complete Poems,* ed. Alicia Ostriker (New York: Penguin Books, 1977), 652.

Bibliography

Aberbach, David. *Surviving Trauma: Loss. Literature and Psychoanalysis.* New Haven and London: Yale University Press, 1989.

Ackroyd, Peter. *Blake: A Biography.* New York: Ballantine Books, 1977.

Baird, John D., and Charles Ryskamp, eds. *The Poems of William Cowper.* 3 vols. Oxford: Clarendon Press, 1980–95.

Bentley, G. E., Jr. "Blake, Hayley and Lady Hesketh," *Review of English Studies.* n.s. 7 (1956).

———. *Blake Records.* Oxford: Clarendon Press, 1969.

———. *The Stranger from Paradise: A Biography of William Blake.* New Haven: Yale University Press, 2001.

Bishop, Evelyn M. *Blake's Hayley.* London: Gollanez, 1951.

Blake, William. *William Blake, The Complete Poems.* Edited by Alicia Ostriker. New York: Penguin Books, 1977.

Brink, Andrew W. *The Creative Matrix: Anxiety and the Origin of Creativity.* New York: Peter Long Publishing, 2000.

———. *Loss and Symbolic Repair: A Psychological Study of Some Poets.* Hamilton, Ontario: Cromlech Press, 1977.

———. "William Cowper and the Elusive Object." Hamilton, Ontario: Cromlech Press, 1971.

Byrd, Max. *Visits to Bedlam: Madness and Literature in the Eighteenth Century.* Columbia: University of South Carolina Press, 1974.

Cagle, William R. "Cowper's Letters: Mirror to the Man." In *The Familiar Letter in the Eighteenth Century.* Ed. Howard Anderson, Philip B. Daghlian, and Irvin Ehrenpreis. Lawrence: University of Kansas Press, 1966.

Cecil, David. *The Stricken Deer, or the Life of William Cowper.* London: Constable, 1929–30.

Clark, J. C. D. *English Society 1688-1832.* Cambridge: Cambridge University Press, 1985.

Clifford, Alan C. *Atonement and Justification: English Evangelical Theology, 1640–1790, An Evaluation.* Oxford, Clarendon Press, 1990.

Cotton, Nathaniel. "Visions in Verse for the Entertainment and Instruction of Young Minds." In *The Poetical Works of Nathaniel Cotton.* London: R. Dodsley, 1751.

Cowper, William. *Memoir of the Early Life of William Cowper, Esq. with Introduction.* London: R. Edwards, 1816.

Cross, David A. *A Striking Likeness: The Life of George Romney.* Aldershot; Brookfield, VT: Ashgate, 2000.

Davis, Michael. *William Blake: A New Kind of Man.* Berkeley and Los Angeles: University of California Press, 1977.

Faiver, David, and Christine Gerrard, eds. *Eighteenth-Century Poetry: An Annotated Anthology.* Oxford: Blackwell, 1999.

Grierson, Herbert J. C., and J. C. Smith. "Cowper." In *A Critical History of English Poetry.* London: Chatto & Windus, 1944.

Harding, F. J. "Dr. Nathaniel Cotton of St. Albans, Poet and Physician." *Hertfordshire Countryside* 23 (1969): 46–48.

Hartley, Lodwick. "The Stricken Deer and His Contemporary Reputation." *Review of English Studies.* n.s. 9 (1958): 650–55.

Hayley, William. *The Life and Posthumous Writings of Cowper, Esq.* 4 vols. London: Joseph Johnson, 1806.

———. *The Life of George Romney, Esq.* London: T. Payne, 1809.

———. *Memoirs of the Life and Writings of William Hayley, Esq.* Ed. John Johnson. 2 vols. London: Henry Colburn and Co., 1823.

Hiatt, Roger L., Sr., M.D. "The Spectrum of Child and Parent Response to Eye Disease." *Annals of Opthalmology* 21 (1989): 325-30.

Hill, B. "My Little Physician at St. Albans: Nathaniel Cotton 1705–1788." *Practitioner* 199 (1967): 363–67.

Hindmarsh, D. Bruce. *John Newton and the English Evangelical Tradition.* Oxford: Clarendon Press, 1996.

Hopkins, Donald R. *Princes and Peasants: Smallpox in History.* Chicago and London: University of Chicago Press, 1983.

Huang, Roderick. *William Cowper: Nature Poet.* London: Oxford University Press, 1957.

Hunter, Richard, and Ida Macalpine. *Three Hundred Years of Psychiatry: 1535–1860.* Oxford: Oxford University Press, 1982.

Hunter, Richard, and J. B. Wood. "Nathaniel Cotton, M.D., Poet Physician." *Kings College Hospital Gazette* 36 (1957): 120–29.

Irving, William Henry. *The Province of Wit in the English Letter Writers.* Durham, NC: Duke University Press, 1955.

Jackson, Stanley W. *Melancholia and Depression from Hippocratic Times to Modern Times.* New Haven and London: Yale University Press, 1986.

Johnson, John. *Poems by William Cowper, Esq. Together with His Posthumous Poetry and A Sketch of His Life.* Boston: Phillips, Sampson & Co., 1849.

Kidson, Alex. *George Romney 1734-1802.* Princeton, NJ: Princeton University Press, 2002.

King, James. *William Cowper: A Biography.* Durham, NC: Duke University Press, 1986.

King, James, and Charles Ryskamp, eds. *The Letters and Prose Writings of William Cowper.* 5 vols. Oxford: Clarendon Press, 1976–86.

Madan, Falconer. *The Madan Family.* Oxford: Oxford University Press, 1933, chap. 8.

Martin, Bernard. *John Newton. A Biography.* London: Heineman, 1950.

Monthly Review. n.s. 79 (1816): 296.

Nicholson, Norman. "The Evangelical Revival." Chap. 3 in *William Cowper.* London: John Lehmann, 1951.

Ober, William B., "Madness and Poetry: A Note on Collins, Cowper, and Smart." In *Boswell's Clap and Other Essays: Medical Analyses of Literary Men's Afflictions.* Carbondale: Southern Illinois University Press, 1979.

Paley, Morton D. *The Continuing City: William Blake's Jerusalem.* Oxford: Clarendon Press, 1983.

———. "Cowper as Blake's Spectre." *Eighteenth Century Studies* 1 (Spring 1968): 245–46.

Porter, Roy. *Mind-Forged Manacles: Madness in England from the Restoration to the Regency.* Cambridge, MA: Harvard University Press, 1987.

Porter, Roy, and Dorothy Porter. *Patient's Progress: Doctors and Doctoring in 18th Century England.* Stanford, CA: Stanford University Press, 1989.

Quinlan, Maurice. *William Cowper: A Critical Life.* Minneapolis: University of Minnesota Press, 1953.

Redford, Bruce. *The Converse of the Pen: Acts of Intimacy in the Eighteenth-Century Familiar Letter.* Chicago: University of Chicago Press, 1986.

Ryskamp, Charles. *William Cowper of the Inner Temple, Esq.: A Study of His Life and Works to the Year 1768.* Cambridge: Cambridge University Press, 1959.

Scull, Andrew T. *The Most Solitary of Afflictions: Madness and Society in Britain, 1700–1900.* New Haven: Yale University Press, 1993.

Southey, Robert. *Southey's Life of Cowper.* 2 vols. Boston: Otis, Broaders, 1839.

Stone, Lawrence. *The Family, Sex, and Marriage in England 1500–1800.* New York: Harper Torchbooks, 1979.

Storr, Anthony. *The Dynamics of Creation.* New York: Ballantine Books, 1993.

———. "Sanity of the True Genius." In *Churchill's Black Dog, Kafka's Mice and Other Phenomena of the Human Mind.* New York: Grove Press, 1988.

———. *Solitude: A Return to the Self.* New York: Ballantine Books, 1988.

Tanner, Lawrence E. *Westminster School: A History.* London: Life, 1934.

Wardrop, James. *Essays on the Morbid Anatomy of the Human Eye.* Vol. 1. Edinburgh: Constable, 1808.

Wright, Thomas. *The Life of William Cowper.* 1892. Reprint, Folcroft, PA: Folcroft Library Editions, 1973.

Index

A

abandonment, WC's fears of
at end of Lady Hesketh's visit, 147
endurance of friendship and, 136
fear of Mary Unwin's death and,
188–189
God's, 61, 98
image of deserted house/deserted
person, 154
in letter to Lady Hesketh, 142
moving away of the Newtons, 78–79
poem about, 129–130
in poems, 231
solitary mansion image, 209–210
Abbott, Lemuel, 181, 182
Aberbach, David, on pathological grief, 9
Adelphi (WC), 46
See also autobiographies, WC's
ambitions, WC's, 105, 135
Anglican Church, 3, 5
animals/pets, 71–74, 113, 122, 150–152,
158
Anonymous, gifts from, 137, 146
See also Cowper, Theadora (cousin)
attachment/loss issues, 3, 9, 28–29,
81–82
See also abandonment, WC's fears of
Austen, Lady Ann
break with, 107–108
health of, 103
inspiration for "The Task" by, 106–107
poem about, 102
reconciliation with, 101–103
relationship of WC and Mary Unwin
with, 89–92
Authentic Narrative (Newton), 48
authorly secrets, 110–111
autobiographies
WC's, 34
Adelphi, 46

Memoir, xii, 24, 32, 33, 61
religious struggles, 39
suicide/madness, 35
William Hayley's, 215–216

B

Bagot, Walter, 11–12, 146, 148, 166
Balls, Harriet (cousin), 17, 167–168
Balls, Richard, 17
Bentley, G. E., on William Hayley,
215–216
biographers, WC's
Andrew Brink (*See* Brink, Andrew)
David Cecil, 33
James King, 15
Lodwick Hartley, 117, 129
Robert Southey, 112, 183
speculation on Mary Unwin–WC
relationship by, 58
Thomas Wright, 32–33
William Hayley (*See* Hayley, William)
Bishop, Evelyn, 177, 217
Blake, William, 214, 219–222, 223–227
Bodham, Ann (Rose), 167–168, 169,
170, 181
Boerhaave, Hermann, 10, 37
Bowlby, John, 82
breakdowns. *See* depression/insanity
Brink, Andrew, 70
on attachment/loss, 9
on "The Cast-away," 117
fullness of WC's biography, 112
Loss and Symbolic Repair, 82, 85, 117
on poem, "To Mary," 197
Storr on, 81–82
on WC's writing of verse, 80
on writing verse, 116
Buchanan, John, 203
Bull, William, 102, 108, 109–110,
181–182, 183

Acknowledgments

My journey with William Cowper was made with support from many wonderful people including my children—Nancy Bell Rollings, Barbara L. de Boinville, and Clay Risk, M.D. I am deeply grateful to Frances Eddy for her friendship, inspiration, and expertise and to Sharon Goldinger of PeopleSpeak for her high professional standards throughout the project. This book could not have been completed without the helpful staff of the Library of Congress and the Reference and Quiet Study Room at Little Falls Library, Montgomery County, Maryland.

About the Author

Louise Risk earned a degree in chemistry from Bryn Mawr College and later pursued biblical studies, including New Testament Greek, at Wesley Theological Seminary in Washington, D.C. She worked as a researcher at the National Library of Medicine for FACT (Food Animals Concerns Trust), a nonprofit group linking animal husbandry practices and human health.

Risk is also the author of *A House on the Hudson,* which examines 140 years in the history of a Victorian country home. The hymns of William Cowper sparked an interest in the poet's life and work that culminated in this book.